Social Activism in Women's Tennis

Analyzing the key players and political moments in women's professional tennis since 1968, this book explores the historical lineage of social activism within women's tennis and the issues, expressions, risks, and effects associated with each cohort of players.

Drawing on original qualitative research, including interviews with former players, the book examines tennis's position in debates around gender, sexuality, race, and equal pay. It looks at how the actions and choices of the pioneering activist players were simultaneously shaped by, and had a part in shaping, larger social movements committed to challenging the status quo and working towards increased economic equality for women. Taking an intersectional approach, the book assesses the significance of players from Althea Gibson and Martina Navratilova to Venus and Serena Williams, illuminating our understanding of the relationship between sport, social justice, and wider society.

This is important reading for researchers and students working in sport studies, sociology, women's studies, and political science, as well as anybody with an interest in social activism and social movements. It is also a fascinating read for the general tennis fan.

Kristi Tredway is a Postdoctoral Fellow in the Bloomberg School of Public Health at Johns Hopkins University, USA.

Routledge Research in Sport, Culture and Society

Critical Research in Sport, Health and Physical Education
How to Make a Difference
Edited by Richard Pringle, Håkan Larsson and Göran Gerdin

Soccer and the American Dream
Ian Lawrence

Social Justice in Fitness and Health
Bodies Out of Sight
Laura Azzarito

The World Anti-Doping Code
Fit for Purpose?
Lovely Dasgupta

Deleuze and the Physically Active Body
Pirkko Markula

Capitalism, Sport Mega Events and the Global South
Billy Graeff

The Nordic Model and Physical Culture
Edited by Mikkel B. Tin, Frode Telseth, Jan Ove Tangen and Richard Giulianotti

Sport and Mediatization
Kirsten Frandsen

Social Activism in Women's Tennis
Generations of Politics and Cultural Change
Kristi Tredway

For more information about this series, please visit: www.routledge.com/sport/series/RRSCS

Social Activism in Women's Tennis
Generations of Politics and Cultural Change

Kristi Tredway

LONDON AND NEW YORK

First published 2020
by Routledge
2 Park Square, Milton Park, Abingdon, Oxon OX14 4RN

and by Routledge
52 Vanderbilt Avenue, New York, NY 10017

Routledge is an imprint of the Taylor & Francis Group, an informa business

© 2020 Kristi Tredway

The right of Kristi Tredway to be identified as author of this work has been asserted by her in accordance with sections 77 and 78 of the Copyright, Designs and Patents Act 1988.

All rights reserved. No part of this book may be reprinted or reproduced or utilized in any form or by any electronic, mechanical, or other means, now known or hereafter invented, including photocopying and recording, or in any information storage or retrieval system, without permission in writing from the publishers.

Trademark notice: Product or corporate names may be trademarks or registered trademarks, and are used only for identification and explanation without intent to infringe.

British Library Cataloguing-in-Publication Data
A catalogue record for this book is available from the British Library

Library of Congress Cataloging-in-Publication Data
A catalog record has been requested for this book

ISBN: 978-0-367-41671-3 (hbk)
ISBN: 978-0-367-81562-2 (ebk)

Typeset in Times New Roman
by Wearset Ltd, Boldon, Tyne and Wear

Dedication

This book is dedicated to Rosie Casals who has saved me more than once. First, she was my coach when I was a professional tennis player, helping this working-class, half-American Indian kid hone my athletic skills on the court and develop social skills off the court. Arriving at her tennis court the first time as a cocky and self-absorbed 18-year-old, she told me: "You will never accomplish anything until you learn how to work hard." (When she asked me what my goals were that first day, I am certain that I rolled my eyes, thinking that it was so obvious, of course, given that I thought I was a gift from the goddesses to women's tennis, and said: "I'm going to be number one in the world." It's then that this response from her came.) Rosie's statement has stuck with me still, guiding my ambition and my work ethic. She crafted me into a person who belonged in the middle class, and in a historically white and upper-class sport, despite my upbringing. Second, after I blew out my knee, which ended my tennis career, she told me: "Go to college until you figure out what you want to do for the rest of your life." Reluctant at first, I became the first person in my family to attend, and, ultimately, graduate from college, solidifying, really, my newfound positioning in the middle class. And, finally, Rosie was my gatekeeper for this study, providing me with access to players that I would not have had without her, along with sending supportive emails that I was doing good work. Thanks Rosie! You are the best! I owe you everything!

Contents

Acknowledgments viii
Prologue: A practice of self-reflexivity xi

Introduction 1

1 The Trailblazers: Setting the stage for social activism in women's tennis 33

2 The Founders: The Original 9, "women's lob" feminism, and the social movement that launched women's professional tennis, 1968–1975 40

3 The Joiners: The era of Evert and Navratilova, 1974–1990 67

4 The Sustainers: The corporatization of women's tennis, 1987–present 93

5 The Throwbacks: Individual players fighting for broader social justice issues 121

Conclusion 162

Epilogue 171
Appendix: Methodological considerations—"Questions please." Press conference participation as a qualitative research method 173
Bibliography 189
Index 204

Acknowledgments

I want to begin by acknowledging two people who saw me begin this work, but did not get to see me finish. My mom and my grandfather passed away too soon to see me earn a PhD and to see this book go into publication, and far, far too soon for me as a person. I miss them both terribly. I thought that with losing them, and my grandmother over 20 years ago, that I would lose my American Indian identity in some way, but I have not. They are still with me, along with all that they taught me.

First and foremost, I want to thank the current and former players who gave me their time for interviews. I continually found encouragement with their interest in my questions, and hence this project. These players include: Rosie Casals, Judy Tegart Dalton, Chris Evert, Julie Heldman, Svetlana Kuznetsova, Andrea Petkovic, Kristy Pigeon, Pam Shriver, Sam Stosur, Renee Stubbs, Serena Williams, and Venus Williams, and many others through press conferences. Without their input, this project would not have been possible. I also want to thank the tournaments and organizations that gave me press credentials for this project: The Family Circle Cup (now the Volvo Cars Open), the Western & Southern Open, the Citi Open, Greenbrier Champions Tennis Classic, and the Washington Kastles. Also, Courtney Nguyen, Ben Rothenberg, and Nick McCarvel deserve a big shout-out for showing me the ropes when I first arrived in the press room.

Thank you to Simon Whitmore at Routledge who saw the value in this book project on sport and social activism. Rebecca Connor, and previously Cecily Davey, were excellent at liaising between Simon and me while also keeping me focused on the end product. I want to also thank Anika Parsons for her keen editorial eye throughout this manuscript and Emma Critchley for her management of this project from edits to proofs.

I have been influenced by many different professors while a student at the University of Colorado and the University of Maryland. Most notable, though, are three people: Alison Jaggar, Vine Deloria, Jr., and Patricia Hill Collins, arguably the greatest feminist philosopher, American Indian scholar, and scholar of intersectionality, respectively, that the world has known. A commonality among Jaggar, Deloria, and Collins is that their work, both in teaching and writing, is epistemically inclusive of various ways of knowing, along with an understanding of the power attached to whose knowledge is counted or not, what political and cultural issues are on the horizon, seeing the interconnections between many different social groups and political and cultural concerns, and a sense of social justice, in that the work is important and needed in people's everyday lives, not just in academic circles. The work is not for accolades, though those have come anyway because their work is excellent, but for offering compassion, understanding, and possible solutions to people. The strength of these three for me is that they pushed me beyond intellectual levels that I did not know were possible. I am far greater as an intellectual for having been their student. The hard part for me now is becoming a scholar who is worthy of this lineage, and, if not becoming, at least continually trying to become that scholar.

This research project began as my PhD dissertation and the members of that committee were the first to read this study when it was in a much more raw form. David Andrews, as the chair, Patricia Hill Collins, Nancy Spencer, Laurie Frederik, Shannon Jette, and Jennifer Roberts, gave tremendously useful guidance and inquisitive questioning that made this project much better. This study was financially supported by the Graduate School at the University of Maryland with the Ann G. Wylie Dissertation Fellowship, the Department of Kinesiology at the University of Maryland with the Sally J. Phillips Dissertation Fellowship, the Dolph Briscoe Center for American History at the University of Texas with the William and Madeline Welder Smith Research Travel Award, and St. Mary's College of Maryland with a Faculty Development Grant. This financial support was hugely beneficial for continuing work on this project.

I also want to thank the feminist sport sociologists who took me under their wings years ago, especially Jaime Schultz, Holly Thorpe, and Jayne Caudwell. Without their friendship and network of support, this path I traveled would have been much, much more difficult.

My tried and true friend through my PhD program and even more now is Stephanie Cork. She was always available with support for me and this project. Plus, she is as smart as they come. As she pushed me from behind to graduation, I pulled her toward that same finish line which she recently crossed.

This project was not without a bit of a bumpy road, physically. I want to give a shout-out to Natalie (Farmer) Hopkins, Melissa Camp, Arati Patel, Kathleen Settle, Chandra Baker, and their teams, for keeping my body as healthy as it can be.

I had fantastic colleagues at St. Mary's College of Maryland. The Department of Sociology provided me with a supportive home and I will always be thankful to Louis Hicks, Elizabeth Osborn, Andrew Cognard-Black, and Helen Daugherty for that. Mike Wick, Katie Gantz, and Christine Wooley from the Provost's office provided a nurturing environment where I could hone my professorial skills, and I always appreciate that. Others from the college I want to thank for their friendship and support are Tuajuanda Jordan, Jessica Malisch, Brian O'Sullivan, Katy Arnett, David Morris, Kathy Koch, Rose Keith, and FJ Talley.

Half or more of this book was written at the kitchen tables of the homes of Ray and Peggy Sullivan in Burlington, Vermont, and Key Biscayne, Florida. The Sullivans are like family to me and they continually treat me as such. Their support and friendship mean the world to me.

I feel like my friends and family have supported me far more through the years than I have them. I especially want to acknowledge my brothers, Kerry and Kevin, as well as Denise, my sister-in-law, and my two nieces, Jessica and Mallory. My dad and my sister, Judy, are also super-supportive and they remind me that blood is more powerful than time. I need to give a shout-out to Betty, as well, who not only has treated me like one of her own, but she taught me how to write effectively. I took that training and ran with it!

I want to thank Angela, my wife of 20 years. I watched her research and write a dissertation, gain a tenure-track job, get tenure, and then become a full professor. All the while, her continual comment: "Why would you ever want to get a PhD?" kept me honest with myself and kept my political commitments in the forefront.

And, finally, my daughter, Ella, is an inspiration. It is often good to see through her eyes: she only sees the good, has only friends and no enemies, sees the world as a site for adventure and exploration, and never sees language as an impediment when communicating with others. My most difficult task in life is raising a little person who will grow up to become a Black woman who is secure, confident, and has many tools for understanding and navigating the world.

Prologue
A practice of self-reflexivity

From July 1988 to October 1992, I was a professional tennis player. Though I blew out my knee before I could play in any of the Grand Slam events, my whole life was about women's tennis. It was where I belonged and I was a part of something. It's that "something" that I am always eager to explore and identify.

I started kindergarten in 1975, the year Title IX, the federal legislation which banned inequality in schools based on gender, was fully implemented in California, the first state to do so. Title IX has had, arguably, its largest impact on women's and girls' sports of any legislation in the US (see, for example, Brake, 2010). Title IX gave me full access to sports and is the catalyst for me becoming a professional tennis player. Being a professional tennis player moved me from the working class to the middle class. Being in the middle class made college a viable option after my playing career was over. This experience plays a significant part in my analysis since, at a personal level, tennis has provided me with an enormous amount of cultural capital that I would not have, had I not been a professional tennis player.

I first began thinking of girls and sport as a ten-year-old baseball player in Little League, in the summer of 1980. Baseball was my first true love and I was so excited to be playing. After try-outs for teams, I was placed on the B-1 team. This was the top team in the B level, with the A level being even higher. I didn't think much of it, happily thinking that that was where I was placed, based on my skills that they observed. The day that the placements were made, a middle-aged male coach who helped place the players on teams walked up to me – I guess to make small talk – and said: "You were good enough for the A-team, but there has never been a girl on that team before." He laughed it off and walked away. I was left confused, because I did not understand how a person would not be placed on the team best suited for their skills. My first gender-based social activism occurred when I was focused on, and successful at, hitting a home run at each of my at-bats whenever we played against the A-team. Anything less than a home run would have felt like a failure, and all that I had as a ten-year-old were feelings, not feminism or theories of social activism. By the next year, I understood this exclusion as structural, and not just interpersonal discrimination. My brother had continually told me that I could be a Major League Baseball player if

I kept practicing, which I did. At some point at the age of 11, I realized that there were no women in Major League Baseball, and there still aren't! I didn't speak to my brother for months because I felt tricked into believing that I had a shot. Later, with the help of a junior high school PE teacher who told me to choose between golf or tennis, the only professional sports at the time for women, all of those feelings were channeled into tennis.

Besides women's professional tennis, my life since my tennis career has been most marked by social activism, along with identity politics and intersectionality. It makes sense that this book engaged all of these components of my life. My own intersectionality of identities has been developed independently and interdependently for more than two decades.

My family is made up of working class, American Indians who moved from Oklahoma to California during the "Dust Bowl." They are the unwritten side of John Steinbeck's work. I am the oldest daughter of the oldest daughter of the oldest daughter all the way back to before "The Trail of Tears" of 1830, the forced removal of American Indians in the Southeast, to what would become Oklahoma. Within this matrilineal culture, I am the heir. My mother was the first in our family to graduate from high school and I was the first to attend college. After my undergraduate degree, a double-major in Women's Studies and Philosophy at the University of Colorado, I stayed at Colorado and earned a master's degree in American Indian religious traditions through the Department of Religious Studies. I was able to accomplish this only two generations from my grandfather being reprimanded for speaking Choctaw at school.

Outside of American Indian contexts, I don't look American Indian, but people do always assume (correctly, of course) that I am a lesbian because my gender (seemingly appearing masculine) is outside of our culture's norm. Though I appear white, most of my social interaction style can be traced directly to American Indians. In American Indian traditions, I am considered a boundary-crosser – I have jumped from the working class to the middle class, I have college degrees, and I was a pro tennis player – the highest-ranking American Indian in the history of women's tennis.

Through sex, gender, sexuality, race, and class, I have been marked, and I understand things, in very particular ways. This practice of self-reflexivity has been descriptive, which is the most common kind across academic disciplines. What makes this project more rigorous and critically engaged is that I put my self-reflexivity to work while in the field and in my writing. As Sandra Harding (1987) asserts:

> The best feminist analysis ... insists that the inquirer her/himself be placed in the same critical plane as the overt subject matter, thereby recovering the entire research process for scrutiny in the results of research. That is, the class, race, culture, and gender assumptions, beliefs, and behaviors of the researcher her/himself must be placed within the frame of the picture that she/he attempts to paint.
>
> (p. 9)

Putting my self-reflexivity to work included engaging with how my informants responded to me and how I was able or unable to gain access.

For me, the personal and the political are merged. I can see how our society places economic value on bodies that are organized hierarchically. As with all of my work, this project emanates from a feminist perspective. Within academic research, male-centeredness of both the researcher and the subjects is dominant. Angela McRobbie, an early member of the Centre for Contemporary Cultural Studies at the University of Birmingham, has noted that seeing women and girls is not the hard part. Indeed, "the difficulty is, how to understand [their] invisibility" (McRobbie & Garber, 1976/2006, p. 177). McRobbie, in thinking through how the personal is political among female researchers, states that:

> One of the central tenets of the women's movement has been that the personal is political. Similarly, feminists recognise the close links between personal experience and the areas we choose for study – our autobiographies invade and inform what we write. Even if the personal voice of the author is not apparent throughout the text, she will at least announce her interest in, and commitment to, her subject in an introduction or foreword. Although few radical (male) sociologists would deny the importance of the personal in precipitating social and political awareness, to admit how their own experience has influenced their choice of subject-matter (the politics of selection) seems more or less taboo.... The absence of self and the invalidating of personal experience in the name of the more objective social sciences goes hand in hand with the silencing of other areas, which are for feminists of the greatest importance.
>
> (McRobbie, 1980, p. 113)

Indeed, the primary concern that Sandra Harding raises is that "women's research and scholarship often has been ignored, trivialized, or appropriated without the credit which would have been given to a man's work" (1987, p. 4).

Sherryl Kleinman asserts that "as nonfeminist colleagues told me, doing feminist research means that the researcher 'has an agenda.' It also implies that other researchers do not" (2007, p. 2). I believe that every researcher has an agenda, whether it is under the guise of a politicized framework like feminism, or of refraining from so-called politics while keeping one's own identity markers invisible, thus feeding into the strength of the status quo. Both are political projects. Indeed, I am frank in stating that I have an agenda. I want to uncover and understand inequality so that I can work more productively to eradicate it. Feminism permeates everything that I write, think, and do. Intersectionality is positioned in my mind the same way. As a political activist, I have not only theorized about feminism and intersectionality, I have lived it and expressed it in publicly political ways. In many ways, this will not be explicitly stated in my writing, nor can people know through my writing what I do through my everyday actions. Yet, as part of my personal politics, feminism spans these dimensions of myself. My scholarship is always both personal and political.

Introduction

The term "women's lob" was coined in the early 1970s by Gladys Heldman, the founding editor of *World Tennis* magazine, to describe the particular style of feminism used in women's tennis at the time (King & Starr, 1988, p. 120). The term is a play on "women's lib," the slang term for the women's movement, and the lob shot in tennis in which the ball is hit high in the air and over the opponent's head, or the opponent hits an overhead smash back. The Original 9, nine women who joined together in 1970, pressured the governing bodies of tennis to offer equitable pay for women as they did for men. Their push for equal prize money, along with the creation of the Women's Tennis Association (WTA) to ensure that prize money continued to grow, led to what became modern-day women's tennis. "Women's lob" drew upon two main components from the broader women's liberation movement: 1) equal pay for equal work; and, 2) access to an economic livelihood through a sustained and consistent offering of tournaments for women. The other goals of the women's liberation movement – such as abortion rights, men sharing in housework and the raising of children, and access to education – were not relevant to the Original 9, though these might have been personal goals of individuals in the Original 9. Indeed, "women's lob" could be seen as equal parts feminism and corporatization, since it was solely focused upon the prize money for women players and the offering, as well as marketing, of women's tennis events.

Utilizing professional women's tennis as the empirical site of this analysis, I examined social activism within sport. Given that professional tennis is the most lucrative sport for women, and thus the most powerful, and that it has been home to many social activists and actions, women's tennis seemed like a robust empirical site to use. Within this empirical site, my overarching research question was: Within the periodic evolution of social activism in women's tennis, what were the issues, expressions, risks, and effects of its various generational iterations? As pioneering social actors in women's tennis, the actions and choices of the Original 9 were simultaneously shaped by, *and* had a part in shaping, larger social movements committed to challenging the status quo and working towards increased economic equality for women. Other players followed the Original 9 as agents of change within women's tennis, who were also shaped by, and had a part in shaping, society at large. This study is an analysis of the Original 9 and the emerging generations of players who followed them, with an eye on the issues they faced and what their social activism looked like.

Suzanne Lenglen, the French tennis champion, railed against the tennis establishment's structure of amateurism in 1926, arguing that she and others could not afford to compete without prize money. Althea Gibson, winner of five Grand Slam singles titles in the late 1950s, struggled to make a space in the whiteness of tennis to exist as a Black woman. She, too, advocated for prize money in tennis, especially since, given her race, she most likely made minimal money under the table to play tournaments, if any. Then, once there was prize money in 1968, with money no longer paid under the table, the disparity between men and women became visibly stark. Ann Haydon Jones, a winner of three Grand Slam singles titles, boycotted the British Hard Court Championships, the first tournament of the "open era," due to the disparity. The efforts of Lenglen, Gibson, and Haydon Jones failed, though, in large part because they each operated as individuals. They were not powerful enough to sway the governing bodies of tennis at the time.

Subsequent efforts of social activism by players in women's professional tennis continued to be centered on equality and representation. Furthermore, the social activism since 1968 can be seen as comprising four distinct generational cohorts of social activists:

- The Founders cohort: These social actors begin the movement, which, in the context of women's tennis, is equality through equal prize money;
- The Joiners cohort: These social actors are the next generation who continue the movement for equality begun by the Founders cohort and, in the case of women's tennis, add issues of representation;
- The Sustainers cohort: This cohort is marked by both a lull in social activism and a regrouping to the demands of heightened corporatization of women's tennis with its prescribed representation;
- The Throwbacks cohort: This cohort is marked foremost by social activism, which comes about by a weakening of the category of sex, more buy-in from male players to women's concerns, and an increase in the use of social media by players.

Interestingly, the Founders cohort is the only generation that used collective activism rather than individual expressions of activism. The individual nature of tennis, as it is primarily a one-on-one sport, may provide the context for individual expressions of social activism, or those who operate more individualistically may be drawn to tennis because of its more individualized, rather than team, format.

Theoretical overview

While analyzing the social activism within women's tennis, my overarching theoretical framework engages intersectionality, with its linkage to articulation, along with the theoretical constructs of identity, and the structures and dimensions of power which undergird both. Other theories and concepts will be engaged, as needed, in each of the chapters.

Social movements and generational cohorts

The literature on social movements is extensive, especially in regards to organization and leadership. What is of importance in this study is the literature on generational cohorts within social movements. This area has garnered far less attention. Indeed, Joseph DeMartini writes that:

> compared to the literature on the origins of social movements, relatively little work has been directed towards an understanding of the long-term consequences of social movement participation and the factors that might explain the maintenance or dissolution of commitments associated with such participation.
>
> (1983, p. 195)

Concurring with DeMartini, Nancy Whittier notes, "empirical work on differences between cohorts is considerably scantier than that of enduring characteristics of one cohort" (1997, p. 763). Hence, the importance of this project.

The German (later British) social theorist, Karl Mannheim, put in motion an analysis of social generations in his 1927 paper, "The Problem of Generations" (1952). According to Mannheim, "the social phenomenon 'generation' represents nothing more than a particular kind of identity of location, embracing related 'age groups' embedded in a historical-social process" (1952, p. 292). To Mannheim, generational cohorts in society come to be in the following manner:

> (a) new participants in the cultural process are emerging, whilst (b) former participants in that process are continually disappearing; (c) members of any one generation can participate only in a temporally limited section of the historical process, and (d) it is therefore necessary continually to transmit the accumulated cultural heritage; (e) the transition from generation to generation is a continuous process.
>
> (1952, p. 292)

Thus, generational cohorts have a natural cycle of emergence and dissipation.

Furthermore, as may be obvious, memories from the previous generations are passed down from the most immediate previous generation to the current generation. Mannheim explains:

> the fact that the transition from one generation to another takes place continuously tends to render this interaction smoother; in the process of this

interaction, it is not the oldest who meet the youngest at once; the first contacts are made by other 'intermediary' generations, less removed from each other.

(1952, p. 301)

Whittier, agreeing with DeMartini, claims that there are two dominant strands in social movement research: political process approaches, or how movements respond to specific political openings, and organizational approaches, which are primarily focused on origins and continuity (1997, p. 760). However, Whittier, drawing on Karl Mannheim, sees a third path, a generational approach which "draws on theory about political generations and cohort replacement ... a generational model of continuity and change in social movements" (1997, p. 760). Furthermore, a given political generation is "comprised of individuals (of varying ages) who join a social movement during a given wave of protest" (Whittier, 1997, pp. 761–762).

A distinct feature of generations that Whittier draws out is that "generational politics and collective identity [are] located in action and interaction – observable phenomena – rather than in individual self-conceptions, attitudes, or beliefs" (1995, p. 16). Defining social movements, Whittier refers to them as "clusters of organizations, overlapping networks, and individuals that share goals and are bound together by a collective identity and cultural events" (1997, p. 761). Though there are the collective identities and collective memories that Mannheim speaks of, another Mannheimian concept that Whittier explains is that "social movements change in part through the entry of recruits. Shifts in political opportunity provide an impetus for change; generational processes of recruitment and cohort turnover are one micro-level mechanism by which such change occurs" (Whittier, 1997, p. 761). With this model, Whittier makes clear that the cohorts are not clearly defined, the politics are always moving forward, and people enter the politics at the point when they enter the social movement. Explaining this process of incremental change within a social movement, Whittier notes:

Social movements are composed of multiple cohorts of personnel at any given time, including both long-time participants and new recruits. Core participants remain committed and mobilized. ... The enduring commitment of long-time activists is an important internal process promoting movement *continuity*. In addition, recruits enter movements at varying rates. Although new entrants share basic assumptions and goals with their predecessors, often they also differ in important ways. Consequently recruitment and personnel turnover help produce change in social movements. These two personnel processes – the persistence of committed long-time participants and the entry of recruits – bridge a theoretical concern with the political processes that shape recruitment and cycles of protest with an analysis of interaction in micro-mobilization contexts and the construction of collective identity.

(1997, p. 761)

Introduction 5

In the ways Whittier explains, social movements continue to have new concepts and ideas drawn in with new recruits, while there also continues to be a strand of collective identity and collective memory that the older activists instill in the younger members. The collective identity is an important feature. Whittier explains:

> When individuals are immersed in a social movement, they internalize a new self-definition as part of a collectivity that interprets the world politically ... Collective identity consists of three related processes: delineation of group boundaries, construction of an oppositional consciousness or interpretative frameworks for understanding the world in a political light, and politicization of everyday life ... Because collective identity is an attempt to make sense of external events, experiences, and the movement context, cohorts construct different identities as the external environment and the movement context change. ... Differences in collective identity are observable in practices such as norms of self-presentation, interactional styles, and internal discourse in the movement.
>
> (1997, p. 762)

Indeed, as Whittier explains, "members remain politically committed and active over the years because they internalize a collective identity that links their sense of self to membership in a politically defined and active group" (1997, p. 763). Thus, people may have no real knowledge of the politics that preceded their entry point, yet all of the members of the social movement, regardless of their generational affiliation, are unified by a belief in the fundamental aims of the movement.

For this study specifically, I will be looking at how social activism has changed across the more than 40 years that women's tennis has been a professional sport. Rather than a seemingly natural lineage of history in this regard, social activism in women's tennis has been shaped by a variety of complex social processes from within and outside of women's tennis. In their important qualitative investigation into the social movement of men organizing to end violence against women, Michael Messner, Max Greenberg, and Tal Peretz reformulated Whittier's framework in order to frame this particular social movement (2015). For Messner, Greenberg, and Peretz, there are the Movement Cohort, the Bridge Cohort, and the Professional Cohort of the men's anti-violence movement.[1] Though this framework is useful as an elaboration on Whittier's framework, which they do not adequately acknowledge as the basis for their own, I am choosing to primarily rely on Whittier's framework for this study.

Beginning any long-standing social movement is the aptly named "Founders" cohort of social movement actors. In describing the Founders cohort, Whittier states that "they entered the movement after initial activism had begun, but before lasting institutions had developed. They transformed the ideas, dissatisfaction, and ad hoc organizations begun by [the Trailblazers] into lasting ... institutions" (1995, p. 62). The Founders cohort, guided by grassroots feminist principles, put in place the original call for action. So, too, did they mentor those who joined the movement after this point.

This cohort was followed by the "Joiners" cohort, who acted as an intermediary between the Founders cohort and what was ushered in after the Joiners cohort, the Sustainers cohort. "The primary role," of the Joiners cohort, according to Whittier, "was to expand existing organizations. Although most founders continued to play central roles in the organizations they had begun, participants drew a distinction between the 'Old Guard' or 'founding mothers' and newer members" (1995, p. 63). Indeed, grassroots feminism was waning because the concepts of feminism had been taken up by universities and other mainstream organizations, but without the political impetus grounding the concepts. Thus, a lineage of the social movement was being created and strengthened.

The Sustainers cohort emerged "as the social and political climate because more conservative and feminist organizations foundered," asserts Whittier (1995, p. 71). Indeed, Whittier further explains that the main task of the Sustainers cohort was to pass on the ideas of the movement to those who entered after them; however, "in sharp contrast to joiners, sustainers were largely pessimistic about the prospects for sweeping social change" (1995, p. 71). The Sustainers cohort references the current era, where many of the things that the Founders cohort was working towards have been realized – and the movement has been mainstreamed to some extent – but the movement now has, maybe, a new set of goals. Again, the movement seemed to be already in place. The goal, then, is to keep it on course, moving forward, but there are seemingly no greater political goals to work towards.

Undergirding my analysis of social activism is my understanding of intersectionality and how people operate within specific contexts and domains of power. Rather than only "a theory of marginalized subjectivity" or "a generalized theory of identity" (Nash, 2008, p. 10), intersectionality facilitates an understanding of specific contexts in which identities exist. The specificity is important, because no identities are the same in each context. Indeed, beyond simply identities, intersectionality can be used to understand the specificity of a particular location, a space that has a particular underpinning social milieu that has been historically created over time. Also, intersectionality can be used to understand the specificity of how one operates, what one does, or how one performs, within the social milieu. Thus, through understanding who, where, and what is done and how, intersectionality can do its most productive work.

Intersectionality is a particular knowledge project that facilitates our understanding of the lived experiences of those who are affected by race, class, gender, sexuality, ethnicity, nationality, and other identities, and how social inequalities are organized, operate, and can be challenged in the social world. Theories of intersectionality also investigate how various identity markers interconnect to shape identities, social institutions, representations, social issues, and social policies. Furthermore, frameworks of intersectionality have an implicit and often explicit commitment to social justice.

"The term intersectionality references the critical insight that race, class, gender, sexuality, ethnicity, nation, ability, and age operate not as unitary, mutually exclusive entities, but as reciprocally constructing phenomena that in turn shape complex social inequalities," asserts social theorist Patricia Hill Collins (2015, p. 2). Put another way, Collins states that:

> intersectionality refers to particular forms of intersecting oppressions, for example, intersections of race and gender, or of sexuality and nation. Intersectional paradigms remind us that oppression cannot be reduced to one fundamental type, and that oppressions work together in producing injustice.
> (2000, p. 18)

More broadly speaking, studies using intersectionality explain the experiences of people with particular and multiple subjectivities, and how those subjectivities operate within various domains of power. Further codifying intersectionality, Collins claims that:

> Intersectional scholarship and/or practice seemingly pivot on a loose set of shared ideas, namely, (1) how race, class, gender and sexuality constitute intersecting systems of power; (2) how specific social inequalities reflect these power relations from one setting to the next; (3) how identities of race, gender, are socially constructed within multiple systems of power; and (4) how social problems and their remedies are similarly constructed within intersecting systems of power.
> (2011, p. 88)

It is this understanding of intersectionality that will be used in this study.

For the purposes of this study, identity is understood as the distinctive characteristic(s) belonging to an individual or shared by all members of a group. Identity will be further understood as "produced, consumed and regulated within culture – creating meanings through symbolic systems of representation about the identity positions which we might adopt" (Woodward, 1997, p. 2) or, I must add, have forced upon us.

Identities

I will be using British cultural theorist Stuart Hall's analysis of identity because it more readily lends itself to the complexities that will arise with an intersectional analysis. Hall, in defining identity, states that:

> I use "identity" to refer to the meeting point, the point of *suture*, between on the one hand the discourses and practices which attempt to "interpellate", speak to us or hail us into place as the social subjects of particular discourses, and on the other hand, the processes which produce subjectivities,

which construct us as subjects which can be "spoken". Identities are thus points of temporary attachment to the subject positions which discursive practices construct for us.

(Hall, 1996a, pp. 5–6; italics in original)

Identity, then, is the discursive construction of subject formation. Identity is not found in the body or, for Judith Butler, on the body, but in the discourse. As such, an identity is fleeting. As the discourse changes, so does the understanding of the identity. Hall clarifies the discursive construction of identity when he writes:

Precisely because identities are constructed within, not outside, discourse, we need to understand them as produced in specific historical and institutional sites within specific discursive formations and practices, by specific enunciative strategies. Moreover, they emerge within the play of specific modalities of power, and thus are more the product of the marking of difference and exclusion, than they are the sign of an identical, naturally-constituted unity – an "identity" in its traditional meaning (that is, an all-inclusive sameness, seamless, without internal differentiation).

(Hall, 1996a, p. 4)

Indeed, identity is known through shared characteristics within a group. However, representations of groups of people based on identities, either their own, or identifications placed upon others, exist in our culture, and affect individuals and groups of people, regardless of how much poststructuralists want to claim that identities and subjectivities, because they are discursively brought into being, do not exist.

Hall provides an example of the discursive creation of identities by relying on Judith Butler's understanding of the creation of sex. Hall states that:

In *Gender Trouble* (1990) and more especially in *Bodies That Matter* (1993), Judith Butler has taken up, through her concern with the "discursive limits of 'sex'" and with the politics of feminism, the complex transactions between the subject, the body and identity. ... Adopting the position that the subject is discursively constructed and that there is no subject before or outside the Law, Butler develops a rigorously argued case that "sex is, from the start, normative. ... In this sense, then, sex not only functions as a norm, but is part of a regulatory practice that produces (through the repetition or iteration of a norm which is without origin) the bodies it governs, that is, whose regulatory force is made clear as a kind of productive power, the power to produce – demarcate, circulate, differentiate – the bodies it controls. ... 'Sex' is an ideal construct which is forcibly materialized through time."

(Hall, 1996a, p. 14; quoting Butler, 1993, p. 1)

For Butler, though, identities are not only discursively created; they are performed. The repetitive performance brings identities – Butler especially focused on gender performance – into being. Furthermore, Butler is describing how the identity of sex is produced, consumed, represented, and regulated, similar to Stuart Hall's and Kath Woodward's understanding of identity formation and maintenance.

To be certain, there is cause to be wary of what is produced in the discursive realm. In regards to Black women, Nikol Alexander-Floyd warns us that:

> A postmodern avoidance of identity and a postfeminist deployment of feminism ... problematizes identity by suggesting that we all are said to have ruptured identities and fragmented bodies. This approach de-legitimizes the study of racism, sexism, and the structural bases of inequality and activism and further threatens black women's scholarly authority on black women's subjectivity.
>
> (2012, p. 2)

The same could be true of other scholars who study the very identity groups to which they belong. Within the discursive realm, the construct of racism has been replaced by discussions of race. Within academic circles, it is debated back and forth whether race exists or not; however, it is racism that has real implications in the lives of people. The same is true of sexism, which is now similarly discussed only as gender issues. Those controlling the dominant discourses are the ones who stand outside of subjugation based on identities. Indeed, their "'whiteness' is understood as comprising material, cultural, and subjective components, as well as cultural practices that are frequently 'unmarked' and 'unnamed'" (Douglas, 2005, p. 259). Their privilege is shown in the discourse being shifted to abstract concepts that really have no answers, rather than tangible social problems that affect large segments of society.

Identity is tied to representation and difference. There are discursively created symbolic boundaries between identities. An identity, then, requires another identity in order to exist, yet neither are static entities; both are discursively constructed and maintained. When identities are created in the discursive realm, they are brought into being and joined with the elusive "other." Hall asserts that:

> Above all, and directly contrary to the form in which they are constantly invoked, identities are constructed through, not outside, difference. This entails the radically disturbing recognition that it is only through the relation to the Other, the relation to what it is not, to precisely what it lacks, to what has been called its constitutive outside that the "positive" meaning of any term – and thus its "identity" – can be constructed.
>
> (Hall, 1996a, pp. 4–5)

This "othering" through identification is both positive and negative. The positive aspects include people forming affinity groups based on particular identities. These groups offer safety and community to its members. The negative aspects include marginalization from the dominant culture which can include racism, sexism, homophobia, and a variety of other discriminatory practices. Furthermore, this "othering," according to Hall,

> is a way of marking how deeply our histories actually intertwine and interpenetrate; how necessary "the Other" is to our own sense of identity; how even the dominant, colonizing, imperializing power only knows who and what it is and can only experience the pleasure of its own power of domination in and through the construction of the Other. The two are the two sides of the same coin. And the Other is not out there, but in here. It is not outside, but inside.
>
> (1996c, p. 342)

Beyond the discursive construction of identities, Hall speaks of the historicity of identities. To Hall,

> cultural identity ... is a matter of 'becoming' as well as 'being.' It belongs to the future as much as to the past. It is not something which already exists, transcending place, time, history, and culture. Cultural identities come from somewhere, have histories. But, like everything which is historical, they undergo constant transformation.
>
> (1998, p. 225)

Furthermore, Hall elaborates that:

> far from being eternally fixed in some essentialised past, they are subject to the continuous 'play' of history, culture and power. Far from being grounded in a mere 'recovery' of the past, which is waiting to be found, and which, when found, will secure our sense of ourselves into eternity, identities are the names we give to the different ways we are positioned by, and position ourselves within, the narratives of the past.
>
> (1998, p. 225)

Identities to Hall, then, are both discursively constructed in the present-day and subject to the ebb and flow of power in the historical materialist sense.

Identity politics are often a merging of an identity and public performance. Woodward (1997) asserts that:

> identity politics involve claiming one's identity as a member of an oppressed or marginalized group as a political point of departure and thus identity becomes a major factor in political mobilization. Such politics involve celebration of a group's uniqueness as well as analysis of its particular oppression.
>
> (p. 24)

Kimberlé Crenshaw (1989, 1991) is often credited with naming intersectionality which allowed it to enter "as a named discourse within the academy" (Collins, 2011, p. 88). Of Crenshaw's work, Patricia Hill Collins claims that:

> A close reading of Kimberlé Crenshaw's 1991 article does two things: (1) it identifies several main ideas of intersectionality that reappear within subsequent intersectional knowledge projects; and (2) it provides a clearer view of the interrelationship of structural and symbolic boundaries in the development of intersectionality as a knowledge project, especially what persisted, what became muted, and what disappeared.
>
> (2011, pp. 92–93)

As referenced previously, Collins asserts that "the term intersectionality references the critical insight that race, class, gender, sexuality, ethnicity, nation, ability, and age operate not as unitary, mutually exclusive entities, but as reciprocally constructing phenomena that in turn shape complex social inequalities" (2015, p. 2). Indeed, as Sumi Cho, Kimberlé Crenshaw, and Leslie McCall (2013) have theorized, the work of doing intersectionality has three primary engagements: a theoretical and methodological paradigm, a framework for analyzing power relations, and political interventions using an intersectional lens. Studies using intersectionality – through specific theoretical and methodological engagements coupled with political interventions – seek to make clearer the complex social inequalities that exist within equally complex power relations and structures. Furthermore, in doing intersectional research, as Sylvia Walby warns, "the challenge is to include these inequalities in the center rather than the margins of social theory" (2007, p. 451).

Kathy Davis claims that "'intersectionality' addresses the most central theoretical and normative concern within feminist scholarship: namely, the acknowledgement of differences among women" (2008, p. 70). Elaborating further, and reifying Collins' theorizing, Davis asserts that:

> Intersectionality brings together two of the most important strands of contemporary feminist thought that have been, in different ways, concerned with the issue of difference. The first strand has been devoted to understanding the effects of race, class, and gender on women's identities, experiences, and struggles for empowerment. ... Gradually, however, the focus shifted to how race, class and gender interact in the social and material realities of women's lives to produce and transform relations of power.
>
> (2008, pp. 70–71)

Indeed, a fundamental tenet of intersectionality is that the social struggle is across relationships with different levels of power. For example, a person might be marked as the "other" in one context, but is part of the core in another context.

Directly addressing intersectionality without using the word, Hall reifies the necessity for the use of "and" when working with intersectional identities when he discussed those people who are both Black and British. Hall states:

> Blacks in the British diaspora must, at this historical moment, refuse the binary black or British. They must refuse it because the "or" remains the sight of constant contestation when the aim of the struggle must be, instead, to replace the "or" with the potentiality or the possibility of an "and". That is the logic of coupling rather than the logic of a binary opposition. You can be black and British, not only because that is a necessary position to take in the 1990s, but because even those two terms, joined now by the coupler "and" instead of opposed to one another, do not exhaust all of our identities. Only some of our identities are sometimes caught in that particular struggle. The essentializing moment is weak because it naturalizes and de-historicizes difference, mistaking what is historical and cultural for what is natural, biological, and genetic. The moment the signifier "black" is torn from its historical, cultural, and political embedding and lodged in a biologically constituted racial category, we valorize, by inversion, the very ground of the racism we are trying to deconstruct. In addition, as always happens when we naturalize historical categories (think about gender and sexuality), we fix that signifier outside of history, outside of change, outside of political intervention.
>
> (1996b, p. 475)

This "and" to which Hall refers adds complexity beyond the mere addition of two identities. Furthermore, in a call for work that is truly using intersectional analyses, Hall asserts that:

> The point is not simply that, since our racial differences do not constitute all of us, we are always different, negotiating different kinds of differences – of gender, of sexuality, of class. It is also that these antagonisms refuse to be neatly aligned; they are simply not reducible to one another; they refuse to coalesce around a single axis of differentiation. We are always in negotiation, not with a single set of oppositions that place us always in the same relation to others, but with a series of different positionalities. Each has for us its point of profound subjective identification. And that is the most difficult thing about this proliferation of the field of identities and antagonisms: they are often dislocating in relation to one another ... Dominant ethnicities are always underpinned by a particular sexual economy, a particular figured masculinity, a particular class identity. There is no guarantee, in reaching for an essentialized racial identity of which we think we can be certain, that it will always turn out to be mutually liberating and progressive on all the other dimensions.
>
> (1996b, p. 476)

Hall could not have made a clearer statement for the case of intersectionality unless he had actually used the term "intersectionality."

A constant struggle for theorists of identities and intersectionality is the balancing act between the avoidance of reifying the idea that identity groups are based on identification and opposition, but not fully drinking the poststructuralist Kool-Aid by obliterating identities altogether. Leslie McCall asserts that:

> Whereas the multicultural and identity-politics perspective tends to maintain group boundaries uncritically in order to revalue them and the deconstructive perspective seeks to eliminate them, the alternative perspective described here seeks to complicate and use them in a more critical way. Feminists of color have steered a middle course, consistently engaging in both theoretical and empirical studies of intersectionality using finer intersections of categories.
>
> (2005, p. 1780)

Though I disagree that the multicultural and identity politics perspective is uncritical, McCall's articulation of the path that theorists of intersectionality have to be vigilant in taking is clear. Indeed, "the point is not to deny the importance – both material and discursive – of categories but to focus on the process by which they are produced, experienced, reproduced, and resisted in everyday life" (2005, p. 1783). One way to do this is to use the categories of race and gender as "'anchor' points – though these points are not static" (Glenn, 2002, p. 14). Denying that the categories exist is only afforded to those who are not marked negatively by subjective categories; however, thinking that categories offer a firm foundation is also shortsighted. Using identity categories as "anchor points" seems an excellent place to begin theorizing about intersectionality. Indeed, Stuart Hall asserted something very similar when he said, "identities are ... points of temporary attachment to the subject positions which discursive practices construct for us" (Hall, 1996a, pp. 5–6). It would not be a stretch to make the claim that "points of temporary attachment" are the same as "anchor points."

The matrix of domination

Being attentive to the complexities of social structures is a focus of intersectionality, yet it is often ignored in many analyses that use intersectional approaches. Identities are produced and maintained through particular domains of power, and people are living their daily lives in response to these domains. The particular politics and power relations in place to regulate identities is best understood through Collins' domains of power, which is also known as the matrix of domination (2000). The matrix of domination shows how "the intersecting oppressions of intersectionality are organized" (Collins, 2000, p. 18). The four domains of power are: structural, cultural, disciplinary, and interpersonal (Collins, 2009, pp. 53–54):

- The structural domain: The institutional structures of a society. Institutional structures are deeply embedded and are very slow to change. The disciplinary domain: The legal structure of a society.
- The cultural domain: The structure of every-day, common-sense understandings in our society. This domain is the intermediary between the structural domain and the interpersonal domain. Through common discourse, one might understand that more Black people live in poverty than white people, and that this has to do with Black people when, in reality, it has far more to do with the structural domain.
- The interpersonal domain: This domain involves the interactions between individuals.

Each of these domains is able to exert power on individuals, locations and social milieus, in different ways and to differing degrees because they are contextually dependent.

Looking at racism specifically, "racism is simultaneously structured and resisted *within* each domain as well as *across* all four domains," asserts Collins (2009, p. 54). When we think of a domain of power, we think of the structural domain with its institutional structures and system of law. However, within the confines of today's color-blind racism, the structural domain is viewed as being completely fair to all people regardless of race, as is cultural and disciplinary domains. Collins warns us that

> it is vitally important to notice that in most people's minds, especially if they believe that a color-blind society is a reality, the first three domains – the structural, the cultural, and the disciplinary – often disappear. As a result, their understandings of race and racism get collapsed into the interpersonal domain.
>
> (2009, p. 54)

Thus, racism is seen as individuals being overtly or covertly prejudiced against people of color. Color-blind racism ignores any social or structural biases that exist in our society.

The world is made up of various relations of power, each contextual. Our own place as individuals is also contextual across each of the relations of power we experience. Though each relation of power is contextual on its own, each one is always interrelated to other relations of power. Also, the world has unjust social inequalities that are either disempowering or empowering, and these social inequalities are complex, both at the interpersonal and cultural level, but also at the disciplinary and structural level. The matrix of domination is the framework for doing intersectionality, where, by using it, I know that I have covered all of the bases where power lies.

As a framework, the matrix of domination is used to analyze how intersectionality operates within different contexts and across different power structures. Indeed, Collins further explains that:

When examining structural power relations, intersectionality functions better as a conceptual framework or heuristic device describing what kinds of things to consider than as one describing any actual patterns of social organization. The goal is not to prove intersectionality right or wrong, nor to gather empirical data to test the existence of intersectionality. Rather, intersectionality provides an interpretive framework for thinking through how intersections of race and class, or race and gender, or sexuality and class, for example, shape any group's experience across specific social contexts. The existence of multiple axes within intersectionality (race, class, gender, sexuality, nation, ethnicity, age) means neither that these factors are equally salient in all groups' experiences nor that they form uniform principles of social organization in defining groups.

(Collins, 1998, p. 208)

The matrix of domination is the empirical tool for the theoretical framework of intersectionality. The matrix of domination might seem too rigid with only four domains; however, these four domains encompass all the contexts in which there are power imbalances and domination.

In this way, it could be said, the matrix of domination is operating as a type of modernist project. It is grounded. Likewise, it could be said, intersectionality is a postmodernist project. It is concerned with theory and discourse. However, as has been shown, intersectionality can operate fluidly across the spectrum of modernist and postmodernist scholarship.

Race, class, gender, and sexuality underpin the origins of the sport of tennis. Tennis emerged as a recreational sport of choice among the leisure class in England and France around 1870. It was at this time that, according to historian Elizabeth Wilson, "a confident upper class and an expanding bourgeoisie with money and leisure to spare were refashioning social, cultural and educational life" (2014, p. 9). Of those playing tennis, tennis historian Robert Lake claims that, "these were upper-middle-class gentlemen playing outdoor versions of established aristocratic racket games on private lawns, among social equals and usually as part of grand social occasions," which provided for these men a "conspicuous, status-enhancing social function" (2014, p. 15). In the 1880s, however, those from the upper-class aristocracy left tennis for even "more exclusive pursuits like golf and polo" (Lake, 2014, p. 17), leaving the bourgeois elites in charge of the growing game of tennis. As Lake explains:

The cultural expressions of upper-class taste sought by the most aspirational upper-middle-class players had a lasting impression upon the sport. From its very beginnings, principally because of its noble heritage ... and also due to its earliest upper-class enthusiasts, lawn tennis attracted those seeking to improve their social positions. All the features that characterised the sport, including the general atmosphere and tone of its clubs and parties, its associated fashions and cultural accoutrements, its rules and etiquette and a sense of how lawn tennis should be played, reflected the general motivations of social mobility for the upper-middle classes.

(2014, p. 17)

The sport's whiteness and sex segregation mirrored the social stratification of the upper class. The people who had access to spacious lawns for tennis nets, or who could afford memberships at tennis clubs, were exclusively people in the upper class. Men wore white pants and long-sleeve shirts that were easy to move in while playing; however, women wore bulky multi-layered dresses that covered them from their wrists to their ankles while their corsets often dug into their ribs, constraining their athletic movements. Thus, tennis became a site for particular intersections of race, class, and sex. Within this milieu of whiteness, upper-classness and male-domination, as well as unquestioned heteronormativity, the issues that emerged for women involved equality and representation. To understand modern-day tennis, these historical constructs of tennis must be understood.

Feminist theories

Feminist theories have at their core the purpose of illuminating and understanding relations between women and men from within our patriarchal culture and, coupled with feminist ethics, provide a prescription for a remedy. This statement is not as easily understandable as it may seem on the surface. Some of the questions that have pulled feminist theories in many different directions include: Which women? Are all women included? Who decides who is included? Are all men the "enemy"? Are all patriarchal cultures the same? Can the remedy be utilized by everyone? What about children, the innocent bystanders to the relations between women and men? and many more questions. These questions, by the way, are primarily coming from women. The feminist sport scholar Susan Birrell asserts that:

> Feminist theory is a self-reflexive theoretical practice that changes because those who produce and use the insights the theories offer are constantly unsatisfied with their scope, their focus or their limitations. Thus some of the harshest critics of feminist theory are feminists themselves, that is, those who make "inside the paradigm" critiques.
>
> (Birrell, 2000, p. 62)

Thus, the most poignant critiques against feminist theories have come from women themselves.

Some professional tennis players, such as Andrea Petkovic (Family Circle Cup, 2014), outright claim to be feminist, but what does feminism mean in the Sustainers cohort? The Founders cohort was guided by the principles of second-wave feminism, specifically, liberal feminism. The era of the Joiners cohort was a calling out of the white, middle-class nature of second-wave feminism, which had been a loose set of various economic-based variances to feminism (i.e., liberal feminism, Marxist feminism, socialist feminism), with the incorporation of identity-based variances, most notably LGBTQ (lesbian, gay, bisexual, transgender, queer) politics. During the Sustainers cohort, feminism had to exist within neoliberal frameworks. There could be debate whether the feminism of this era is third-wave feminism, postfeminism, and/or neoliberal feminism, or are these three concepts different names for the same concept?

Second-wave feminism

Second-wave feminism is, at its most basic, a discussion between liberal feminism and radical feminism. As Birrell defines it:

> Liberal feminism is based on the humanist ontological position that men and women are more alike than different. Despite their inherent similarities, however, women and men come to live different lives, with different experiences, different opportunities and different expectations, because society erects barriers that restrict their equal participation in society.
> (Birrell, 2000, p. 64)

Consequently, proponents of liberal feminism propose eradicating the barriers in society that keep women and men from participating equally. Radical feminism, on the other hand, counters liberal feminism. According to Birrell, with liberal feminism:

> Men and women ... are essentially different. The patriarchal system men have established (and which continues to benefit all men, even those pro-feminist men who would like to see the system changed) has failed dramatically; what is needed is another vision of the world emanating from the insights of women. Radical change entails a fundamental societal transformation, not just equal access to the system that already exists. ... The way to accomplish this is not through legislation but through revolution. Another radical solution is for women to establish their own separate spaces and practices outside the purview of patriarchy.
> (Birrell, 2000, p. 64)

Debate between liberal feminists and radical feminists was in whether proposing legislation in the (male-dominated patriarchal) legal system, or complete revolution, was the answer.

Liberal feminism and radical feminism focused on sex, with women as the primary subject, often to the exclusion of other identity features that may cause oppression, such as race, class, gender, sexuality, religion, and nationality. Enter Marxist feminism into the second-wave feminism debates; however, Marxist feminism, as one might guess with Marxism, seemed to favor class over sex, or any other category. Feminists addressing this critique shifted Marxist feminism into socialist feminism, which offered a more equitable theoretical path to walk. According to Birrell, "socialist feminist theory privileges neither capitalism nor feminism but acknowledges class and gender [sic] as mutually supporting systems of oppression: capitalist patriarchy is the proper subject for analysis and social action" (2000, p. 66).

Ruptures to second-wave feminism

What has been described thus far has been the debates among predominantly white women. The first feminist attempts to include racially-marginalized women were to add "women of color" and stir, so to speak, the feminist theories already in place. Building upon the feminist theorizing laid out by the Combahee River Collective statement in 1977, written primarily by Barbara Smith, Demita Frazier and Beverly Smith, Cherríe Moraga's and Gloria Anzaldúa's edited volume, *This Bridge Called My Back: Writings By Radical Women of Color* (1981), Angela Davis in *Women, Race and Class* (1983), bell hooks with *Feminist Theory: From Margin to Center* (1984), Audre Lorde with *Sister Outsider* (1984), Gloria Anzaldúa in *Borderlands/La Frontera: The New Mestiza* (1987), Patricia Hill Collins with *Black Feminist Thought: Knowledge, Consciousness and the Politics of Empowerment* (1990), and others, the focal point for racially marginalized women needed to be these women themselves, with the theorizing building out from that center.[2]

Similar to the writing of racially-marginalized feminists inserting race into the discourse of feminism, lesbians inserted sexuality into the discourse. Lesbian feminism also ranged from lesbian inclusion in feminist theoretical debates to lesbian separatism, where lesbians, and, in these debates, preferably all women (Frye, 1978), should form communities in which there are no men, thus removing patriarchal structures from the equation. Lesbian feminism was catapulted into the limelight after Betty Friedan's expulsion of Rita Mae Brown and Ivy Bottini from the National Organization of Women, citing the increasing growth of the "lavender menace." Theorists of lesbian feminism include women who were also working within Black feminism, such as Audre Lorde, Gloria Anzaldúa, and Barbara Smith. Lesbian feminism was also guided by the writings of the political action group Radicalesbians beginning in 1970, the work of Rita Mae Brown with *Rubyfruit Jungle* (1973), Charlotte Bunch in *Lesbianism and the Women's Movement* (1975), Adrienne Rich with her essay "Compulsory heterosexuality and lesbian existence" (1980), and Sheila Jefferies and others as the Leeds Revolutionary Feminist Group with the essay, "Love your enemy?: The debate between heterosexual feminism and political lesbianism" (1981).

With the writing from these aforementioned scholars, there was no protection for second-wave feminism as it had stood, and the theorizing from these women and others have only made completely clear that, in order to see the entire visual field, one must stand next to the person who is farthest from the center. Black feminism has been best at a sustained argument in this regard.

Third-wave feminism vs. postfeminism

For a look at third-wave feminism and postfeminism, I will use Leslie Heywood and Angela McRobbie, respectively. I have put these two together, in conversation, because Heywood's descriptions of postfeminism are starkly opposed to McRobbie's descriptions of postfeminism.

In the first sentence of *Third Wave Agenda* (1997), Heywood, along with Jennifer Drake, claim that third-wave feminism is often labeled as postfeminism. Heywood and Shari Dworkin, in *Built to Win* (2003), claim that the objectification thesis brought into being by second-wave feminists fails to account for the complexity of today's female athletes. Heywood and Dworkin contend that many female athletes do not feel objectified by sexualized representations because they feel ownership over their bodies. They agree that female athletes have to rely on their looks rather than their skill in order to garner endorsements, but this they dismiss to the freedom of each athlete to choose for herself and that athlete's claim of ownership over her own body. This individualism of each person is the undoing of community.

Angela McRobbie, in her article "Post-feminism and Popular Culture" (2004), asserts that there never was a third-wave feminism; that we went directly from the very politically-charged second-wave feminism to postfeminism which, to her, is a dismantling of all of the gains made by second-wave feminists. McRobbie would assert that postfeminism is a claim to our current state, not a label that people can claim to be. Postfeminism, to Angela McRobbie, is the "active process by which feminist gains of the 1970s and 80s come to be undermined" (2004, p. 255). It's an undoing of second-wave feminism. What occurs with postfeminism is that feminism is seen as outdated, old, and not needed anymore. Indeed, feminism becomes a Gramscian "common sense."

McRobbie claims that postfeminism emerged from the joining of neoconservative values in regards to gender, sexuality, and private life, with liberalization in regards to choice and diversity (2004, pp. 255–256). She sees the dismantling beginning in 1990, when Judith Butler's feminist critique *Gender Trouble* was published. At this time, magazines for women and girls emerged. In these magazines, pseudo-feminist arguments were waged. The readers think that they understand the finer details of feminism, but they are really far from that. Indeed, with the money and the power that players in women's professional tennis have and are able to attain, it might be difficult for some to understand the need for feminism.

Angela McRobbie and Stéphanie Genz have views of postfeminism which seem like polar opposites. McRobbie, as has been shown, views postfeminism as a sort of anti-feminism or a non-feminism, where feminism is viewed as a spent force that is no longer needed (McRobbie, 2004). Genz, however, sees postfeminism as an attempt to rejoin femininity with feminism (2006). To her, second-wave radical feminists discredited femininity and, now, women want to be both feminine and politically engaged. This would be Genz's view of postfeminism; femininity merged with liberal feminism.

20 *Introduction*

Genz accuses second-wave feminists – and Betty Friedan explicitly – for focusing on professional, paid work as the route to autonomy. To Genz, this caused second-wave feminists from having a politics for minimum wage service-sector workers who can barely make ends meet. Instead, this focus on professional labor led to our modern-day consumerism, according to Genz. She goes on to critique second-wave feminism for recognizing that a culture could be resisted, but not seeing that the culture itself could change. Postfeminism, to Genz then, sees this changed culture and is able to be a type of feminism that can operate within it.

Postfeminism vs. neoliberal feminism

Catherine Rottenberg, in her article, "The Rise of Neoliberal Feminism" (2014), explains the pervasiveness of the seemingly unlikely linkage of feminism and our neoliberal context. She asks: "What does it mean, many longtime feminists are asking, that a movement once dedicated, however problematically, to women's liberation is now being framed in extremely individualistic terms, consequently ceasing to raise the spectre of social or collective justice?" (Rottenberg, 2014, p. 419). Neoliberal feminism, with its focus on individualism and rejection of social justice, is, thus, very similar to third-wave feminism and postfeminism. Similar to third-wave feminism, and in line with individual choice having primacy, there is no critique of neoliberalism by neoliberal feminists, as there had been of liberalism by liberal feminists. Rottenberg explains:

> Unlike classic liberal feminism whose raison d'être was to pose an immanent critique of liberalism, revealing the gendered exclusions within liberal democracy's proclamation of universal equality, particularly with respect to the law, institutional access, and the full incorporation of women into the public sphere, this new feminism seems perfectly in sync with the evolving neoliberal order. Neoliberal feminism, in other words, offers no critique – immanent or otherwise – of neoliberalism.
>
> (Rottenberg, 2014, p. 419)

Indeed, rather than neoliberalism creating a female subject in the Foucauldian sense. Neoliberalism, according to Rottenberg, has created the feminist subject.

It makes sense that neoliberalism creates new subjects; however, how can there be a merging of feminism and neoliberalism? Rottenberg explains how the feminist subject within neoliberalism exists:

> Individuated in the extreme, this subject is feminist in the sense that she is distinctly aware of current inequalities between men and women. This same subject is, however, simultaneously neoliberal, not only because she disavows the social, cultural and economic forces producing this inequality, but also because she accepts full responsibility for her own well-being and self-care, which is increasingly predicated on crafting a felicitous work–family

balance based on a cost-benefit calculus. The neoliberal feminist subject is thus mobilized to convert continued gender inequality from a structural problem into an individual affair.

(Rottenberg, 2014, p. 420)

This feminist subject understands inequality, but, rather than there being structures in place that keep those inequalities alive, the inequalities are viewed as individual disagreements or preferences.

Aligning with Angela McRobbie's version of postfeminism and the continual unraveling of feminism until it has no substance, Rottenberg asserts that the same is true of neoliberal feminism. She asserts:

> My claim, therefore, is that the contemporary convergence between neoliberalism and feminism involves the production of a new kind of feminism that is eviscerating classic mainstream liberal feminism. This neoliberal feminism, in turn, is helping to produce a particular kind of feminist subject. Using key liberal terms, such as equality, opportunity, and free choice, while displacing and replacing their content, this recuperated feminism forges a feminist subject who is not only individualized but entrepreneurial in the sense that she is oriented toward optimizing her resources through incessant calculation, personal initiative, and innovation. Indeed, creative individual solutions are presented as feminist and progressive, while calibrating a felicitous work–family balance becomes her main task. Inequality between men and women is thus paradoxically acknowledged only to be disavowed, and the question of social justice is recast in personal, individualized terms.
>
> (Rottenberg, 2014, pp. 421–422)

Thus, words and meanings that were political have become benign. This feminism is coupled with action, or with an eye on political and social change.

The white and heteronormative nature of neoliberal feminism is readily apparent as one would suspect with neoliberalism. Rottenberg describes this new neoliberal feminist subject:

> The production of neoliberal feminism makes cultural sense, since it becomes one more domain that neoliberal governmentality colonizes and remakes in its own image. ... No longer concerned with issues, such as the gendered wage gap, sexual harassment, rape or domestic violence, ambitious individual middle-class women themselves become both the problem and the solution in the neoliberal feminist age. And by tapping into what Sara Ahmed has termed the current "happiness industry" (Ahmed, 2010), neoliberal feminism attempts to ensure that the new feminist subject is and orients herself towards the goal of finding her own personal and felicitous work–family balance.
>
> (Rottenberg, 2014, p. 432)

This neoliberal feminist subject is clearly white, middle class, and heterosexual, since other women, feminists included, are still concerned with the wage gap, domestic violence, and equality.

If this is the current state of feminism, this neoliberal feminism, then it is clear how McRobbie could claim that we are in a state of postfeminism, where feminism no longer exists. Thus, are third-wave feminism, postfeminism, and neoliberal feminism the same thing but, seemingly, separated by terminology?

Redistribution and/or recognition

Further complicating this understanding of feminism is that of social stratification and the different power structures for each identity. Nancy Fraser (1997) argues that identity politics strive for either redistribution or recognition. For example, class as an identity marker seeks redistribution of wealth and goods. Identities based on sexuality seek recognition. Fraser asserts that race and gender seek both redistribution and recognition. Race and gender are what Fraser calls bivalent collectivities. That is, race and gender are differentiated in society through political and economic structures, as well as social and cultural structures. Nira Yuval-Davis (2011), however, claims that redistribution and recognition are operating on different social stratum. The two concepts cannot be equated as operating within similar levels of power.

Moving beyond the waves of feminism

Jayne Caudwell, in her article "Sport Feminism(s): Narratives of Linearity?", asserts that arguments for or against second- or third-wave feminisms are ineffective for our understanding of sport. She proposes a theory of "sporting feminism" that traverses the various so-called feminist waves. Caudwell asserts that with the use of waves to describe feminist theory, an entire generation of women is pitted against another generation of women in order to establish a linearity. Furthermore, Caudwell asserts that this emphasis on the wave metaphor overly simplifies theoretical expansion of feminist theory.

Caudwell claims that the wave metaphor was created by third-wave feminists. It created a binary between second-wave feminism and third-wave feminism. This binary diminishes the accomplishments of second-wave feminism in an effort to strengthen third-wave feminism. Furthermore, Caudwell counters Heywood's claim that third-wave feminists saw the "multiplicity of identity," as if second-wave feminists never did. Disregarding all of the scholarship of Black and Chicana feminists, among others, and focusing only upon the theoretical framework established by white second-wave feminists, Heywood's claim might be true.

Research methods and design

For this research on social activism in women's professional tennis, I used multiple qualitative methods. These methods included semi-structured questionnaires and interviews with members of the Original 9 and other former players, observation of participation at tournaments, which included getting to speak to current players through press conferences, and narrative analysis. These form the largest portion of the qualitative data collected for this research.

This study, too, was designed as a feminist study from the start. Sandra Harding asserts that feminist research must begin with the questions that women want answered. She explains:

> If one begins inquiry with what appears problematic from the perspective of women's experiences, one is led to design research *for* women. ... That is, the goal of this inquiry is to provide for women explanations of social phenomena that they want and need, rather than providing for welfare departments, manufacturers, advertisers, psychiatrists, the medical establishment, or the judicial system [or, I would add, other men] answers to questions that they have. The questions about women that men have wanted answered have all too often arisen from desires to pacify, control, exploit, or manipulate women. Traditional social research has been *for men*. In the best of feminist research, the purposes of research and analysis are not separable from the origins of research problems.
>
> (1987, p. 8; italics in original).

Thus, through speaking with the women who were, and are, activists within women's tennis, and conducting continual member checking with my informants, this study is, indeed, a feminist study of women's tennis that is *by* those in women's tennis.

To be sure, this study was *not* an ethnography. I did not immerse myself in women's tennis, following the tour from city to city, week to week, across the globe for a year or more, which would easily identify an ethnography.[3] Nor did I simply see what themes emerged from my experience in the field. I used interviews and questionnaires to gather data from former players specific to their involvement in social activism. And, in the field with current players, through the acquisition of media credentials, I observed the tournament environs as a member of the press, and I was able to interview – through one question, at the most, for each press conference – current players.

Interviews and questionnaires

According to Shulamit Reinharz, "for a woman to be understood in a social research project, it may be necessary for her to be interviewed by a woman" (1992, p. 23). This project used multiple techniques for gathering data from former players in women's professional tennis: semi-structured interviewing, survey research, and structured questions for clarification purposes. Reinharz explains the techniques as follows:

> Semistructured or unstructured interviewing ... is a qualitative data-gathering technique. It differs from ethnography in not including long periods of researcher participation in the life of the interviewee and differs from survey research or structured interviewing by including free interaction between the researcher and interviewee. Survey research typically excludes, and interview research typically includes, opportunities for clarification and discussion. Open-ended interview research explores people's views of reality and allows the researcher to generate theory.
>
> (1992, p. 18)

Specific components of the interview process I conducted with members of the Original 9 were individualistic semi-structured interviews. I asked questions specific to social activism, with its catalysts and risks, in women's tennis, but tried to make the questions as open as possible to allow each person the opportunity to provide their own story.

For the most part, I used questionnaires to gather qualitative data from former players. The questionnaire worked really well, because it began the conversation and I could email follow-up questions to specific responses if needed. In this way, I counter Reinharz's assertion that "survey research typically excludes ... opportunities for clarification and discussion" (1992, p. 18). All of my informants knew beforehand that I might follow up for clarification on responses they provided. Email allows for this to easily occur.

In addition, for one former player, who said that my questionnaire did not work for how she would like to engage with my project, we had a Skype interview.[4] For this informant, I used the questionnaire as a guideline during our conversation. Also, I conducted one interview via the telephone. I dislike the telephone for interviews because it is very difficult, besides being illegal in the US (which is partially why it is so difficult), to record the conversations.

Of the Original 9, I was able to gather data from five of the nine women: Rosie Casals, Judy Dalton, Julie Heldman, Kristy Pigeon, and Billie Jean King.[5] Other former players that I interviewed were Pam Shriver and Rennae Stubbs, and I secured a one-on-one interview with Svetlana Kuznetsova, a current player, when she played the 2014 Citi Open in Washington, D.C.

Questions asked

Because the members of the Original 9 live all over the United States, and one lives in Australia, it was not financially feasible to interview each of the women in person. In crafting a questionnaire for the Original 9, I wanted the questions to be open-ended, but specific to the topic of the social activism in which they were involved. The 11 questions were:

- What was the impetus for the Original 9 forming?
- What compelled you to join the Original 9? Describe your feelings when you decided to join the Original 9.

- What were you thinking the gains of the Original 9 would be? Were these gains realized? Were there other gains you hadn't anticipated?
- What were you thinking the risks of joining the Original 9 would be? Were these risks realized? Were there other risks you hadn't anticipated?
- How were decisions made among those in the Original 9?
- What people, politics or ideas influenced your actions with the Original 9, either personally or collectively, or both?
- What was it like to play the Virginia Slims of Houston in 1970? Describe your emotions, the atmosphere, the tournament, and the other players.
- Describe the meeting at the Gloucester Hotel in 1973 in which the WTA was formed? What were your goals for the WTA in 1973? How did you think forming the WTA would help women's tennis?
- What about the culture of women's tennis made it a site for trailblazers in the early 1970s?
- Is women's tennis still a site for trailblazers? Why or why not?
- What else would you like me to know about the Original 9, your participation in the Original 9 and women's tennis more generally, and/or the current state of women's tennis?

From responses to these questions, I could ask for clarification or elaboration on specific responses. In this way, the questionnaire opened up dialogue about specific aspects of the activism of the Original 9.

When I interviewed Pam Shriver, an interview which was conducted over the phone while we both were at the 2015 Family Circle Cup, my questions were more specific to the Joiners cohort, of which she belonged.

In interviewing Rennae Stubbs, who is Australian and a lesbian, I asked her questions specific to Margaret Court's hostility towards LGBTQ people in Australia. Unfortunately, I did not ask her at the time about the Sustainers cohort to which she belonged. The questions I asked her were:

- What were or have been the influence of Kerry Melville and Judy Tegart on Australian tennis, especially women's tennis?
- What lineage or remnants of the Original 9 are still apparent in women's tennis today?
- In regards to Rainbow Flags Over Margaret Court Arena at the Australian Open 2012, I loved that you acted by posting on their Facebook page how activists could behave that would get their point across and not disrupt play. That was excellent.
    - What was the atmosphere like on Margaret Court Arena in 2012?
    - Could you tell that there was a social "movement" happening in the stands?
    - What do you think the risks were for Laura Robson, wearing the rainbow headband?
    - Martina Navratilova also wore a shirt with rainbow piping, but I doubt that there were any risks for her. Or, were there?

26 *Introduction*

- Tennis Australia has publicly stated they feel that Margaret Court's stance against gay marriage is discriminatory. Do you get a sense that Australia is basically taking Billie Jean King's stance that, yes, Court was one of the best players ever and that should be respected, but that her views on gay people are not respectable? So, there is a separation of the two people – Margaret the player and Margaret the minister?

Observation of participation

Observation of participation is a method that I used during my data collection. Participant observation was not. From the start, I knew that I could not play tennis in the tournaments at which I was observing. I could, however, observe players during their matches, walking around the grounds interacting (or not) with fans, and in the players' areas. In this way, I observed the participation of the players, and I was able to speak with players through press conferences at tournaments.

Feminist content analysis

Until recently, it was relatively common for tennis players to write autobiographies and historical accounts while playing on the circuit or, shortly thereafter, in early retirement. I used these autobiographies as cultural artifacts produced by women who played professional tennis (see, for example, Reinharz, 1992). Of note are the autobiographies of Evonne Goolagong (1975, 1993), Billie Jean King (1974, 1982), Chris Evert (Lloyd, 1982, 1986), Martina Navratilova (1985), Pam Shriver (1987), Margaret Court (1976, 1993), Tracy Austin (1992), Monica Seles (1996), Zina Garrison (2001) and Serena Williams (2009). Historical accounts of women's tennis written by tennis players include Virginia Wade's history of women at Wimbledon (1984) and Billie Jean King's history of women's tennis (1988). Included, too, are the books by tennis fashion designer Ted Tinling (1963, 1977, 1979, 1983). Though these books were written for mass audiences, these primary sources figured prominently in my study.

Collection of data and analysis

In the field, I used a professional quality Sony ICD-SX712 digital flash voice recorder for recording press conferences, a Moleskine notebook for old-fashioned pen and paper notes while in the field, and a Sony 5N digital camera with 18–55 mm and 55–210 mm lenses for creating a visual archive. Once home, I used NVivo for Mac on my laptop to organize voice recordings and documents. This software, arguably the leading software for analyzing qualitative data, let me organize all of the interview data from formal interviews and press conferences that I had collected.

Given that I had interview data from only seven people in total – five of the Original 9 (Rosie Casals, Judy Dalton, Julie Heldman, Kristy Pigeon, and Billie

Jean King) along with Pam Shriver and Rennae Stubbs – and smaller sets of questions and answers from current players, I did not code the data in the conventional way. Questions and answers were specific to social activism and, given that there were so few, I did not need to be selective in using them, or creating themes that spanned many different interviews.

Women's tennis: A review of the literature

The literature on women's tennis varies from peer-reviewed articles to books, from autobiographies to theoretical pieces, and from magazine articles to Facebook pages. This review will be limited to articles and books written in the academic arena in an effort to contain the sheer amount of information available. This study is on the culture of women's professional tennis, which began in 1968 with the "open era" of tennis, gained traction when the Original 9 officially joined together in 1970, and was made indisputable with the creation of the WTA in 1973.

Nancy Spencer, the leading sociologist of tennis, has written extensively on diverse issues within women's tennis. Beginning with her doctoral dissertation on Chris Evert and celebrity femininity in women's tennis (1996), Spencer has, most notably, analyzed women's tennis as a subculture (1997), the placement of the Battle of the Sexes within the feminist movement (2000), the rivalry between Chris Evert and Martina Navratilova with the positioning of Evert as "America's sweetheart" and Navratilova as the "other" (2003), and the racism that surrounds the Williams sisters (2001, 2004).

Apart from Spencer, there have been a few other academic writers who have investigated women's tennis. Pamela Forman and Darcy Plymire documented the media coverage of Amélie Mauresmo before and after she came out as a lesbian (2005). Toby Miller documented the media response to Mauresmo as well in his book, *Sportsex* (2001). My own article extending Judith Butler's heterosexual matrix analyzes the issues that Mauresmo faced when she came out, and relies heavily on the newspaper documentation of the previous two works (2014). Jaime Schultz has documented Serena Williams' clothing (2005) and the impact of Billie Jean King (2011). Delia Douglas has worked to uncover the racism surrounding the Williams sisters (2002, 2005, 2012). Susan Ware has produced an account positioning Billie Jean King as the catalyst for the recent boon in women's sports (2011). Lastly, Susan Birrell and C L Cole researched the impact of Renée Richards in women's tennis (1990), and Birrell and Mary McDonald analyzed the impact of King's public outing by her former lover Marilyn Barnett (2012). These academically rigorous accounts of women's tennis will be foundations that this study rests upon.

There are many journalistic accounts of women's tennis. Full-length biographies and historical accounts written by journalists include Grace Lichtenstein's very early volume on women's tennis (1974), Karen Stabiner's account of top-ranked juniors trying to make it on the women's world tour (1986), John Feinstein's *Hard Courts*, which was a study of both men's and women's tennis

(1991), Michael Mewshaw's *Ladies of the Court* (1993), Jon Wertheim's *Venus Envy* (2001), Selena Roberts' analysis of the "Battle of the Sexes" tennis match between Billie Jean King and Bobby Riggs (2005), and Johnette Howard's detailed book on the Chris Evert and Martina Navratilova rivalry (2006). These books, though competitive as national best-sellers, are not necessarily academically rigorous sources.

In sport, social activism has been significant, yet actions have been few and far between. There are the raised fists of Tommie Smith and John Carlos, along with the quiet strength of Peter Norman, at the 1968 Olympics. There was also Muhammad Ali who, because of his religious beliefs, was a conscientious objector of the Vietnam War through his refusal to being drafted in 1967. Ali, at the time of his arrest for draft evasion, was the world heavyweight champion. Also, of note, is Bill Russell of the Boston Celtics who was an outspoken supporter of the American Civil Rights Act during his career. Russell is one of the best NBA players of all time and was on the best team of his era during his activism. In baseball, too, there was, of course, Jackie Robinson, but also Curt Flood, the self-described "well paid slave," who fought MLB's reserve clause which bound a player to his team, thereby ensuring "free agency" which MLB players now enjoy. These examples, however, all fueled the strength of the Black Power movement. Until 1970, riding the wave of the Women's Movement, however, there had not been consistent activism by women in sports. The actions of the aforementioned activist athletes, though, no doubt influenced the Original 9.

Significance of the research

This study is important, because professional tennis is the highest-profile sport in the world for women, yet it is a microcosm of what is going on in society at large. Many facets of women's tennis have been under the gaze of academics, including the culture in general, race, rivalries, biographies, etc. This book, however, will be highlighting two features specifically: 1) the generational cohorts of social activism in women's tennis; and, 2) the intersectional power relations within women's tennis.

Nancy Whittier notes in analyzing scholarship on social movements: "empirical work on differences between cohorts is considerably scantier than that of enduring characteristics of one cohort" (1997, p. 763). This research not only places the Original 9 and many events of women's tennis since then as a social movement, but there is also an analysis of the different cohorts of this social movement. This will add significantly to the discourse of scholarship in the field of social movements.

Women's professional tennis is a place where intersectional power relations are hidden in plain sight, because the power relations are naturalized. These hidden power relations come to the fore when there is social activism against the dominant power. This research uncovers features of how specific identities exist within complex power structures. This study should add to the discourse on intersectionality more broadly, while specific sections of this book will be in dialogue with scholars of women, gender, sexuality, and race.

An important feature of credible research, and a way to be respectful to informants, is member checking. My study had various modes of member checking built into it. First, Rosie Casals and Judy Dalton read sections and chapters as they were completed, and offered insights and critiques. They did this, not as a means for oversight, but because of interest in my work; however, their comments and feedback operated as a member-checking device. Second, during interviews, I was able to lay out the structure of this book – especially the historical framework of social movements – which offered space for those I was speaking to, to either disagree or expand on the concept. This type of member checking was done with Pam Shriver, Venus Williams, Serena Williams, Rosie Casals, and Judy Dalton.

Chapter outlines

The framework of the Trailblazers, Founders, Joiners, Sustainers – the last three formulated by Whittier (1995, 1997) – and Throwbacks cohorts, easily lends itself to the framework of this study on social activism within women's professional tennis. Again, to restate the research question for this study: Within the periodic evolution of social activism in women's tennis, what were the issues, expressions, risks and effects of its various generational iterations? Each chapter offers an analysis of the specific social activism that occurred within that particular cohort of the social movement.

Chapter 1 – The Trailblazers: Setting the stage for social activism in women's tennis

In women's professional tennis, the Trailblazers set the stage for the formidable social activism that occurred, beginning in 1968. The notable women who advocated for women's equality in tennis were Suzanne Lenglen, Althea Gibson, and Ann Haydon Jones. These women are each from different eras of tennis, Lenglen from the 1920s, Gibson, the 1950s, and Haydon Jones, the 1960s. Because the actions of these players were not joined by a collective effort and they remained solo actors, their efforts could be easily dismissed. However, they nonetheless paved the way for the collective social activism that would take place, beginning in 1970.

Chapter 2 – The Founders: The Original 9, "women's lob" feminism, and the social movement that launched women's professional tennis, 1968–1975

In women's professional tennis, the Founders cohort is the social movement begun by the Original 9 in 1970 to advocate for prize money equal to what was offered in men's tennis. I have demarcated the Founders cohort as occurring between 1968, when tournaments became "open" and thus offered prize money, and 1975, with Billie Jean King's last Grand Slam singles title win. The Founders cohort had waned somewhat, however, after the Battle of the Sexes tennis match between Billie Jean King and Bobby Riggs in 1973. At this point, it was clear that women's tennis had arrived as a big-time sporting event and could garner the attention of a sporting spectacle.

Chapter 3 – The Joiners cohort: The Evert-Navratilova era, 1974–1990

The Joiners cohort followed the Founders cohort. This era, most easily identified as the Evert-Navratilova era, has been marked for this study as beginning in 1974, with Chris Evert's first Grand Slam singles title, and ending in 1990, with Martina Navratilova's last Grand Slam singles title win. Those players in the Joiners cohort were greatly influenced by those in the Founders cohort; however, the economics and popularity of tennis was changing as well. The Joiners cohort ushered in an increase in mass-marketing, individual player endorsements, and athletes as celebrities. Despite the massive growth of women's tennis during this time period, there were setbacks; issues emerged that caused a shift in the social movement of women's tennis. Most notably, these include Martina Navratilova's defection from Czechoslovakia in 1975, Renée Richards successfully suing the United States Tennis Association (USTA) to be allowed to play in the US Open as a woman in 1977, despite having been born male, and the public outing as lesbians of Billie Jean King and Martina Navratilova in 1981.

This cohort is the one to which I belonged. My playing career ran from 1988–1992, which places me at the cusp of the Joiners cohort and the Sustainers cohort; however, having Rosie Casals, a member of the Founders cohort, as my coach, kept me firmly placed in the Joiners cohort.

Chapter 4 – The Sustainers cohort: The corporatization of women's tennis, 1987–present

Following the Joiners cohort was the Sustainers cohort. The Sustainers cohort, existing from 1987, with Steffi Graf's first Grand Slam singles title, until the present, is greatly influenced by the further corporatization of women's tennis, along with a distancing from the pioneering history of early women's professional tennis history. Seemingly, this is because the gains the Founders cohort pursued are assumed to have been attained.

The notable events that took place for the Sustainers cohort are Steffi Graf's disavowal of women's tennis history and activism, the stabbing of Monica Seles in 1993, the restructuring of the WTA in 1997–1998, the emergence of the WTA's anti-grunting policies and the "strong is beautiful" advertising campaign, and the color-blind racism that Serena Williams experienced.

Chapter 5 – The Throwbacks cohort: Individuals fighting for broader social justice issues, 1999–present

Building upon the historical framework created by Whittier (1995, 1997), this study identifies the emergence of a Throwbacks cohort, named by Pam Shriver during an interview (2015). This cohort is notable for an increased focus on social justice issues while also navigating the landscape as a member of the Sustainers cohort. It is possible that these players are rogue individuals, and this is not an emerging Throwbacks cohort. When I asked Venus Williams, after briefly explaining the generational cohorts of social activism in women's tennis, if a Throwbacks cohort that was focused on social justice was emerging, she simply said: "High hopes" (V. Williams, press conference interview, August, 2015).

The Throwbacks cohort is distinct for Amélie Mauresmo's unapologetic coming out as a lesbian in 1999, Venus Williams' fight for equal prize money at Wimbledon from 2005–2007, the fan-based social movement of Rainbow Flags Over Margaret Court Arena in 2012, and the emergence of former players from the women's tennis tour coaching men.

Notes

1 In their paper, "Generations, Cohorts, and Social Change," Duane F. Alwin and Ryan J. McCammon (2003) argue emphatically against conflating the term "generation" with the term "cohort." To them, a generation, as referencing kinship and biological replacement within families, shows a flow of the entry of newcomers (newborn children) and the death of elders, and this flow has overlap among all of the people involved (2003, pp. 25–27). A cohort, on the other hand, as Alwin and McCammon have claimed, is the time period to which one was born. Thus, as the argument goes, everyone born at a specific time will be a cohort, responding similarly to various effects (2003, pp. 27–28). Nancy Whittier, along with Michael Messner, Max Greenberg, and Tal Peretz, are using generation and cohort interchangeably. For clarification, I am writing of "generational cohorts" as I, too, see the two terms as interchangeable within the social movement literature. In women's tennis, the players are not related biologically (apart from the three sets of sisters – the Williams sisters, the Rodionovas, and the Chans), yet there is a flow of newcomers and an exiting of elders rather than a distinct ending of one cohort and a beginning of another.
2 Of note is an absence of American Indian feminism. In 1997, I asked Angela Davis, given that there was no American Indian feminism, if I could lean on Black feminism until it emerged. She said yes, and I am still waiting, still leaning on Black feminism.
3 This would have been ideal, of course, but I did not have $100,000 to spend on this study.
4 I felt great as a researcher that she was comfortable enough with me to tell me that my questions didn't work for her. It took a lot of work to build up the rapport that I have with all of the players, past and present. We ended up having a long chat, almost a whole hour, via Skype.
5 Data from Billie Jean King came in the most unconventional way. King published an article, "The Legacy of the Original 9," on *The Players' Tribune* website, a site where athletes post their own writing that speaks to the questions I posed to her, on August, 26, 2015. Rosie Casals assured me that this article was King's response to the questionnaire I had given her.

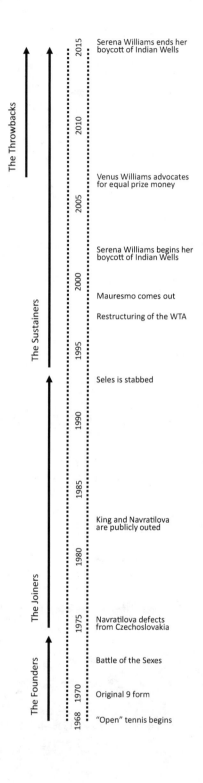

1 The Trailblazers

Setting the stage for social activism in women's tennis

In women's tennis, the Trailblazers set the stage for the formidable social activism that occurred, beginning in 1970. Sociologist Nancy Whittier describes Trailblazers, to whom she refers as initiators, as having "developed and made visible a critique of the status quo, formed initial organizations and networks, and articulated the issues that initially mobilized feminists into action" (1995, p. 59). The notable women who advocated for women's equality early in tennis were Suzanne Lenglen, Althea Gibson, and Ann Haydon Jones. These women are each from different eras of tennis, Lenglen from the 1920s, Gibson, the 1950s, and Haydon Jones, the 1960s. Because the actions of these players were not joined by a collective, sustained effort and these women remained solo actors, their efforts were easily dismissed by the establishment. However, they nonetheless paved the way for the collective social activism that would take place, beginning in 1970.

Suzanne Lenglen, the first celebrity of women's tennis

Suzanne Lenglen was born in 1899 in Paris, France, but she spent most of her youth and early adulthood in Nice, at her family's home conveniently located across the street from the Nice Lawn Tennis Club (Little, 1988, p. 2). In 1914, at the age of 14, Lenglen had been a French Championships finalist. However, her career was put on hold until 1919, due to the outbreak of World War I.

Between 1919–1926, Lenglen won six Wimbledon titles, two French Championships, and a gold medal at the Olympics held in Antwerp, Belgium, in 1920. Lenglen shot to fame and celebrity status at Wimbledon in 1919 for two reasons. First, she defeated Dorothea Chambers, who was a seven-time Wimbledon champion, solidifying her reputation in tennis.[1] Second, Lenglen created a stir which forever changed tennis fashion and established Lenglen's celebrity status. During the 1919 Wimbledon championships, Lenglen played in a dress designed by the famous Parisian couturier Jean Patou. According to Ted Tinling, the famous British tennis couturier, Lenglen "appeared in a flimsy, one-piece, cotton 'frock' which was calf-length, with short sleeves, and worn without petticoats" (Tinling, 1977, p. 8). Other players were still playing while completely covered in clothing from their neck to their wrists and ankles. It is difficult to know which caused more of a shock to the tennis world and Wimbledon high society: Lenglen's risqué tennis attire, or her sipping of brandy between sets.

Though no woman at Wimbledon had previously shown her ankles or arms, the dress itself allowed for Lenglen's physicality and athleticism to be less constrained than in traditional tennis fashion. Tinling noted that Lenglen "used to say that skill must come first and clothes must free the body. So she got rid of all the petticoats, stiff with starch as they were then" (Matheson, 1975). The next year, 1920, Lenglen added to her fashion-forward sense when she

> returned to England with the new "bobbed" hairstyle; to keep her hair attractively in place, she conceived what was soon to become the famous "Lenglen bandeau," two yards of brightly colored silk chiffon, tightly swathed around her head. Within weeks the Lenglen bandeau was copied by a million women, and for the next six years there was not a tennis girl who did not attempt some imitation of the Lenglen look.
>
> (Tinling, 1979, p. 21)

There is no documentation of the relationship between Patou and Lenglen beyond the accounts that he designed her tennis dresses. He was, however, known for his sports clothing for women. Charles Creed, of the Parisian couture house which specialized in English tailoring, noted that Patou had a "wonderful flair for publicity" (Evans, 2008, p. 256), and Lenglen's status in tennis and in society certainly would have given Patou considerable publicity.

It was through Lenglen that Ted Tinling's own career in women's tennis was born. Tennis fashion, though, was probably the unifying force between Tinling and Lenglen. Lenglen "was the ultimate 'diva' of sport, and she contrived to bring a taste of highly sophisticated theater to a world previously centered only on a leisurely pastime" (Tinling, 1979, p. 14), and this theater was often created through fashion. Of Lenglen, Tinling noted that she "taught me that tennis was show-biz and clothes had to be dramatic, too" (Matheson, 1975). But he also learned the importance of comfort for the players.

As early as 1926, women had shown discontentment with the pay structure of tennis. Suzanne Lenglen was an eight-time Grand Slam champion,[2] the namesake of the *Coupe de Lenglen* given to the women's champion of the French Open, and the world's first female tennis celebrity. She was also a very early advocate for tennis becoming professional. In 1926, Lenglen stated that:

> In the twelve years I have been champion I have earned literally millions of francs for tennis and have paid thousands of francs in entrance fees to be allowed to do so. ... Where did all this money go? ... Why shouldn't the players get something out of it? It meant years of practice and a life's work for most of us. ... The owners of these clubs at which I so often played were mostly shrewd businessmen and they saw to it that these tournaments netted them a handsome profit. ... Under these absurd and antiquated amateur rulings only a wealthy person can compete. ... Is that fair? Does it advance

the sport? Does it make tennis more popular or does it tend to suppress and hinder an enormous amount of tennis talent ... whose names are not in the social register?

(Little, 1988, p. 83)

Had it not been stated beforehand that these words were spoken by Lenglen in 1926, one might have suspected that Billie Jean King or one of the other well-known activists of women's tennis had made these remarks in 1970, 44 years later. The same words would reflect the growing unrest in women's tennis that finally came to a head in 1970. What Lenglen's words do reflect is the extent of the issue of women making a fair livelihood in women's tennis.

Lenglen turned professional in the fall of 1926, a decision that would keep her banned from subsequent Grand Slam events. She signed to tour the US and Canada for four months in late 1926 and early 1927. For this work, she was paid the huge sum of $50,000 (over $700,000 in current dollars) in addition to a share of the profits (Little, 1988, p. 94). Though Lenglen gained a hefty sum for this tour, she likely would have won many more Grand Slam events had she been allowed to compete in them. When tennis became "open" in 1968, amateurs and professionals competed together for the first time. From 1968, a player could have professional contracts – clothing, rackets, exhibition matches, etc. – and receive prize money from the tournament. Amateur players, usually college players or players still playing in junior events, simply refuse the prize money.

Althea Gibson, breaking down racial barriers in women's tennis

Althea Gibson was born in South Carolina in 1927, but she and her family moved to Harlem, New York, in 1930. In 1941, she won the New York State Championships, the first tournament that she entered. In 1944 and 1945, Gibson won the junior's division of the American Tennis Association's (ATA) national championship. The ATA was the alternative Black tennis association to the white-dominated United States Lawn Tennis Association (USLTA). The following year, 1946, she was a finalist in the women's division of the ATA national championships. Beginning in 1947, Gibson won ten straight women's national championships. Gibson gained the attention of Walter Johnson[3] and Hubert Eaton, Black physicians based in Lynchburg, Virginia, and Wilmington, North Carolina, respectively. Under the guidance of Drs. Johnson and Eaton, Gibson was educated, trained in nutrition and proper hygiene habits, and manners, alongside tennis training. These values helped her more easily transition into the upper class and white world of women's tennis once it was desegregated.

In 1956, a British journalist wrote,

> To pretend that Miss Gibson is just another player is to bilk the truth. She is the first colored player ever to invade a game which is riddled with

snobbery, even if your skin is the same color as the majority of the other players in it.

(Gibson, 1958, pp. 106–107)

In the context of tennis in the United States, racial segregation at tournaments was the standard until Gibson played the US National Championships (now the US Open) in 1950. To understand the blocking of Gibson, a Black woman and long-time champion of the ATA, from the US National Championships until 1950, as racism on the part of the USLTA is to miss half the story. The USLTA had anti-discrimination policies on the books. To qualify to play at the US Open National Championships required gaining ranking points through a series of smaller tournaments; however, most of those smaller tournaments were held at segregated country clubs across the US Though Gibson could qualify to play the tournaments, she was not allowed to enter the grounds of the country clubs because of their racial segregation policies, which made these tournaments available only to white players.

In 1950, under mounting pressure, the USLTA granted Gibson a wildcard to play the US National Championships, thereby bypassing the requirement for ranking points from these sanctioned tournaments. Alice Marble, widely regarded at the time as the greatest player that the US had ever produced, having won five Grand Slam singles titles between 1936–1940, publicly appealed for Gibson to be allowed to play the US National Championships in the July 1950 issue of *American Lawn Tennis* magazine. She wrote:

> If tennis is a game for ladies and gentlemen, it's also time we acted a little more like gentlepeople and less like sanctimonious hypocrites. If there is anything left in the name of sportsmanship, it's more than time to display what it means to us. If Althea Gibson represents a challenge to the present crop of women players, it's only fair that they should meet that challenge on the courts, where tennis is played. ... If she is refused a chance to succeed or to fail, then there is an uneradicable mark against a game to which I have devoted most of my life, and I would be bitterly ashamed.
>
> (Gibson, 1958, p. 60)

With intense lobbying by the ATA, coupled with the letter written by Alice Marble, in mid-August of 1950, Gibson learned that she had been granted a wildcard to enter the US National Championships.

Taking a step back, in order to counter the racial segregation of USLTA-sanctioned tournaments, the ATA was formed in 1916 and became the governing body for sanctioning tournaments that were often held at Black universities and other spaces that were open to Black players. Of particular note, the Peters sisters, Roumania and Margaret, dominated the ATA circuit in singles and doubles from the 1930s through the early 1950s, and Althea Gibson was dominant in the ATA circuit during the late 1940s and 1950s, winning ten straight women's national titles beginning in 1947. Between 1956 and 1958,

Gibson won five Grand Slam tournaments: the French Championships, which is now the French Open, two US Championships, and two Wimbledon titles.

The interlocking social institutions of tennis allowed country clubs to continue to hold USTA-sanctioned tournaments, despite the USTA having established anti-discrimination policies. Being sanctioned means that the tournament counts towards ranking points. At any time, the USTA could have denied sanctioning the tournaments at segregated country clubs; however, they did not. Thus, even though the USTA had anti-discrimination policies, these apparently did not extend beyond the corporate offices. By analyzing these interlocking institutions, we can see the complexity and contextualization that intersectionality offers.

In 1968, the Grand Slam tennis tournaments, which had previously only allowed amateur players to enter, became open to both amateurs and professionals. Prior to the open era, players were paid under the table to compete in tournaments. This system was not equitable, but based on the perceived marketability of the players. Thus, we can assume that white male players were paid more under the table than Black male players. Likewise, white female players were paid much less under the table than white male players, and Black female players were likely not paid at all. For example, Althea Gibson, who had won five Grand Slam titles along with being named Female Athlete of the Year by the Associated Press in 1957 and 1958, often struggled financially to continue her tennis career, which ended abruptly in 1958 due to financial hardship.

Althea Gibson broke the color barrier, desegregating tennis at the highest level, similar to Jackie Robinson's entry into Major League Baseball in 1947. Gibson's efforts paved the way for Arthur Ashe and subsequent Black tennis players, most notably the Williams sisters. Of her Wimbledon victory in 1956, Gibson wrote:

> Shaking hands with the Queen of England was a long way from being forced to sit in the colored section of the bus going into downtown Wilmington, North Carolina. Dancing with the Duke of Devonshire was a long way from not being allowed to bowl in Jefferson City, Missouri, because the white customers complained about it.
>
> (Gibson, 1958, p. 127)

She had indeed entered a completely different world and ensured that other Black players who followed her could, too.

Ann Haydon Jones, the feminist matriarch of women's professional tennis in the "open" era

Ann Jones was born in 1938 in Birmingham, England. She won the British girls championships in 1954 and 1955, and the Wimbledon girls title in 1956. She went on to win three Grand Slam singles titles: the French Open in 1961 and

1966, and Wimbledon in 1969. Jones was also a finalist at the US Open in both 1961 and 1967.

The world's first open tennis event was the British Hard Court Championships, held in Bournemouth, England, April 22–27, 1968. Ann Jones (née Haydon) boycotted the Lawn Tennis Association (LTA) event due to the unequal prize money distribution. The men's singles winner at the tournament, Ken Rosewall, received £1,000 and the women's singles winner, Virginia Wade, would have received £300. However, she was still an amateur, so she was obligated to refuse all of the prize money except expenses.

Jones had won the French Championships in 1961 and 1966, and would go on to win Wimbledon in 1969, and she leveraged the power that she had earned through playing tennis against the LTA. Since the British Hard Court Championships was the first open tennis event, Jones' actions were the first protest against unequal prize money distribution in professional tennis. Linda Timms, in an early article on prize money disparity, wrote:

> The leader of the movement, and the most militant of all, is Ann Jones, four time Hard Court Champion. She promptly declared that she was "seriously considering withholding her entry for Bournemouth as a protest" and that she was confident of support from Christine Truman, Virginia Wade and Angela Barrett – these four between them having won the singles titles there for ten out of the last thirteen years.
>
> (Timms, 1968, p. 34)

Indeed, Truman, Wade, and Barrett did not join Jones in her boycott of the Bournemouth tournament, thus thwarting any possibility for powerful social activism. According to Timms, Jones continued by saying:

> "I feel the protest must be made now," Mrs. Jones said. "In this country, once a precedent is set it immediately becomes a tradition. We are not asking for equal prize money, but it should be at least half of the men's amount, not a third as they are offering now. ... This protest is not a gesture, it is a firm threat. Unless some adjustment is made to the proportion of the prize money before the entries close in April, I will not play. The whole of the men's game is expanding, and the women must not be left behind."
>
> (Timms, 1968, p. 34)

It's shocking that a request for a third of the men's prize money was met with silence. Jones had the vision of what was to come for women in professional tennis, but no other players joined her in her boycott. Thus, a social movement would have to wait.

Ann Jones was the number one seed for the 1969 US Open; however, she withdrew before the tournament began and did not play singles at another subsequent Grand Slam tournament. She reduced her playing schedule in 1970, primarily only playing in England, because she wanted to start a family. In 1971, at the age of 33, because she was pregnant with her first child, Jones officially retired. Though not able to join the Original 9, which she would likely have done, she was certainly a catalyst for the Original 9 nonetheless.

The unequal prize money distribution that Ann Jones illuminated in Bournemouth, England, was replicated in all of the subsequent tournaments of 1968 and 1969. The men's and women's winners of Wimbledon in 1968, Rod Laver and Billie Jean King, earned £2,000 and £750, respectively. There was a slight gain for women, though it was still inequitable, for the men's and women's winners of Wimbledon in 1969, Rod Laver and Ann Jones, who earned £3,000 and £1,500, respectively. There were similar ratios of inequitable prize money distribution at the other Grand Slam events. Disparity was growing at all of the tournaments, not just Grand Slam events, and by 1970, the Italian Open men's and women's winners, Ilie Năstase and Billie Jean King, received $3,500 and $600, respectively. The disparity in prize money between men and women had grown from around 2:1 to almost 6:1 in only two years of open tennis.

It would be easy to start an analysis of social activism in women's tennis with the Founders, primarily the Original 9, who will be the focus of Chapter 2; however, they reaped the benefits of Lenglen, Gibson, and Haydon Jones who came before them. The three had outlined the path for the Original 9 and there were tactics for organizing and pushing back against tournament owners, using the media effectively to get messages across, that had been tested and could be honed further. Ann Haydon Jones most directly affected the Founders, since she was focused on prize money equity and her activism had been only two years before theirs. Althea Gibson was more prominent for the Joiners during the Evert-Navratilova era, the focus of Chapter 3, and the Throwbacks, the women balancing their playing careers with social activism, which is the focus of Chapter 5.

Notes

1 This match was a Challenge Round match. At this time, defending champions played one match which was against the winner of the tournament of all the challengers.
2 Lenglen actually won 12 Grand Slam singles titles: Wimbledon, 1919–1923, 1925; and the French Championships, 1920–1923, 1925–1926. Until 1925, the French Championships was not open to players from outside of France, so her four titles from 1920–1923 are not officially counted in her overall Grand Slam tally. Lenglen would likely have won many more Grand Slam titles; however, when she turned professional in the fall of 1926, she was banned from subsequent Grand Slam events.
3 Johnson would later mentor Arthur Ashe.

2 The Founders
The Original 9, "women's lob" feminism, and the social movement that launched women's professional tennis, 1968–1975[1]

As social activists, Suzanne Lenglen, Althea Gibson, and Ann Haydon Jones were unable to make formidable change on their own. However, in 1970, the collectivity of the Original 9 emerged, and nine top-ranked players joined together for a common cause of equal prize money, becoming successful in stemming the ever-increasing disparity between men's and women's prize money. The emergence of the Original 9 as a collective group for social activism is remarkable, given the historic underpinnings of individualism in tennis.

Guided by the vibrant women's movement of the time, the focus of the Original 9 was solely on equality which would be shown through equal prize money at tournaments. With expert marketing and advertising, as well as couture fashion, the Original 9 were able to begin a women's tennis tour that grew from those nine women in 1970 to 64 players in 1973, and create an organizing body, the Women's Tennis Association (WTA), to govern the new tennis tour.

Equal pay for women was the issue from the women's movement that became the focal point for the Original 9, with a dismissal of other concerns of the women's movement not directly relevant to women's tennis, such as reproductive rights, maternity leave, and domestic violence concerns. Interestingly, too, an overall lack of analysis of issues of class and race led to the unraveling of the women's movement. So, too, were class and race sidelined in women's tennis, despite those being concerns of individual members.

Though individual complaints about the inequality present in women's tennis as compared to men's tennis had permeated the sport as far back as 1926, it was not until 1970 that an organized group effort took shape. Since then, women's professional tennis has had a continual presence of social activism. Beginning any long-standing social movement are the Founders, the original social movement actors. For women's tennis, the Founders were the Original 9, with their protest against unequal prize money distribution between men's and women's professional tennis.

Sociologist Nancy Whittier describes the Founders as those who institutionalize feminist organizing and ideals. As Whittier states, "they entered the movement after initial activism had begun, but before lasting institutions had developed. They transformed the ideas, dissatisfaction, and ad hoc organizations begun by initiators into lasting feminist institutions" (Whittier, 1995, p. 62).

Indeed, the Original 9 followed the one-woman battles waged by Althea Gibson and Ann Haydon Jones, and were existing in a space created by Gladys Heldman in which men and women were culturally equal, just not economically equal (Chapter 1). The Original 9 solidified the expectations of equality into institutional forms via the women's tour and the establishment of the WTA, to both operate as the governing body of the women's tour and as a player's union. The Founders, then, are those who put in place the original call for action. It is their issue that underlies the efforts of subsequent generations, even as the generational cohorts that follow add their own issues for activism.

The Founders cohort in women's tennis (1968–1975) is identified as the era of the Original 9, the origin story of social activism in women's tennis. This era begins with the "open" era of tennis, beginning in 1968, when all players, amateur and professional, began competing against each other in tournaments. The specific expression of this generational iteration of social activism in women's tennis was the forming of the Original 9 and their continued activism for equal prize money for women in the face of great professional risks. The Original 9, with the help of Gladys Heldman, Joseph Cullman and Ted Tinling, created a vibrant women's tour for tennis, and, later, helped form the WTA to govern the women's tour. In spite of threats, the nine women maintained pressure on the governing bodies of tennis while also increasing their numbers, so much so that, by 1973, what had included only nine women had increased to over 60 players who banded together to form the WTA. The feather in the cap for the Founders was Billie Jean King's defeat of Bobby Riggs in the "Battle of the Sexes" in September, 1973. I have demarcated the Founders cohort ending with Billie Jean King's final Grand Slam singles title, which was Wimbledon 1975.

Of note, Nancy Spencer, in her essay "Once Upon a Subculture: Professional Women's Tennis and the Meaning of Style, 1970–1974" (1997), describes the Founders cohort in terms of Dick Hebdige's theory of subcultures (1979). Hebdige outlines the cycle of a subculture "as proceeding from oppression to defusion/diffusion and resistance to incorporation" (Spencer, 1997, p. 365). Thus, in this framework, the unequal prize money that female tennis players faced was the oppression. In resisting that oppression, the women created a tour separate from the men's; a distinct style was formed that diffused through the Virginia Slims tour, which was eventually incorporated into the "establishment" of professional tennis (Spencer, 1997, pp. 365–366). This framework is very useful in explaining the Founders cohort and how the Original 9 came into being, but is more difficult to use to explain the generational cohorts of women's professional tennis. As such, this project uses the generational cohorts model to explain the lineage of social activism in women's tennis which began during this particular moment.

Interestingly, intersectionality is displayed in mainly silent, yet profound, ways for the Founders cohort. The women of the Original 9 were largely homogenized into a seamless group, devoid of class or race issues differing from the status quo, closely aligned with the second-wave feminist tenets of the era. Thus, the working-class backgrounds of Billie Jean King and Rosie Casals, and

Casals' Salvadoran heritage, were pushed to the side in an effort to focus fully on a single-topic social movement for equal prize money. So, too, was the religious background of Gladys Heldman and Joseph Cullman put aside to focus solely on equal prize money without issues that could sidetrack the main focus at hand. To be certain, their Jewish backgrounds informed their actions in profound ways. Ted Tinling, the fashion designer, was gay, and brought an understanding of inequality like Heldman and Cullman; however, these aspects did not overshadow the single-mindedness of all 12 activists to remain focused on the single task of equal prize money. To be sure, the minoritarian statuses of those involved informed their activism, but none of these other issues were allowed to derail them from their singular goal of equal prize money. However, the historically-constructed social milieu of professional tennis was upper class, male, and heteronormative. This is the backdrop to the actions of the Original 9.

Prior to the open era of tennis, players were inequitably paid money under the table based on their marketability for the tournament. Since it was done in this way, nobody knew what the others were being paid. After the open era of tennis began, money was distributed through prize money based on the level one attained in a tournament and, thus, prize money distributions for tournaments were publicly known. In 1970, after two years of increasing inequality with the prize money between men's and women's tournaments, the Original 9 formed.

The Original 9 was a group of nine women – Billie Jean King, Rosie Casals, Julie Heldman, Kristy Pigeon, Judy Tegart, Kerry Melville, Jane Bartkowicz, Valerie Zeigenfuss, and Nancy Richey – who banded together in 1970 to pressure the governing bodies of tennis to offer equitable pay and access to tournaments for women as they did for men. They emerged in and through the women's liberation movement in the US.

The term "women's lob" – merging the slang term of "women's lib" for feminism with the lob tennis shot – was coined in the early 1970s by Gladys Heldman, the founding editor of *World Tennis* magazine, to describe the particular feminism that was being used in women's tennis (King & Starr, 1988, p. 120). The Original 9 drew on two main components of the rhetoric of the broader women's liberation movement of the time: 1) equal pay for equal work; and, 2) access to an economic livelihood.[2] In tennis, this would be shown through equal prize money and an equal number of tennis tournaments offered for men and women. Equal prize money but with an offering of four tournaments for women and 20 for men would not accomplish anything. Thus, both equal prize money and equal number of tournaments had to happen.

Until 1968, men and women competed alongside each other as amateurs at the Grand Slam tennis events – the Australian Championships, the French Championships, The Championships, Wimbledon, held in the UK, and the US Championships. There was essentially no prize money, however, it is likely that many men were making appearance fees. Granted, there were professionals – only men – who made a living playing events created for professional players, but these players were not allowed to play in the Grand Slam events because they were only open to amateurs at the time. In 1968, this all changed. The

Grand Slam tennis events became "open." That is, the tournaments were now open to both amateurs and professionals, and the two competed against each other in the same draws. For the first time, prize money was offered, but with a great discrepancy between men and women. Of note, this is when all of the Grand Slam events altered their names to include the word "Open," to demarcate the change, as in the "French Open," instead of the French Championships. Only Wimbledon retains the older name, The Championships.

The change to open tournaments soon made women players realize that they needed to improve their position in the world of tennis. Prior to 1968, there existed only a small offering of tennis events for women outside of the Grand Slam events, and now they were being short-changed in regards to prize money with the new open Grand Slams. Women players began to feel disgruntled.

What compelled Billie Jean King, Rosie Casals, Julie Heldman, Kristy Pigeon, Judy Tegart, Kerry Melville, Jane Bartkowicz, Valerie Zeigenfuss, and Nancy Richey to join together as the Original 9 was, no doubt, an economic issue. It was partly due to the inequitable prize money, but also due to the number of tennis tournaments available for women outside of the Grand Slam events.

In 1970, the Pacific Southwest Championships in Los Angeles, California, offered prize money disparity of 12:1. This was the final straw. The need to stem the tide was becoming all the more evident. On what the Original 9 wanted, Billie Jean King states:

> We wanted to be paid equally and we wanted to be treated fairly. Originally we had hoped to partner with the men's tennis tour and have a unified voice in the sport on a global basis. But the guys wanted no part of it. And not every women's player wanted to join us. So we went to plan B.
>
> (King, 2015)

It is possible that not all of these nine women considered themselves feminists. Their actions and the outcome of their actions, however, were feminist. They were women focused on ensuring that there would be a future for women in women's tennis and hoping that it would become as lucrative as it is today. Sexuality, class, and race, in the context of 1973, were sidelined as issues during this movement in an effort to keep the social activism by the Original 9 aimed at fighting for unfettered economic equity. "Women's lob" feminism was drawing on the branch of liberal feminism from second-wave feminism. Indeed, Kristy Pigeon noted that:

> Prior to the formation of the Original 9 I had been exposed to the women's rights movement while attending the University of California at Berkeley. In 1968 [while a freshman at Mills College] I attended a lecture presented by Betty Friedan and had a clear understanding of changes that needed to be made to our society. As a professional tennis player there was never a doubt that I needed to support the group's quest for equal prize money.
>
> (Pigeon, interview, November 9, 2014)

The Original 9 were focused solely on changing the rules and culture of professional tennis to ensure fair and equal compensation for work for all women in tennis.

The players frontstage

Originally, the alternate event to the Pacific Southwest tournament, where the men's winner would make $12,500 and the women's winner would make $1,500, was going to include: Margaret Court, Rosie Casals, Nancy Richey, Judy Dalton, Kerry Melville, Peaches Bartkowicz, Patti Hogan, and Valerie Zeigenfuss, and, only for doubles, Billie Jean King (G. Heldman, 1970, p. 16). Court, who was suffering from an ankle injury, was replaced by Kristy Pigeon. Hogan got cold feet, and, with all of the top players barred from competition for participating in this alternate event, became the #1 female player from the US. King filled Hogan's spot in the singles draw. Julie Heldman, suffering from tennis elbow at the time, played one point against King in a preliminary match. Thus, the women who would become known as the Original 9 by playing the Virginia Slims of Houston tournament were: Jane Bartkowicz, Rosie Casals, Judy Tegart Dalton, Julie Heldman, Billie Jean King, Kristy Pigeon, Kerry Melville Reid, Nancy Richey, and Valerie Zeigenfuss.

Jane Bartkowicz, known as "Peaches," was born April 16, 1949 in Hamtramck, Michigan. Bartkowicz had a strong junior career, winning 17 titles including the girl's singles title at Wimbledon in 1964. She was a quarter-finalist at the US Open twice, in 1968 and 1969, and reached a career-high ranking of number 8 in the world in 1969. Bartkowicz was also a member of the winning US Federation Cup team of 1969. She retired from tennis in 1971.

Rosie Casals was born in San Francisco, California, on September 16, 1948 and continued to be raised there. Of Salvadoran descent, her parents returned to El Salvador, leaving Rosie and her older sister, Victoria, with their great-uncle and great-aunt, Manuel and Maria Casals, when Rosie was still a baby. Manuel, affectionately known as "Tío" ("uncle" in Spanish), taught Rosie and Victoria how to play tennis at the Golden Gate Racquet Club, a public tennis facility in Golden Gate Park in San Francisco. Though only 5'2" tall, Rosie's game was aggressive and her overhead smash was her biggest weapon. By the age of 16, she was the top-ranked junior and women's adult-division player in Northern California. By 17, Rosie was ranked #11 of women in the United States. The following year, 1966, Rosie and Billie Jean King began their domination of women's doubles by winning the US Hard Court Championships, the US Indoor Championships, and making the quarter-finals of Wimbledon. In 1967, Casals and King won Wimbledon and the US Open women's doubles crowns. Casals and King ended up winning eight Grand Slam women's doubles championships, all at Wimbledon and the US Open. Casals won one more women's doubles title at the US Open in 1982, teaming with Wendy Turnbull. Casals also won two mixed doubles championships at Wimbledon with Ilie Năstase and one US Open mixed doubles title with Dick Stockton. In singles, Casals was a two-time finalist at the US Open, losing to Margaret Court in 1970 and Billie Jean King in 1971. Casals' Grand Slam tennis career spanned over 20 years, from 1964–1985.[3] Casals was inducted into the International Tennis Hall of Fame in 1996.

Judy Tegart Dalton was born December 12, 1937, in Melbourne, Australia, and still lives there today. Dalton was a late bloomer in tennis. Julie Heldman, in describing Dalton, says:

> She always has a smile, a friendly word, a pat on the back and the time to stop and chat. From her husky build you might surmise that she is a net-rusher (she is) and has a big serve (she does). If she had not been trained under the Australian disciplines of silence and attention to the matter at hand, you would rather expect her to shout "Noice Shot!" when you passed her at net. ... When Judy is playing well, she has the same steamroller power as Margaret Smith [Court].
>
> (J. Heldman, 1968, p. 40)

Apart from the Australian Open, she did not reach the quarter-finals of a Grand Slam tournament until she was 29. Once she found her way into the quarter-finals, however, she became a regular at that level in Grand Slam events. Dalton's highest ranking was number 7, which she achieved in 1968, at the age of 31. Dalton reached the final at Wimbledon in 1968, falling to Billie Jean King in two close sets, 7–9, 5–7. She won eight doubles titles, at least one at each of the four Grand Slam tournaments. Five of those doubles titles were in partnership with Margaret Court, two were with Lesley Turner, and one was with Rosie Casals. Furthermore, Dalton was a member of the Australian Federation Cup team from 1965–1967 and from 1969–1970. Australia won the Federation Cup in 1965 and 1970.

Julie Heldman was born December 8, 1945, in Berkeley, California, to Julius and Gladys Heldman. Following a very strong junior career, Heldman enrolled in Stanford University at the age of 16, where her parents met, graduating in 1966. According to The WT Reporter:

> Julie has a big, natural forehand, a sharp backhand and a lob-volley. ... Julie "retired" in the summer of 1966 because the pressures of trying to win were no longer enjoyable. Thirteen months later she emerged from her chrysalis to play the best tennis of her life.
>
> (1968, p. 59)

Heldman reached a career-high ranking of number five in the world in 1969. Between 1968 and 1974, Heldman reached the quarter-finals or better in each of the four Grand Slam tournaments in both singles and doubles. Furthermore, Heldman played on the US Federation Cup team in 1966, 1969–1970, and 1974, and was the captain of the team in 1975. The US won the Federation Cup in

1966 and 1969. Following her playing career, Heldman graduated from the University of California Los Angeles Law School in 1981.

Billie Jean King was born November 22, 1943, in Long Beach, California, to Bill and Betty Moffitt. King attended California State University, Los Angeles until she joined the tennis tour full-time. King was ranked #1 in the world from 1966–1968, 1971–1972, and 1974. King won 12 Grand Slam singles titles: the Australian Open in 1968, the French Open in 1972, Wimbledon in 1966–1968, 1972–1973, and 1975, and the US Open in 1967, 1971–1972 and 1974. She also won 16 Grand Slam doubles titles, primarily with Rosie Casals as her partner, and 11 Grand Slam mixed doubles titles. In addition, King was a member of the US Federation Cup team as a player in 1963, 1966–1967, and 1976, and as a captain in 1977–1979, and 1996. The US won the Fed Cup seven times with King, in 1963, 1966–1967, and 1976–1979. King was inducted into the International Tennis Hall of Fame in 1987.[4]

Kristy Pigeon was born August 12, 1950. Pigeon won the girl's title at Wimbledon in 1968. That same year, she made it to the fourth round of Wimbledon in the main draw. She repeated her fourth-round appearance at Wimbledon in 1969 as well. Pigeon attended Mills College and then the University of California at Berkeley, where she earned a BA in biology and art. She was pursuing a graduate degree in wildlife biology when she stopped to pursue professional tennis. After her tennis career was over, Pigeon founded the non-profit organization Sagebrush Equine Training Center in Idaho which provides therapeutic and recreational horse riding for children and adults with physical, mental, and emotional impairments.

Kerry Melville Reid was born August 7, 1947, in Mosman, New South Wales, Australia. Reid won the 1977 Australian Open singles title. She was also a finalist at the US Open in 1972, and a semi-finalist at the French Open in 1967, and Wimbledon in 1974. Reid also won two Grand Slam doubles titles, the Australian Open in 1968 with Karen Krantzcke and in 1977 with Mona Guerrant, and Wimbledon in 1978 with Wendy Turnbull. In 1979, Reid was made a Member of the Order of the British Empire (MBE) by the Queen.

Nancy Richey was born August 23, 1942 in San Angelo, Texas. Of Richey, Julie Heldman wrote: "Nancy is the hard-hitting baseliner. She powders the ball cleanly from side to side with better pace and more control than any other woman in the world" (J. Heldman, 1967, p. 18). Richey won two Grand Slam singles titles, the Australian Open in 1967 and the French Open in 1968. She was a semi-finalist at Wimbledon in 1968 and reached the final of the US Open in 1966 and 1969. Richey reached a career-high ranking of number two in the world in 1969. She was also the winner of four Grand Slam doubles titles, partnering with Carole Graebner for the 1965 US Open and the 1966 Australian Open, and with Maria Bueno for the 1966 Wimbledon and US Open titles. Richey won the US Clay Court Championships for a record six consecutive years from 1963 to 1968. She was also a member of the winning US Federation Cup team of 1969. Richey was inducted into the International Tennis Hall of Fame in 2003.

Valerie Zeigenfuss was born June 29, 1949 in San Diego, California. She reached the fourth round at the US Open in 1969 and 1975, and at the French Open in 1972. She and Bartkowicz won a bronze medal in doubles at the 1968 Olympics in Mexico City.

To be sure, there were risks involved for the Original 9. The greatest risk was expulsion from tennis. Billie Jean King explains, "For us, everything was at risk. The USLTA ... threatened us with suspension and expulsion" (King, 2015). Indeed, the risks were very real. The Original 9 were banned from the Federation and Wightman Cups, and were told that they were to be banned from Wimbledon (Casals, interview, November 15, 2014). For the Australians, as King explains, Judy Dalton and Kerry Melville faced even more severe sanctions: "They were told if they signed with us, their playing days were over" (King, 2015). As Dalton explains, "The Australian Tennis Association banned us from playing in our country and also using our Australian endorsed tennis racquets and shoes" (Dalton, interview, November 15, 2014). Kristy Pigeon adds that:

> We also risked being proven wrong and that possibly the public had little interest in watching women play tennis if men were not also playing in the same tournaments. Therefore, our pride and our livelihoods were also at stake. Fortunately, the risks were not realized.
> (Pigeon, interview, November 9, 2014)

With that, Rosie Casals notes, "In many ways it was scary taking these chances but mostly it was exhilarating" (Casals, interview, November 15, 2014).

The backstage: Gladys Heldman, Joseph Cullman III, and Ted Tinling

An argument against equal pay for women's tennis was the belief that women players did not draw the crowds to the tournaments, and that they were less entertaining than men. This kind of prejudicial thinking, alongside arguments that women should not be paid equally, was countered by women players and their supporters, with the argument that women's tennis had as much entertainment value as men's tennis, and the women in tennis were going to prove it.

The players and their supporters soon developed a plan to increase the entertainment value of women's tennis. This was done through a masterful consortium of sorts with the Original 9, Gladys Heldman, publisher of *World Tennis* magazine, Joseph Cullman III, CEO of Philip Morris, and the couture fashion of Ted Tinling. They worked seamlessly together to make women's professional tennis an entertainment spectacle. What is interesting, too, is that these three were socially marginalized – Heldman and Cullman were Jewish, and Tinling was gay – which must have fueled their desire to see women's tennis not only survive, but prosper.

Gladys Heldman: the marketing of the women's professional tennis revolution[5]

Gladys Heldman was a force to be reckoned with. She was charismatic, dominant, and preferred conditions on her own terms that, because they were ethically sound, were usually convincing to others. Gladys was the daughter of George Z. Medalie, a New York City lawyer, US Attorney for the Southern District of New York, and New York Court of Appeals judge, and Carrie Kaplan, a Latin and Greek scholar. Gladys met Julius Heldman, a nationally-ranked junior, college, and amateur tennis player, at Stanford University where she was an undergraduate student and he was a PhD student. They graduated in 1942, she with a BA and Phi Beta Kappa honors in only three years, and he with a PhD in physical chemistry. Gladys and Julius were married two days later. While Julius was a chemistry professor at the University of California, Berkeley, Gladys earned an MA in medieval history there in 1943. She had planned to pursue a PhD in history; however, the births of her daughters, Carrie and Julie, sidelined her from that project.

While staying at home to raise their daughters, Julius recommended that Gladys take up tennis for its social outlets. In 1953, Gladys founded *World Tennis* magazine, which, from the start, was notable for its equal coverage of men's and women's tennis under her guidance. Gladys, now, was on track for arguably becoming the most important person in the history of women's tennis.

A reporter once asked Gladys Heldman if she was the one who created the Virginia Slims Women's Circuit. According to Tinling, Heldman quickly retorted, "No. It was Jack Kramer" (Tinling, 1979, p. 305). Kramer, tournament director of the Pacific Southwest Championships, refused to make the prize money for men and women more equitable. It was the final straw. His refusal compelled Billie Jean King, Rosie Casals, Julie Heldman (Gladys' daughter), Kristy Pigeon, Judy Tegart Dalton, Kerry Melville Reid, Jane "Peaches" Bartkowicz, Valerie Zeigenfuss, and Nancy Richey to form as the Original 9, under the guidance of Gladys Heldman.

Gladys Heldman went to work immediately. She put up $5,000 of her own money and secured the sponsorship of Philip Morris, the cigarette company, through her friendship with the CEO Joseph Cullman III, to support the Virginia Slims of Houston tournament, scheduled to coincide with the Pacific Southwest Championships (G. Heldman, 1970). In exchange for signing $1 contracts, not only were the players protected by antitrust laws from the USLTA, the event became essentially an exhibition tournament instead of one needing sanctions.

Joseph Cullman III: Phillip Morris and the corporate sponsorship of the women's professional tennis revolution

The sponsorship of Philip Morris came easily because they were eager to find an advertising venue for the cigarette created for women, introduced in 1968. Their marketing slogans, especially "You've come a long way, baby!", were a seemingly perfect fit for women's professional tennis. Thus, the Virginia Slims tennis circuit was born. By the end of 1970, the Virginia Slims circuit had offered seven more tournaments, building on the success of the Virginia Sims of Houston, and had gained 31 more players beyond the Original 9. Boasting 40 players, the Virginia Slims circuit was assured to have an entire season of tournaments in 1971.

Joseph Cullman III was not only a person who found himself in the right place at the right time, he was a marketing genius with a philanthropic heart. His great-grandfather, Ferdinand Kullman, a cigar maker in Germany, immigrated to the United States in 1848. His grandfather, Joseph Cullman Sr., had started a small cigar business when he opened a store in New York City. Joseph Cullman Jr. and his brother, Howard Cullman, formed Tobacco and Allied Stocks, Inc. in 1929, which invested in securities of tobacco companies. By December 1929, Tobacco and Allied Stocks held over $3 million worth of stock.

In 1941, Joseph Cullman Jr. purchased the defaulting Benson & Hedges cigarette brand as it floundered into bankruptcy:

> It was called Benson & Hedges, an offshoot of an old British establishment and its principal place of business was a shop on Fifth Avenue that sold monogrammed, gold-tipped and hand-rolled cigarettes to the carriage trade. Mr. Cullman's father [Joseph Jr.] thought the place a suitable outlet for his cigars and bought control for $850,000. For this amount, he also acquired a luxury cigarette produced by Benson & Hedges called Parliament, with a recessed mouthpiece and a cotton filter.
>
> (Kaufman, 2004)

Returning from World War II as a Navy lieutenant and having already graduated from Yale University, Joseph Cullman III, then only 29, took over the management of Benson & Hedges from his father and "as Mr. Cullman [Joseph III] took over, the sales of Parliaments surged despite or perhaps because of their high price and snob appeal" (Kaufman, 2004).

In 1954, Philip Morris and Benson & Hedges negotiated a merger and Joseph Cullman III became executive vice president of Philip Morris. Philip Morris wanted the filter tips that Parliaments had:

> This was a time that filter-tipped cigarettes were just being introduced by other companies. Philip Morris had no filters and its management thought that Parliaments might prove useful, particularly if health concerns with cigarette smoke were to intensify. In 1954 the company turned over stock valued at $22.4 million to Mr. Cullman's father for his interest in Benson & Hedges. Philip Morris obtained Parliaments and Benson & Hedges.
>
> (Kaufman, 2004)

Quickly rising through the ranks of Philip Morris, Joseph Cullman III was CEO and chairman of the board of directors from 1957 to 1978.

As for the company he joined, its fortunes were to rise even more steeply under his direction. In 1961, Philip Morris was dead last in sales among the six major American producers. By 1972 it was in second place and in 1983 it overtook Reynolds Tobacco, which had been the industry leader for the previous 25 years. It earned so much cash that it was driven to use its huge cigarette profits to seriously diversify, acquiring giants like Jacobs Suchard, Miller Beer and Kraft General Foods and becoming the largest consumer products company in the world.

(Kaufman, 2004)

This change in fortunes came about with Cullman III working closely with the Leo Burnett advertising agency to create the Marlboro Man. In January 1955, the Marlboro cigarette was introduced (Cullman, 1998, p. 93).

Sales of Marlboro were increasing in the North, but were stagnant in the South, where whispers that Philip Morris was a Northern tobacco company and filled with racial integrationists, both of which were true, kept sales low. Indeed, Philip Morris' Richmond, Virginia, facilities "were more integrated than any other in the industry" (Cullman, 1998, p. 95), and their New York City office had a Black sales executive and were poised to hire more (Cullman, 1998, p. 95). Philip Morris also had several Jewish people in visible positions, including Cullman, and, during this time, "when Jews were prominent in the civil rights struggle and segments of the white South identified Jews as radicals, trouble-makers, and – let's not be afraid to use the word – 'nigger lovers' Philip Morris was, unsurprisingly, singled out for retribution" (Cullman, 1998, p. 95).

In regards to tennis, in line with his hiring and management practices at Philip Morris, Cullman writes of being interested in increasing the diversity and changing the upper-classness of the sport. He states:

> I became interested in tennis as a "project" in the 1960s, when the sport was dominated mostly by club types who played at restricted clubs. ... I was not happy with the lack of diversity – racial, religious, gender, and economic – of the players and those in the stands. There were a few outside the mold earlier – very few. ... More change was on the way, in the form of Pancho Gonzales, Althea Gibson, Arthur Ashe, Manuel Santana, Billie Jean King, and a host of other minority and women players. It was something like the situation Jackie Robinson faced in baseball after the war. I appreciated that it takes time for people to change attitudes, but tennis wasn't moving fast enough until the Marlboro CBS-TV national sponsorship changed things.
>
> (Cullman, 1998, pp. 173 and 175)

Truth be told, it was not solely Marlboro advertising that began to create a change in people's attitudes, but the television broadcast of the US Championships more broadly. Cullman explains further:

Now for my role in tennis, and my attempts to address some of the sport's problems. In 1968, I had become part of the tennis "establishment." I was active in helping get the US Championship held at Forest Hills nationally televised for the first time on CBS and sponsored by Marlboro. This national TV broadcast of the US championships changed tennis from a white shoe club sport to a sport for all Americans. In 1969 and again in 1970 I served as chairman of the US Open.

(Cullman, 1998, p. 174)

Indeed, the televised aspect of the US Championships is what changed people's perceptions, not Marlboro's involvement per se. It was Cullman's foresight to bring tennis to the masses through television that changed people's perception. Marlboro, through Cullman's positioning as the CEO of Philip Morris, was just the vehicle he used to put his ideas into action.

In 1968, Philip Morris created Virginia Slims, a cigarette longer and more slender than a regular cigarette, which was meant to appeal to women, as a balance to the Marlboro mystique of manliness. The question for Cullman was how to advertise this new cigarette to women. The slogan for Virginia Slims, "You've Come a Long Way, Baby," was a perfect fit for women's professional tennis.

Ted Tinling: Fashion design for the women's professional tennis revolution[6]

Ted Tinling was the clothing mastermind for women's professional tennis. Although he worked as a chair umpire and player liaison at Wimbledon, his most notable contributions to tennis were the on-court "couture" styles which he created for women players. Tinling "was a familiar figure at tournaments with his lanky 6-foot-7-inch frame, bald head and often modish apparel" (Thomas, 1990). In addition to being openly gay, donning a one-carat diamond earring in his left ear (long before it was an aesthetic symbol for gay men), he had a personality that was much larger than his sizeable frame. He was "gargantuan, bald and boldly opinionated" (Finn, 1990). Bud Collins, the tennis writer and historian, affectionately dubbed Tinling "the leaning tower of pizzazz" (Collins & Hollander, 1994). Tinling outfitted almost all of the great female tennis players in a fashion career that spanned four decades from 1947–1988, which he documented in three books: *White Ladies* (1963), *Love and Faults: Personalities Who Have Changed the History of Tennis in My Lifetime* (1979), and *Tinling: Sixty Years in Tennis* (1983), which is a reprint of *Love and Faults* with an additional four previously unpublished chapters. Tinling also wrote a small pamphlet for The Wimbledon Lawn Tennis Museum, *The Story of Women's Tennis Fashion* (1977).

Tinling's most memorable fashion creation was the daring bloomers of Gussie Moran, worn at Wimbledon in 1949. Wimbledon was "the tournament with which he waged a tempestuous lifelong love affair" (Finn, 1990). Tinling and the All England Club (where Wimbledon is played) were locked in a continual tussle over the requirement of players to wear only white; this sparring continued for over four decades. Martina Navratilova's 1979 Wimbledon singles title win was the last time a Tinling dress won a Grand Slam event. Indeed, Tinling's dresses were worn by Wimbledon champions in 12 of the 20 years from 1959–1979. In 1984, Rosie Casals was the last player in the main draw at Wimbledon to wear a Tinling dress. In the early 1980s, with the emergence of lucrative contracts from sports clothing manufacturers, the need for a tennis couturier was waning.

Tinling began his career in fashion design before World War II, making embellished wedding gowns for the British upper class. But after the war, rather than focusing solely on gowns, he shifted his interest to tennis clothing. His efforts would forever alter the place of women in the sport of tennis. Through the creation of feminine, and sometimes hyper-feminine, tennis attire, Tinling was one of the chief marketing agents for the burgeoning women's professional tennis scene. In many respects, he also veiled this scene from naysayers who would choose to belittle and dismiss female athletes with assertions of a lack of femininity, or worse, manliness, through physical expressions of skill and power.

As a teenager, while living in the French Riviera (for his chronic and severe bronchial asthma), Tinling met and became a close confidante with the tennis great, Suzanne Lenglen. At the Nice Lawn Tennis Club, where Lenglen played, Tinling was called upon to be chair umpire for one of Lenglen's daily matches. He was just 14 at the time. After the match, Lenglen's father requested that Tinling call all of his daughter's matches, and the club organizers, "accustomed to being scared to death of Suzanne's tantrums, were greatly relieved at this prospect" (Tinling, 1979, p. 12). As Tinling explained further:

> There is always one lad in every stable who, by some unaccountable bond of telepathic sympathy, can hold the bridle of the star runner in peace and calm. For two teenage years I was that "stableboy" to the greatest tennis star ever known.
>
> (Tinling, 1979, p. 12)

It is this relationship with Lenglen that propelled Tinling's interest in couture fashion.

London Fashion House. Tinling began formal studies of dress design in London, beginning in 1927. In 1931, he had a large enough following to open up his own business and, within a year, was able to move to Mayfair, the upscale fashion district of London, and show his first collection of women's dresses. By 1938, Tinling had a reputation in London that rivaled that of other designers in haute couture, especially for lavish wedding dresses. During that year, he created 14 dresses for weddings at St. Margaret's at Westminster Abbey, which at the time was the church for the most important high-society weddings in England.

In many respects, Tinling's personal dandy style guided his fashion aesthetics. Indeed, "the self-proclaimed virtues of queerness and queer style lie in its shameless celebration of the artificial and the flamboyant – the decorative remainder to a stratified and utilitarian idea of society" (Geczy & Karaminas, 2013, p. 82). To this end, Tinling's creations seem to display an almost hyper-femininity, using sequins and beads, each one hand-stitched, that glittered across a room, or, in the case of Tinling, across a tennis court.

Between 1927–1939 and 1947–1949, the gap accounting for his service in World War II, the All England Club employed Tinling to serve as a player liaison during the two weeks of the Wimbledon Championships. The position required him to escort players from the locker rooms to Centre Court and court number 1. In 1947, following the war, Tinling returned to London to resume his work in fashion design. He quickly became frustrated. The post-war rationing of goods and products in England stifled his fashion creativity. It was then that Tinling began to focus on women's tennis fashion. Tennis was a world that he already intimately understood, and tennis dresses required much less fabric than elaborate wedding gowns.

He did not drop wedding gown design entirely, however. Between 1950 and 1980, he created 14 wedding gowns for tennis players including one for Christine Truman in 1967 (British Pathé, 1967a), and, his most notable wedding gown, Chris Evert's dress for her marriage to the Englishman John Lloyd in 1979.

Pushing Boundaries at Wimbledon. Tinling was always pushing the boundaries of tennis fashion, especially the white only clothing rule at Wimbledon, which he continually tried to defy. Albert Camus asserted: "The dandy creates his own unity through aesthetic means. … He only maintains himself through defiance" (Geczy & Karaminas, 2013, p. 73). This continual bucking of authority was a trademark of Tinling's and made him the perfect fashion designer for the soon to emerge Virginia Slims tour. As early as the 1940s, Tinling was striving to change the perception that women's tennis was "boring" compared to men's tennis, and he did this by bringing attention to the players through his fashions on the court.

As a marketing tool for women's tennis, Tinling's dresses struck the right tone for highlighting the femininity and gracefulness of the players. Tinling notes that:

> Designing for personalities seen daily by millions of viewers, it is my first task to assess accurately what particular feature or characteristic in these personalities the public has already decided it likes best. Then I have to dream up styles which I think will illustrate these features exactly – certainly blend with, and not contradict, the fans' pre-conceived notions.
>
> (Jones, 1971, pp. ix–x)

It can never be known to what extent Tinling's fashions crafted positive perceptions of female athletes; however, there can be no doubt that they buffered against many of the perceived threats of women's physical strength and power through sport.

54   *The Founders*

Tinling's first tennis creation was a dress for Joy Gannon for the 1947 Wimbledon tournament. This dress had a distinct feature that could only be seen from up close. Indeed,

> the dress had an unusual feature: a narrow blue and pink hem that went all but unnoticed by tournament officials, but not by the players. There was soon such a clamor for even more colorful outfits that Wimbledon officials ruled that only white could be worn for the 1949 tournament.
>
> (Thomas, 1990)

What catapulted Tinling to tennis fashion fame was his design of the controversial ruffled lace bloomers for Gertrude "Gorgeous Gussie" Moran at the 1949 Wimbledon Championships, which could be seen underneath the shortest dress to have ever graced Centre Court at that time. Not only was the dress banned from Wimbledon for the subsequent rounds of play, Tinling was fired as player liaison for the tournament, a position he had held since 1927. Tinling asserts that

> the furore [Gussie Moran] created across the world, once again revolutionised the entire field of sportswear, illustrating, as Lenglen did so convincingly, that to be functionally attired need not deprive women of their fundamental birthright to look attractive and pretty.
>
> (Tinling, 1977, p. 16)

Despite having lost his job as player liaison, this bold fashion move catapulted Tinling's status as the premier fashion couturier for women's tennis.

The next year, in 1950, Tinling further pushed the boundaries of acceptable tennis fashion with his dress designs for Beverly Baker. These dresses had clear insets around the hem that allowed more of Baker's thigh to show than was acceptable. They were immediately condemned in England as being "indecently transparent" (Tinling, 1977, p. 16).

Tinling was greatly influenced by Christian Dior's "New Look" of 1947.

> This style was widely held to represent, as Teddy Tinling expressed it, "an international hunger for a return to femininity and sexual attraction." Tinling was determined to bring femininity back to the court and believed this was an advance for the women players.
>
> (Wilson, 2014, p. 149; quoting Tinling)

To be sure, there was debate over whether making players more sexually attractive was an advancement.

During the mid-1950s, Tinling was still restricted to creating all white tennis fashions. As Tinling notes:

> restricted, as we were, to all-white on the outside, I felt the compromise of some pretty, pastel "underneaths" would be appealing and that lacy petticoats

under tennis dresses would be attractive and acceptable to everybody concerned. In this second respect I was once again wrong.

(Tinling, 1977, p. 19)

Apparently, when Wimbledon proclaimed all white, they meant everything, even the undergarments, needed to be completely white. Of note, the first Grand Slam event where color on clothing would be allowed did not occur until the 1972 US Open, and that was to increase television visibility.

The extent to which Tinling tennis designs entered the realm of popular culture can be seen in the collection of Pathé fashion films.[7] Most notable of these is "Wimbledon Fashion Preview" (British Pathé, 1967b) which shows top English tennis stars like Ann Haydon Jones and Virginia Wade modeling Tinling fashions and "Tennis Fashions" (British Pathé, 1953) in which the Americans Maureen Connolly and Julie Sampson display Tinling creations.

Tinling created unique outfits for each individual player. Evonne Goolagong gives some insight into the process Tinling used for his fashion creations when she wrote:

> Teddy Tinling was about forty years older than me. He was an extraordinary-looking fellow, more than 2 metres (6–1/2 feet) tall and thin as a rake. In tennis, Teddy was couturier to the stars. He had been the last word in tennis fashion since he designed American player Gussie Moran's lace panties that caused so much trouble at Wimbledon in 1949. Now each year he selected a group of women – some of them established stars, some rising – and designed a range of tournament dresses for them.
>
> (Goolagong & Jarratt, 1993, p. 149)

In other words, Tinling was selecting real live mannequins for his tennis dress creations. Goolagong was hand-picked early by Tinling. She explained their first meeting:

> After I'd won a couple of minor tournaments in England, Teddy contacted Mr. Edwards [her coach] and arranged for a fitting session at his studio in London. I was knocked out by the man. He was absolutely charming and he knew everything there was to know about women's tennis. He boasted he had dressed "every Wimbledon champion from Suzanne Lenglen to Evonne Goolagong". I laughed, but he said, "Your day is coming, my dear".
>
> (Goolagong & Jarratt, 1993, p. 149)

Indeed, Goolagong became an elite player, winning two Wimbledon singles titles (1971, 1980), along with one French Open title (1971) and four Australian Open titles (1974–1977). Though Goolagong never won the US Open, she was a four-time finalist there (1973–1976).

Unfortunately, in the 1960s, tennis fashions began to move away from couture-inspired clothing. Ready-to-wear tennis clothing was taking over the market.

In the 1960s, the "Fred Perry-sponsored look, consisting of short-sleeved, white knitted shirts, worn with either kilted skirts or with tailored shorts, found a steadily increasing following" (Tinling, 1977, p. 20). This look was simply the men's polo shirts and shorts only slightly recrafted for a woman's body. However, these large companies – such as Lacoste, Ellesse, Fred Perry, and Sergio Tacchini – had the resources to offer players lucrative contracts to wear their clothing. Tinling could only offer one of a kind, personally tailored couture tennis dresses, but no lucrative clothing endorsements.

Leaving England; Moving to Philadelphia. In 1975, just after the conclusion of Wimbledon, Tinling left England and established his dressmaking shop in Philadelphia, Pennsylvania. Of the move, he said, "I'm leaving England for good. They can get on with Wimbledon looking like a vicarage garden party. I'm tired of outdated white" (Matheson, 1975). Yet it was not only Wimbledon that discouraged Tinling. It was all of England, as Tinling asserted:

> In America they said they wanted only the best. They took me up because they thought I was tops. They think of me as young – though I am 65. But in Britain nobody wants to know. My business is up for sale but nobody wants to buy. When I once asked all five leading colleges of fashion in London to send a student to help out during Wimbledon week, all refused. An amateur took the job. A Greek boy. Now he has his own boutique. I've never been asked to lecture on fashion in Britain, though I am a couturier of the old school and know my craft through and through. ... I find myself getting contentious all the time. England is not ready for the BIG TIME, the life style I find so invigorating. I need to be buoyed up to work. Then there is the financial aspect. Most of my income comes from overseas. My clothes are made under license in many countries. I am so heavily taxed bringing my profits on foreign earnings back to sterling I am always the loser.
>
> (Matheson, 1975)

By this time, Neiman Marcus and other high-end American department stores carried a line of Tinling tennis dresses. Tinling designed the dresses, and then they were mass-produced from his original. Some were also replicas of the dresses the stars of women's tennis were wearing. The dresses for the players, though, were made exclusively by hand for each player.

Philadelphia was the host city of Billie Jean King's World Team Tennis (WTT) team, the Philadelphia Freedom, the same "Philadelphia Freedom" of Elton John's 1975 hit tribute to Billie Jean King. He was a huge fan of the Philadelphia Freedom team, as King explained:

> I remember I got him one of our uniforms, made by Ted Tinling, our designer, who was English as well. I had Elton fitted at a hotel, and he would come to the matches and sit on the bench in his uniform and he'd just

go nuts and scream at me to do better. It was hysterical! It was great. He was really intense…so enthusiastic.

(EltonJohn.com, 2018)

Nine years after moving to Philadelphia, in 1984, Tinling described his delay in moving to the US as his only regret in life. He said:

I don't deal in regrets, but the single regret I have in all my life is that I didn't move to America right after the war. But I was chicken then, and I needed someone to tell me I'm good. I always do. In England, you see, you're taught that it's immodest to speak up about yourself. You shouldn't flaunt. There is the assurance that if you are capable at something it will show itself. But in America there is this enormous determination to make an identity – a desire to be somebody out of 220 million.

(Deford, 1984)

Tinling dressed the stars of tennis, helping create their on-court personas, but he had a desire to be a star himself in the world of fashion.

In a surprising turn of events that showed the turning tide of Tinling's reputation in England, in 1982, Wimbledon asked him to return as the liaison between the tournament officials and the players. It took Wimbledon 33 years to develop an appreciation for Tinling. In 1986, Tinling was inducted into the International Tennis Hall of Fame.

In May 1990, Tinling traveled to England to see his physician regarding recurring and worsening respiratory complications, similar to those which first provided him with the opportunity to meet and become the confidante of Suzanne Lenglen in the French Riviera. He passed away in his sleep on May 23 at the age of 79.

Of Tinling, Martina Navratilova said, "Ted was such an integral part of the tennis community, it's hard to imagine it without him. … He was one of a kind, and he will be missed. Wimbledon will not be the same without him" (Bonk, 1990). Rosie Casals asserted that Tinling's

personality was as colorful as he dressed and dressed us. He could praise you with his quick words or dress you down with his acid tongue. He was someone who could make you laugh with a word and a look. He was definitely special and I'm so glad I got to know him and that he got to dress me. He loved stars and he was a star in his field of couturier.

(Casals, interview, 2015)

Agreeing with Casals, Chris Evert noted that "when he complimented you, you were on top of the world…but sometimes when he insulted you, he could level the mightiest of egos. He was never afraid to utter the unspoken" (Finn, 1990). According to Billie Jean King, too: "Ted has been everything in the sport of tennis. ... He lived through so much history, he was a walking encyclopedia. He was always on the cutting edge" (Bonk, 1990).

Tinling's dresses were always individualized for the particular player who would be wearing the dress. He made over 50 dresses for Judy Dalton alone across the two decades of her career. Her favorite dresses were one embellished in the green and gold of the Australian flag, a couple that displayed Dalton's star sign, and the dress made especially for her appearance in the final at Wimbledon in 1968 which "had lace and purple ribbon trimmings" (Dalton, interview, 2015). Tinling instructed Dalton to keep the dresses because they would be of interest someday. A few of Dalton's dresses are on display at the National Sports Museum in Melbourne, Australia, the Wimbledon Museum, and her tennis club, the Royal South Yarra Lawn Tennis Club in Toorak, Australia (Dalton, interview, 2015). The International Tennis Hall of Fame, of which Tinling was inducted in 1986, also holds a variety of his dresses from various players and from his estate. King's winning "Battle of the Sexes" dress is in the Smithsonian's American History Museum collection. Clearly, Tinling's couture fashions were works of art, but they are also cultural artifacts for the women's sporting revolution.

Tinling's mark upon women's tennis, and popular culture more generally, is indisputable. His compulsion to push the limits of fashion, no matter how much the powers that be are offended, made him a couturier that will never be replicated. This mindset may have been created through his own marginalization as a gay man. His dandy flair was both a performance and a push against convention. He obliterated convention by inscribing it, especially conventional gender norms, on his clothing to such an extent that it was torn apart and made into something new. What was new was the female athlete in all her glory. He appreciated superstars; however, these superstars were elite-level professional athletes. Tinling's fashions, with their veil of femininity, allowed female athletes to compete unencumbered by cultural expectations. This would be Tinling's greatest feat.

The accomplishments of the Original 9

Players were frequently on morning radio shows or at stores doing direct advertising. As Kristy Pigeon described, "I can remember getting up at 5AM to do radio talk shows and sitting in the sports section of KMart talking to passers by. In addition, we frequently did clinics to drum up ticket sales for our tournaments" (Pigeon, interview, August 31, 2015). Billie Jean King has said the same; that players

> must get up early to give clinics and interviews because that is what makes our tournaments successful. Sometimes it's a pain, but it's part of the bargain. It makes the sponsors want us. We ask for big prize money, but we do a lot more than just play tennis to get it.
>
> (The WT Reporter, 1971, p. 40)

This, no doubt, had a tremendously adverse effect on the tennis accomplishments of each of the Original 9; however, the players were all suffering for the cause in similar ways. Even so, the accomplishments of the Original 9 were far-reaching.

The Virginia Slims circuit, 1970–1973

Growing disparity between the prize money offered to men and women came to a head as the Pacific Southwest Championships, with Jack Kramer as tournament director, offered the men's singles champion $12,500 and the women's singles champion $1,500 (G. Heldman, 1970, p. 14). In an attempt to find a more common ground, Gladys Heldman told Kramer, "The girls are talking about boycotting your tournament because of the low prize money," to which Kramer responded: "That's fine with me. ... I'll take the $7,500 and throw it in the men's singles" (G. Heldman, 1970, p. 14). Ultimately, rather than a boycott of the Pacific Southwest tournament – for fear it would adversely affect the lower-ranked players who would play the tournament anyway – consensus was formed around organizing an eight-woman tournament elsewhere during the same week as the Pacific Southwest tournament.

Joseph Cullman III was eager to support the fledgling women's tennis tour with Virginia Slims sponsorship. Describing the original tournament in Houston, Cullman wrote:

> The women's tournament, to be held at the Houston Racquet Club, was originally to be called the Houston Invitational, but when Gladys – who was a good friend of mine – told me what was going on and that she was looking for corporate support, I saw a unique opportunity to support women's tennis. I saw the Houston tournament as a chance to support the women's game and as a unique sponsorship opportunity for Philip Morris. So we put up $2,500 and had the name of the event changed to the Virginia Slims Invitational. The tournament, which had total prize money of $7,500, was won by Rosie Casals and marked the birth of the women's professional tennis tour.
> (Cullman, 1998, p. 176)

In response to the formation of this alternate tournament to the Pacific Southwest Championships, "the USLTA responded by taking away the eligibility cards of those players who competed in Houston, which meant they could no longer play in USLTA sanctioned events" (Cullman, 1998, p. 176). Not only were the players barred from playing in USLTA-sanctioned tournaments, which included the US Open, the USLTA could block the players from playing in the other Grand Slam events.

To protect the players, Gladys Heldman paid each of the players one dollar in exchange for signing contracts as professional players. In this way, the Virginia Slims of Houston, held September 23–27, 1970, did not need to be sanctioned, because it was not being counted for ranking points. It was as if the players were playing an exhibition tournament, but it certainly felt real to them. As mentioned previously, the eight players who originally opted to play the Virginia Slims of Houston were: Margaret Court, Rosie Casals, Nancy Richey, Judy Dalton, Kerry Melville, Peaches Bartkowicz, Patti Hogan, and Valerie Zeigenfuss, with Billie Jean King as a ninth player, but only for doubles (G. Heldman, 1970, p. 16). Court pulled out of the tournament due to an ankle injury[8] and was replaced by Kristy Pigeon. Hogan refused to sign the contract, but did offer to live with any sanctions from the USLTA that the others had to live with. Julie Heldman, suffering from tennis elbow at the time, played one point against King in a preliminary match. Thus, the Original 9 were formed.

The Virginia Slims Circuit was born when,

> within a week after the first Virginia Slims Invitational [in Houston] in November 1970, we were able to announce that Virginia Slims would sponsor eight women's tournaments, each in a sixteen-draw format beginning in January 1971. And the rest is tennis history. ... By the end of 1971 there were sixty-four women competing in tournaments for about $225,000.
> (Cullman, 1998, p. 177)

Furthermore,

> in 1972, with Virginia Slims' continued support, two $100,000 events took place, one in Boca Raton, Florida, and the other in Hilton Head, South Carolina. That same year Billie Jean King became the first female athlete in history to win $100,000 in prize money – a lot of money at that time – in a single year.
> (Cullman, 1998, p. 177)

Indeed, women's tennis was growing at an incredibly rapid pace, not only in terms of prize money distribution, but in the increase in players as well. Cullman sums the history of the tour up nicely when he says, "the Virginia Slims Tour, which culminated annually with the women's championship at Madison Square Garden, became one of the most successful promotions in women's sports history and lasted for more than twenty years" (Cullman, 1998, p. 177).

Adding to the entertainment value of women's tennis and the success of the Virginia Slims tour were the tennis fashions created for each player by Ted Tinling. At the time he helped establish the Virginia Slims tennis circuit, Cullman named Tinling the official clothing designer for the tour. As such, by the mid-1970s, Tinling was overseeing a $500,000 per year budget for dresses for the Virginia Slims players (Thomas, 1990). Tinling described his method for creating individualized dresses for each player when he stated that:

> You see, when you dress a player you must take into account both her personality and the way she hits a ball. I would never dare dress a player without seeing her play. And sometimes the person and the player can be

quite contradictory. I originally objected when Billie Jean wanted frillier dresses, but I went along with her and put her into the sequin business – I called it my firefly collection – because she was big enough to pull it off. They said she looked like an aging rock queen, but in the context of her majesty, that was a compliment.

(Deford, 1984)

Tinling crafted each dress to the personality, and special requests, of its owner, and no two dresses were alike.

Dresses, and the Virginia Slims tour, were never without controversy, especially, it seemed, at Wimbledon. In 1972, Rosie Casals was forced to change her Tinling dress mid-match to a dress that was predominantly white (Tredway & Liberti, 2018). The dress she had been wearing was white with a purple pattern across the front that Wimbledon officials believed spelled "VS," Virginia Slims, the primary sponsor of women's tennis. Casals later jokingly quipped that this dress became so famous that it got a place in the International Tennis Hall of Fame before she did. A few days later, Casals arrived for her match wearing a white dress with the Virginia Slims icon "Ginny" embroidered on the front. What disturbed Wimbledon officials most was that "Ginny," in her traditional pose, is holding a racket in one hand and a long-stem cigarette in the other. Two reprimands in two days led Wimbledon officials to seriously reconsider whether she should be allowed to play at Wimbledon in the future, which she was. Casals responded by stating:

Capt. Gibson [the head referee] said he couldn't allow such blatant advertising but they can't have it both ways. ... If they won't allow Virginia Slims advertising then they shouldn't allow the Fred Perry leaf on shirts, the British Leyland cars that take the players to their hotels, or the Commercial Union results board giving the placings to date in the Grand Prix organized by the firm.

(Evening Independent, 1972)

Indeed, Casals was not advertising cigarettes. She was advertising the Virginia Slims circuit. Its ever-growing success, however, disrupted the tennis establishment which was still controlled by men.

The formation of the Women's Tennis Association, 1973

A growing need for a players' union matched the growth of professional tennis. In 1968, Billie Jean King wrote about the ability for a players' union to buffer against discrimination, especially racial discrimination.[9] She asserted:

Players of the World, speak out! You have a responsibility to the future of the game. If the players form a union, they could become an active factor in tennis. Now a club-oriented organization runs the game from a narrow-minded perspective. The players must not endorse this situation by default.

How many tournaments would be staged in clubs which discriminate on racial or an ethnic basis if the players as one unified body decided not to participate? A players' union motivated by more than just self-interest could be a plus factor to the game.

(King, 1968, p. 32)

The WTA would not be formed for another five years, but it is clear that King could see its value.

In January 1973, according to Billie Jean King, the politics of women's tennis was contentious because of "our decision to sign contracts with Gladys [Heldman] that called for the founding of a Women's International Tennis Federation [WITF], and Gladys's lawsuit, which I later joined, seeking an injunction to prevent the USLTA from disrupting our tournaments" (King, 1988, p. 142; see Leagle.com (1973) for the details of Heldman's lawsuit). According to Rosie Casals, the conceptualization of the WITF had become, by June of 1973 when it was actually formed, the WTA (Casals, personal correspondence, 2016). Heldman's lawsuit, however, failed in court as there was no proof of injurious actions from the USLTA, only threats of such actions.

The WTA was formed by 64 women, including most of the Original 9, during a secret meeting at the Gloucester Hotel in London a few days before the start of Wimbledon in June 1973. There were two main outcomes of the meeting. First, the WTA Tour was created through the merging of the North American-based Virginia Slims tennis circuit and the European-based International Lawn Tennis Federation's Women's Grand Prix circuit. Second, the WTA was formed as a governing body for the WTA Tour which existed apart from the International Tennis Federation (ITF) and the smaller national tennis organizations like the USLTA. Francoise Durr, in describing the meeting, said:

Sitting in that room at the Gloucester Hotel, I felt like we were going to make history. Well, we hoped that was what we were going to do, but we couldn't be sure. So we locked the door and we said we would not leave until we'd created an association of some kind. Some of the women were more nervous than others. But my good friend Betty Stove, who was very tall, stood guard – and nobody left. Of course Billie Jean was the main force behind it all, but Rosie Casals was right there and me too. ... I'm glad we held our nerve because when more people come together it only makes your position stronger. Afterwards I remember feeling a real sense of achievement. When you are on the court, you have to take things into your own hands – you are playing for yourself. But after taking the decision to create the WTA as a group, we were very happy. The men were making more money and it was time to show what we could do too.

(Newman, 2013)

One condition of the meeting from the start was, in feminist fashion, that forming the WTA would be agreed upon by consensus, or not at all. If all of the players were not in agreement, then the push to form the WTA would not proceed.

Once the WTA was formed, Peachy Kellmeyer, a former tennis player who, in 1966, successfully sued to overturn the rule that women could not receive collegiate athletic scholarships, which helped pave the way for the passage of Title IX, became the WTA Tour director, placing her in charge of the tournaments, which she was from 1973–1976. From 1977–1981, Kellmeyer was the executive director of the WTA, second in command behind the CEO.

After the formation of the WTA, Gladys Heldman, who would have been the leading contender for executive director of the new organization, fell into the background. One of two things occurred: either Heldman was exhausted from the long struggle getting women's tennis to that point, or she was pushed out. Her daughter, Julie Heldman, in speaking with me, feels that she was pushed out, as a casualty of the politics (J. Heldman, 2015). If all of the political baggage could be foisted onto Heldman, the new WTA could emerge as a non-political, thereby seemingly more legitimate, organization in professional tennis.

The Battle of the Sexes, 1973

After more than three years of working to get women's professional tennis off the ground and independently viable, another spectacle was about to occur. Possibly knowing that women's professional tennis had arrived, Bobby Riggs had, for months, asked Billie Jean King to play against him. Riggs was well-known in tennis circles for having won the Wimbledon singles title in 1939 and the US Championships, prior to it becoming the US Open, singles titles in 1939 and 1941. King always refused Riggs' offers since she could see no gains in beating, essentially, an old man in a tennis match. Riggs persisted, and eventually convinced Margaret Court, then the #1 player in the world, to play against him. Dubbed "the Mother's Day Massacre," Court, who was not prepared to face the theatrics of a match with Riggs, lost 6–2, 6–1, a resounding defeat. King knew what she had to do. She had to play Riggs, and beat him. The future of women's tennis was under threat and winning could put women's tennis on the right path.

Tinling created King's dress for this event which has become the leading symbol for women's athletic equality. What he created was a dress "in mint green with a royal-blue insert across the bodice, matching her royal-blue tennis shoes, and embroidered with rhinestones and sequins in a 'VS' [Virginia Slims] design" (Tinling, 1977, p. 25). The dress King actually wore for the event was the back-up dress that Tinling had made in case there were problems with the primary dress. Of the job, Tinling asserted:

> I had the job of designing the all-important dress for the Great Challenge [the Battle of the Sexes match]. I was particularly delighted because, that year, every major championship in the world had already been won by a

> player wearing a T.T. [Ted Tinling] design. I thought Billie Jean would beat Riggs and this would be MY Grand Slam.
>
> (Tinling, 1979, p. 290)

Competition, then, was not only between the players. It was on the players.

The original dress for the match was made

> of truly beautiful and unusual fabric, which was composed of opalescent cellophane stitched in wavy stripes onto thin nylon net. By candlelight [which is all the lighting there was when Tinling showed the fabric to King due to a power outage] all its rainbow shades shimmered like an oil slick in the sun. Billie Jean was ecstatic. "I love it. I love it," she cried.
>
> (Tinling, 1979, p. 290)

Tinling's years in fashion, however, had taught him to always be prepared. He told Margaret Goatson Kirgin, his assistant from 1959 until Tinling's death in 1990, that they must make a standby dress for the event. With so little turn-around time, Tinling decided to recreate King's winning Wimbledon dress into one with color instead of the all-white.

When the day of the match came, King rejected the first dress, because when she rubbed her palm on it, she did not like the feel of the cellophane: "'I have never felt anything like this before,' she said. 'I could not risk upsetting my concentration with this strange sensation on my hand'" (Tinling, 1979, p. 291). The details of the standby dress, however, could only be seen from close by, whereas the fabric from the primary dress was shimmery and could be seen from far away. To be visible from the upper seats at the Houston Astrodome, Tinling felt he needed to add 200 rhinestones and 200 sequins to the back-up dress. He sewed these on by hand up to the minute that King's entourage left for the arena. Only after the rhinestones and sequins had been hand-stitched, Tinling felt that "Cinderella Standby could really go to the ball" (Liebowitz, 2003).[10]

King soundly beat Riggs 6–4, 6–3, 6–3. The women's sports revolution had arrived. As evidenced by the media and corporate hype, the entertainment value of women's tennis had become realized. Tinling achieved his Grand Slam in 1973 and added the "Battle of the Sexes" – the most important tennis match to date – to the other feathers in his cap.

Of the Battle of the Sexes match between King and Riggs, Patricia Bradley asserts that "the biggest television audience that had ever turned in for a feminist-related event had nothing to do with organized feminism" (2003, p. 273). Through media hype, quite possibly everyone in the US had not only heard of the Battle of the Sexes, but knew enough about it to have chosen a side. Ted Tinling noted that, "previously Joe [Cullman of Philip Morris] had been a lone prophet of marrying big business with women's tennis. Now big business was dotted all the way around the arena, sharing in a media happening of gargantuan proportions" (Cullman, 1998, p. 177). As evidenced by the media and corporate hype, the entertainment value of women's tennis was realized.

Bradley contends that the King-Riggs Battle of the Sexes match put an end to second-wave feminism. The match was able to do so, according to Bradley, because "once a national audience was established, feminism was vulnerable to the takeover of those parts useful to media" (Bradley, 2003, p. 283), which is what occurred, ushering in postfeminism. According to Angela McRobbie, post-feminism is an action which, on the surface, appears to use and strengthen feminism, but, in fact, these actions undermine its core. McRobbie asserts that "post-feminism ... refer[s] to an active process by which feminist gains of the 1970s and 80s come to be undermined" (McRobbie, 2004, p. 255). How it undermines feminism, McRobbie explains, is that:

> post-feminism positively draws on and invokes feminism as that which can be taken into account, to suggest that equality is achieved, in order to install a whole repertoire of new meanings which emphasise that it is no longer needed, it is a spent force.
> (McRobbie, 2004, p. 255)

When the Battle of the Sexes match is looked upon as the moment when women's equality with men was attained, feminism is seen as having not had a systematic and organized political movement behind it and, if equality has been attained, there is no more need for feminism.

A significant parallel to feminism and the Battle of the Sexes tennis match occurred earlier with racial equality and the March on Washington in 1963. The March on Washington is considered the pinnacle of acceptable Black activism, and acceptance of racial integration is believed to have followed the success of the March on Washington, but it did not. Furthermore, the 2008 election of Barack Obama is viewed as the beginning of post-raciality, but it was not, and the Black Lives Matter social movement shows that.

Conclusion

The era of 1968–1973 in women's tennis was politically contentious. Without second-wave feminism, it is safe to say that the Original 9 would never have come into being. Yet, according to Patricia Bradley, the Battle of the Sexes, the ultimate media and corporate spectacle of entertainment for the Original 9, is what ended second-wave feminism, not just in women's tennis, but second-wave feminism at all levels (Bradley, 2003, p. 283). This is a bold assertion from Bradley, but one that needs to be kept in mind.

The Founders cohort in women's tennis comprised a short period of time; however, events happened rapidly to map the course for women's professional tennis. In 1968, there was one woman, Ann Haydon Jones, who made a stand against inequitable prize money for men and women. Then, in 1970, nine women, the Original 9, made a stand. By the end of 1971, 64 women were making a stand. There is power in numbers. Ann Haydon Jones, with only a one-person protest, was easily ignored, and the members of the Original 9 were threatened by the governing bodies in tennis; however, nothing could be done to admonish 64 women who were joined in consensus for the creation of the WTA. The structure for which the Original 9, Gladys Heldman, Joseph Cullman III, and Ted Tinling built the foundation, not only stood the test of time, but expanded into a global enterprise for sports entertainment. The history of women's tennis shows the power that one person has that can influence nine people, and then snowball into a full-fledged and viable women's tennis tour of 64 people.

Notes

1. This chapter, minus the theoretical framework and the specifics on Gladys Heldman, Joseph Cullman III, and Ted Tinling – essentially a chapter on the history of the Original 9 – has been published as a book chapter in *The Routledge Handbook of Tennis: History, Culture and Politics*, edited by Rob Lake.
2. The other goals of the women's liberation movement – such as abortion rights, men sharing in housework and the raising of children, access to education, etc. – were seemingly not relevant to the Original 9, at least not publicly, though these might have been personal goals of individuals in the Original 9.
3. Of note, Casals began coaching me in 1988, so she had only recently retired.
4. Her younger brother, Randy Moffitt, became a Major League Baseball pitcher, playing for the San Francisco Giants (1972–1981), the Houston Astros (1982), and the Toronto Blue Jays (1983).
5. I received a William and Madeline Welder Smith research travel award from the Briscoe Center for American History at the University of Texas (www.cah.utexas.edu/research/smith_travel.php) to conduct archival research of Gladys Heldman's papers which are housed there. Julie Heldman, who boxed up the papers, told me that I wouldn't find much of interest because Gladys destroyed much of the tennis-specific documents when she was angled out of women's tennis.
6. Some of this section appears in *Fashion, Style & Popular Culture*, in my article titled, "'The Leaning Tower of Pizzazz': Ted Tinling, Couturier for the Women's Professional Tennis Revolution," published in 2016.
7. Pathé films were short film clips shown before feature films in movie theaters.
8. I would love to ask Court if this was a real injury, or if she got cold feet about being a member of a social movement. It's a complete shock that she was a member of the original list. Billie Jean King said that Margaret Court "was one of the first ones to be asked. I wish she would have joined [the Virginia Slims circuit]. I still hope so because it would be good for everyone, especially the spectators" (The WT Reporter, 1971, p. 40).
9. At this time, Arthur Ashe is in the limelight as the #2 ranked male player in the world, so the issues he faced were widely known. Also, in 1966, 13 Black boys protested when they were banned from the segregated country club in Richmond, Virginia, where the USLTA Mid-Atlantic boys under-14 sectional tournament was being held. This event would still be discussed at this time.
10. The original dress was lost soon after the match. Whether it was misplaced at the Astrodome or left in a hotel room, nobody knows. It simply has not been seen again. The "Cinderella Standby" dress, however, the one King wore to beat Riggs, is in the Smithsonian Institute's Museum of American History.

3 The Joiners

The era of Evert and Navratilova, 1974–1990

The Founders cohort had been marked by a group of women collectively working towards equal prize money in women's tennis. Beginning with the Joiners cohort, however, the most prevalent social activism in women's tennis, as it was prior to the Founders cohort, was individual activism rather than collective action. This activism did, however, affect broader social issues and groups of people, rather than it being individual activism for purely personal gains.

The Joiners cohort can be viewed as continuing the work towards equality through equal prize money that the Founders cohort began, but also for the introduction of the representation of women generally, alongside distinct socially marginalized groups. Sociologist Nancy Whittier explains that, for the Joiners cohort, "their primary role was to expand existing organizations" (1995, p. 63), like the WTA and ITF. Likewise, "although most founders continued to play central roles in the organizations they had begun, participants drew a distinction between the 'Old Guard' or 'founding mothers' and newer members" (1995, p. 63). Thus, the Joiners cohort keeps in place and extends the issues of the Founders while also adding issues important to their own generations into the matrix of activism. The Joiners cohort in women's tennis continued to push for equal pay, which was the primary issue of the Founders, but the Joiners cohort also ushered in identity politics, specifically in regards to sex, sexuality, gender, and nationality. For example, during this era, Renée Richards, formerly Richard Raskind, fought to be allowed to compete as a woman at the US Open in 1976, Martina Navratilova defected from the Soviet-controlled Czechoslovakia in 1977, and the public outings of Billie Jean King and Navratilova occurred in 1981.

The social activists in the Joiners cohort showed a response to the critiques of the lack of diversity within the women's movement, but from within women's tennis. As such, as the women's movement splintered into various groups, such as lesbian feminism and Black feminism, and even began questioning what the previously taken-for-granted category of "woman" was, differences from the whiteness, upper-classness, and heteronormative underpinnings in tennis came to the fore.

The Joiners cohort (1974–1990) is identified as the era of Chris Evert and Martina Navratilova. This era begins with Chris Evert winning her first Grand

68   *The Joiners*

Slam title in 1974. Between the 1974 French Open and 1990's Wimbledon, Evert and Navratilova won 36 of the 66 Grand Slam singles titles (or 55 percent) available. The two, along with other players from this era, were greatly influenced by the Original 9, but they also saw the ushering-in of cross-marketing and, relatedly, the increased celebrity status of players. In this way, they bridge the Founders cohort and the current era, the Sustainers cohort. I have marked this cohort's end in 1990, the last year Martina Navratilova, at the age of 33, won a Grand Slam singles title, her ninth Wimbledon singles title.

As previously mentioned, the Joiners cohort acts as an intermediary between the Founders cohort and what was ushered in after the Joiners cohort, the Sustainers cohort. Grassroots feminism, which had propelled the Original 9, was waning for the Joiners cohort because the concepts of feminism, for the most part, had been taken up by universities and other mainstream organizations – without the political impetus grounding the concepts – though there were members of feminist social organizations that were now working within universities.

This is what occurred in women's tennis. Though second-wave feminism was waning throughout the Joiners era, the Founders cohort had put in place a solid feminist foundation from which to build. The Founders cohort had been focused on gaining equal prize money and a collection of tournaments for players to choose from. They had, in order to focus fully on these economic gains, jettisoned any identity markers that might have thwarted their efforts to gain economic parity with men. For the Joiners cohort, with the lingering Cold War fears and the emergence of LGBTQ politics, identity markers became front and center.

All of the women who play tennis professionally are marked by sex; a person has to be a woman to play women's tennis, though, in this chapter, the concept of "woman" will be contested. Intersectionality emerges during the Joiners cohort in more public ways than had been shown during the Founders cohort. Other identities intersect with the category of sex to produce other effects. During the Founders cohort era, other identity politics emerged, especially in regards to sex, gender, sexuality, and nationality. Interestingly, Martina Navratilova was an example of all of these intersections. Navratilova was marked by sex (though the public discourse bantered the question of whether she was a man), but also by gender (that she is too masculine), sexuality (she is a lesbian), and nationality (she is from Czechoslovakia, one of the countries of the former Soviet Bloc). All of these identities are marginalized, and, often, these identities are intertwined, and even mistaken for one another, in the discourse surrounding her. Even with all of these identities emerging publicly during the Joiners cohort, it must be noted that issues of race did not emerge at this time simply because there were no top-ranked Black players. The identity politics that emerged during this time period are the most obvious strand; however, tennis is still operating within the social milieu of its historical underpinnings, namely upper-classness, whiteness, and heteronormativity. With the rivalry between Evert and Navratilova, too, we see the intersectionality of performances, namely, the style of play each used in tennis. Evert's baseline play was deemed feminine and demure, staying at the baseline waiting for the ball to arrive. Navratilova, on the other hand, was understood as masculine and aggressive, displaying her dominant serve-and-volley game in which she rushed the net.

The success of Chris Evert and Martina Navratilova: The potential of the Original 9 is realized

In 1971, a 16-year-old amateur from Florida entered women's tennis by storm. Chris Evert was who Billie Jean King had hoped for, a girl-next-door who could become the new face of women's tennis. When Evert arrived in women's tennis, she noted that:

> well, the women treated me like shit. They were not nice. I was the first one. I was the guinea pig. ... The women made it blatantly clear that I was not their favorite, and that I was intrusive. It was, "How dare you come in, take all our money and get on the cover of *Newsweek*?"
>
> (Roberts, 2005, p. 84)

Indeed, Evert was the guinea pig for women's professional tennis and all that the Original 9 set out to fight for. If women's tennis could not succeed with a player like Evert, the all-American girl-next-door, it was just not going to be successful.

In the summer of 1971, at the beginning of the US Open, King gathered many of the pros together "for a lecture of Evert Envy" (Roberts, 2005, p. 85). Johnette Howard explained the meeting:

> Unbeknownst to Evert, King had ... called a meeting of her fellow players earlier in the tournament – "Yep," King booms with that trademark, explosive laugh of hers, "another meeting! HAH!" – and chided them for giving young Evert the cold shoulder. "I said, 'All right, you guys. How many of you said hi to Chris Evert?'" King recalls. "A couple of them said, 'Well, *she's* not very nice. ... She's such a snob. ... She's standoffish too.' I said, 'You guys, she is *sixteen years old*! And I don't even care how she behaves. We are older. We welcome the younger players. Didn't we talk about doing all this work to give the younger generations an opportunity? Look at her – she is *it*! You are going to be passing the baton to her. She is our next star! We have *got* to have her. So I don't even care if you like her. It's not about 'like,' it's about doing the right thing. And besides, *I* like her.'" Then King told them: "What you guys are really upset about is, she's kicking our asses."
>
> (Howard, 2006, p. 50)

This was not to say that King was afraid of Evert. It meant that King could see that a new era of women's tennis was unfolding.

Evert made it to the semi-finals at the 1971 US Open, where she faced King. If King lost, would it mean the end of the women's tennis tour? King asserted:

> My head started going through the history of what we'd done and I just felt if I lost to Chris, everything we had tried to build was going to go down the drain. They'll say, "Amateur Wins US Open" and "She's better than professionals." Then we could not or might not have had our own tour. And if we don't have a tour, we are screwed, we are finished. I thought, "I have to win. I have to win this match." It's one of the hardest moments I ever had. The only time I cried about a match before or since.
>
> (Howard, 2006, p. 49)

King won 6–3, 6–2. Evert left the US Open with a newfound celebrity status. King helped ensure the strength of the women's tour by reaching the final, where she defeated Rosie Casals to win the championship. Afterwards, King stated, "After all our work to start a tour, we're going to be okay. A star was born this week" (Howard, 2006, p. 51).

Two years later, in 1973, Martina Navratilova played Wimbledon and, at the insistence of the Czechoslovakia Tennis Federation, the short-lived USTA pro circuit instead of the Virginia Slims circuit. As such, Navratilova did not get to know King until 1974. During one of their first conversations, King told Navratilova what she saw in her:

> "You know, you could be the greatest player ever," King said. Navratilova stammered, "Really?" ... Navratilova was still carrying the twenty extra pounds she had gained during her first visit to America. She did not look like a world-beater. "Yeah, Martina, you could be the best player ever – I mean in the history of the game," King said. "God has given you this extraordinary talent. You're an amazing athlete. But if you don't work hard you are not going to make it."
>
> "Are you serious?" Navratilova said, still studying King's face and waiting for the punch line. "I am serious." King nodded. "Just think about it." Then they fell silent.
>
> (Howard, 2006, p. 53)

King had seen Evert's sheer determination and competitive nature. Now, with Navratilova, she had seen the unfettered athleticism. These two styles would become the two styles from which all subsequent players modeled their play.

Together, Evert and Navratilova were two sides of the same coin. Evert had the poise and comportment of a champion. Navratilova had the sheer athletic ability of a champion. However, Evert and Navratilova were opposites in other ways: baseliner and serve-and-volleyer, right-hander and left-hander, the Ice Maiden and the one who cried on court after losses, respectively. In terms of identity markers, Evert and Navratilova were opposites as well: American and Czech, heterosexual and lesbian, feminine and perceived masculine, even Republican and Democrat, respectively. Yet, they are best friends.

These opposites drove the WTA Tour to success. The combined success of Evert and Navratilova ensured that the WTA Tour would remain vibrant and even strengthen through time. Navratilova ended her career having won 167 singles titles, including 18 Grand Slam singles titles. Evert won 154 singles titles, including the same number of Grand Slam singles titles as Navratilova at 18. With a total of 321 singles titles, other players during this era, it is safe to say, rarely won tournaments. Together, they played each other 80 times, with Navratilova having a slight lead at 43 wins. If you think of famous rivalries in sport, none come near to having 80 separate matches. Muhammad Ali and Joe Frazier fought against each other (wait for it!) three times. In tennis, Bjorn Borg and John McEnroe played against each other 14 times. No rivalry in any sport compares to the 80 matches of Navratilova versus Evert.

Martina Navratilova's defection from Czechoslovakia, 1975

Cold War fears surrounded Martina Navratilova when she joined the world of women's professional tennis. Cold War fears played out in depictions of Chris Evert as the pretty, blonde, feminine American who needed to be protected from the women like Navratilova, women that the USSR and Soviet satellite countries produced (see, for example, Spencer, 2003). Many in the West believed that female athletes from behind the Iron Curtain were on State-issued steroids, or not even female at all, but impersonating women. Navratilova's aggressive play and sturdy stature only fed into the dichotomous politics surrounding these two.

Navratilova defected from Czechoslovakia after losing to Chris Evert, the eventual champion, in the semi-finals of the US Open in 1975. Already in the US, she sought political asylum from the Immigration and Naturalization Service office in New York City. Only three people knew her intentions that day: Chris Evert, Billie Jean King, and Rosie Casals. Within a month of her request for asylum, she was granted a permanent residency card for the US. In 1981, Navratilova officially became a US citizen.

The precipitating events for Navratilova's defection began in 1948, following World War II, when her maternal grandparents were forced by the Soviets to surrender their family estate in Czechoslovakia – including 30 acres, vast apple orchards, and a clay tennis court – and move into a small house shared with strangers. Navratilova's forebears lived on the second floor, where Navratilova was born, in the small house overlooking what had been the family's grand estate, in 1956.

George Vecsey, who co-authored Navratilova's autobiography (Navratilova & Vecsey, 1985), claimed that Navratilova, through her family, had memories of nice things, and remembered that they were comfortable. He stated that:

> She may not have had hot water until whenever, but the memory of having nice things goes beyond that. ... On her mother's side, they once had money. They used to look at that house with other people living in it with bitterness. It was part of their family heritage. And there was this sense in

Martina, from a very early age, that things *did* belong to her, that she deserved to have certain things in life economically, psychologically.

(Howard, 2006, p. 59; italics in original)

These memories, according to Vecsey, propelled Navratilova toward success.

Growing unrest in Czechoslovakia was galvanizing into what became known as Prague Spring. Elected as the first secretary of the Communist Party in January of 1968, essentially a presidential role of a satellite nation under the control of a more powerful country, Alexander Dubček began decentralizing the government, creating more autonomy for Czechoslovakia, which allowed for more freedoms for Czechoslovakians. Of the short era of Prague Spring, Navratilova, who was only 11 at the time, said:

You would have to have been deaf, dumb, and blind to miss what was going on. ... People were trying to recapture the old energy they used to have before the war. There was a feeling of excitement in the air. People were holding mass open-air meetings in the town square, promising to work harder to help rebuild Czechoslovakia, wanting only some small incentive, some reward, some freedom. Sometimes you'd go out in the morning and all the Russian banners would be turned around on the buildings as a modest protest.

(Howard, 2006, p. 60)

On August 21 of that year, Russia invaded Czechoslovakia, thereby rolling back the attempts at decentralizing the government and silencing any forms of protest against Russian policies. Navratilova asserted that:

There was a lot of talk that the Russians would come in. ... We never believed it would come to that, and life went on pretty much as usual. ... Nobody was shooting but you had the feeling it could start any minute.

(Navratilova & Vecsey, 1985, p. 50)

Indeed, Navratilova explains that: "I was such a kid that my first reaction [to the Russian invasion] was disappointment over the cancelation of the tournament" (Navratilova & Vecsey, 1985, p. 50). It was not until the collapse of the communist regime with the Velvet Revolution in 1989 that Czechoslovakia became truly autonomous.

In her first taste of the West, Navratilova first played tennis outside of Czechoslovakia in 1969 at a tournament in West Germany. In 1973, Navratilova made her debut in the US with the winter circuit early in the year. By the end of 1974, Navratilova was ranked #9 in the world. However, given that she was not allowed to keep her prize money because she was a citizen of communist Czechoslovakia, Navratilova did not turn pro until after her defection in 1975.

In defecting to the US, Navratilova's actions were not without provocation, nor were they hastily made. After the French Open in 1975, the Czechoslovakian tennis association, led by Antonin Bolardt, complained that she spent too much on her hotel in Paris, which was chosen by Navratilova because it was the same hotel where the American players were staying (Navratilova & Vecsey, 1985, p. 92). They threatened to keep her from playing Wimbledon, the next Grand Slam event of the year. At the last minute, Navratilova and, surprisingly, her parents and sister, were allowed to travel to England so that she could play Wimbledon. With the entire family out of Czechoslovakia, Navratilova's feelings that she wanted to defect grew even stronger. She could defect to the US with her entire family. When Navratilova lost in the quarter-finals, her family had to make a quick decision. In a move surprising to many, the entire family traveled back to Czechoslovakia. Hana Mandlíková, who was also playing the Czech national championships following Wimbledon, described the surprise at seeing Navratilova: "There were stories going around that they had defected. ... People looked as if they had seen a ghost" (Howard, 2006, p. 71). Yet, again, though, the Czechoslovakian tennis association threatened to keep her from playing the upcoming US Open, and they did keep her from traveling to a tournament in France scheduled to be held a few weeks after Wimbledon (Navratilova & Vecsey, 1985, p. 93). This was the last straw, the last threat that Navratilova would allow to be levied against her. She made up her mind to defect to the US on her own.

Navratilova received permission to play the US Open in 1975. She said, however:

> even with the permission to leave the country, I could feel their control tightening. They were treating me like a little girl ... when I was already a professional athlete, and they wouldn't give me permission to play Team Tennis. I had no idea when I'd get out again.
> (Navratilova & Vecsey, 1985, pp. 93–94)

Indeed, prior to the US Open, Navratilova said, "this can't go on, I told myself. Every time you go home, you're going to wonder if they'll ever let you out again. It's time to make your move" (Navratilova & Vecsey, 1985, p. 95). Losing to Evert in a semi-final match at the US Open, Navratilova went directly to the Immigration and Naturalization Service office in New York City to request political asylum.

The next morning, Navratilova discovered that her defection had become a media sensation when CBS News contacted her for an interview. According to Joel Drucker,

> figuring it was all about tennis, [Navratilova] agreed to conduct it at the tournament later that day. But five minutes later came a call from Vera Sukova [the coach of the Czechoslovakian women's national team] asking, "Why did you do it?"
> (Drucker, 2015)

Navratilova quickly contacted her manager, Fred Barman, who had arranged the meeting with the Immigration and Naturalization Service office in New York City, who, in turn, contacted Jeanie Brinkman, public relations director for the Virginia Slims tour. Brinkman spoke of that moment saying, "the story was out … so it was time to let everybody know" (Drucker, 2015). Brinkman arranged a press conference, at which Navratilova continually stated, "I wanted my freedom" (Drucker, 2015).

Navratilova continued to exhibit fear of retaliation from Czechoslovakian authorities. Brinkman recounted a story to Drucker of the evening following the press conference. As Drucker explained:

> That evening, Navratilova dined with Brinkman and Fred Barman in Greenwich Village. Joked the bartender, a friend of Brinkman's, "Hey, Brinkman, the KGB were just here looking for you." Navratilova ran out of the restaurant and spent the next two days in Brinkman's apartment. Said Brinkman, "I had a call from the FBI saying that my phone was tapped and that there was a car in front of my apartment if I needed anything. It was very much out of a spy novel."
>
> (Drucker, 2015)

Behind the scandal, then, the FBI was protecting Navratilova from the KGB. This part of the story is never told.

Navratilova was granted a permanent residency card a month after seeking asylum. She lived with the daily threat that she might be kidnapped by the secret police and forced to return to Czechoslovakia. An agent from the Czechoslovakian embassy in the US met with Navratilova, and she recounted that interaction:

> He said, from now on, they'd let me do anything I wanted, as long as I returned before October 30 [1975], when my visa ran out. But if I tried to come back after that date, I'd go to jail for two years. That told me a lot. That they could even think of talking about jail meant I would be in big trouble if I ever set foot in my country again.... We talked for about two hours, and it must have been clear to them that I wasn't going back.
>
> (Navratilova & Vecsey, 1985, pp. 99–100)

Even with a permanent residency card, Navratilova was not completely in the clear until she could apply for US citizenship in five years. Of this period in her life, Navratilova said:

> I never thought of it as a defection. I didn't know what the word meant. I simply believed that one day I'd come to the United States and stay here. Now I had to wait five years to become a citizen, which meant five years of avoiding flights over Communist territory, just in case my plane would be forced to land and I would be taken off it. I wasn't taking any chances.
>
> (Navratilova & Vecsey, 1985, p. 101)

During this five-year span, Navratilova did not play the French Open, nor did she play the Australian Open for four of those five years.[1] She, instead, stayed closer to safety, playing only the US Open and Wimbledon during this time period between 1975 and 1981. Once Navratilova was granted citizenship, she played all of the Grand Slam events each year.

Despite having defected from Czechoslovakia and becoming a US citizen, Navratilova was never able to escape the perceptions that those in the West have of athletes, especially female athletes, from behind the Iron Curtain. This became even more pronounced in the 1980s, when she sculpted her body into peak performance.

In 1966, the International Amateur Athletic Federation (IAAF) instituted the first sex test for athletes, a "nude parade" to verify athletes' sexual organs, at the European Championships in Track and Field. According to Lindsay Parks Pieper:

> Cold War fears infiltrated all facets of culture as panic about the possibility of atomic warfare between the USSR and the USA consumed global attention and severed the world into East and West along the ideological "Iron Curtain". Not surprisingly, sport emerged as a contested arena and the Olympics morphed into a forum to demonstrate national superiority. Accordingly, during the "Cold War Olympics" the medal count gained increasing importance; when the USSR triumphed – largely due to the Russian women's victories – alarm ensued.
>
> (Pieper, 2012, p. 678)

Fear of the superiority of the Soviet female athlete led to anxiety that the Soviet female athletes were not female at all, but males posing as women. Of course, the superiority of the Soviet female athletes was culturally based. The Soviet Union, and likewise its satellites, focused on sport as an arena for success, and young girls were trained similarly to young boys. Within the communist system, there were only members of the proletariat, not distinctions between men and women specifically. Countries in the West did not focus on sports, nor female advancement in the same way, and it showed at the Olympics every four years.

The 1968 Olympics in Mexico City ushered in a different sex test. The buccal smear test, more commonly known as the Barr body exam, was an examination of cells from inside an athlete's cheek to determine chromosomal makeup.[2] This exam was the standard for sport until 1999. Since 1999, sex verification is conducted for an athlete only when there is suspicion that the female athlete is male.[3] Though sex testing is always conducted under the guise of fairness, its underlying impetus is gender patrolling of female athletes. Female athletes are allowed to be strong and powerful, but they must always do so while performing in a feminine manner.

Navratilova's musculature, now a standard feature in women's tennis, coupled with being from a former Soviet satellite and being a lesbian, led many to question her sex. These features – gender, nationality, and sexuality – intersected to create a fear of Navratilova which was unwarranted. Juxtaposed with Chris Evert, these features of Navratilova were even more pronounced.

Renée Richards and the redefining of womanhood, 1977

In 1976, the WTA and the USTA faced an issue that neither could have predicted would arise. The question would be, what does the term "women" in Women's Tennis Association, or women's professional tennis, actually mean? Rather than the identity marker of sex being etched in stone, the fluidity of the term's meanings had to be considered.

Before opting for sex reassignment surgery in 1975, Renée Richards was Richard Raskind. Raskind had been a formidable amateur tennis player, captain of the Yale tennis team, an officer in the US Navy, one of New York City's leading ophthalmologists, and highly ranked in the men's over-35 division of the USTA. After the surgery, as Renée Richards, she relocated to Southern California in order to start her life anew.

While in California, Richards returned to one of her loves: tennis. Now a woman who was 6'2" tall, Richards found great success in tennis and began to enter, and win, tournaments. After defying her friends and peers, Richards decided to enter the La Jolla tennis tournament in California. The unknown Renée Clarke defeated the defending champion in easy fashion (Birrell & Cole, 1990, p. 1). This drew the suspicion of tennis officials and spectators. After a birth certificate was revealed, all those in tennis were now aware of the transformation Richards had undertaken. Her life went from being private, with no one knowing about her surgery, to being very public, with one announcer at the La Jolla tournament telling Richards, "you were a private person before you won the finals in La Jolla" (Drath, 2011).

After the La Jolla tournament, Richards entered the draw at a tournament in South Orange, New Jersey, organized by Eugene Scott, an old friend (Birrell & Cole, 1990, p. 1). With Richards' entry into the tournament:

> The United States Tennis Association (USTA) and the Women's Tennis Association (WTA) promptly withdrew their sanctions from the South Orange tournament. In protest of Richards' participation, 25 of the 32 women originally scheduled to play in South Orange withdrew to enter an alternative tournament hastily arranged and sanctioned by the USTA and the WTA.
>
> (Birrell & Cole, 1990, p. 1)

To clarify, players may have pulled out of the tournament because of Richards' participation, but it is more likely they pulled out because the tournament was no longer sanctioned, meaning it would not count towards ranking points.

When Richards then won a tournament in Connecticut "that qualified her to play on the Avon satellite circuit, a competition level one notch below the women's main professional tour" (Howard, 2006, p. 182), the WTA began to get nervous.

Subsequently, the USTA, the WTA, and the US Open Committee began requiring sex chromosome tests, the Barr body test, for all female competitors at the US Open. This was a definitive test that Richards would surely fail. She refused to take it. Because the Barr body test verifies one's DNA, all athletes, including post-operative trans people, will exhibit the X or Y chromosome that they have had since birth. Refusing to subject herself to the sex testing, Richards was not able to compete in the 1976 US Open and other professional events. Instead, she competed in amateur events and became a star, winning most of them. Afterwards, the WTA used this test for all female athletes in tournaments around the world.

In 1976, Richards was barred from entering the US Open because she had not successfully passed the Barr body chromosome test to prove that she was a woman. Richards had not failed the test; she just simply had not taken the test. Richards sued the USTA, citing the 14th Amendment, arguing that she was not being treated equally (Leagle.com, 1977). She requested an injunction against the USTA to allow her to play the US Open.

At the US Open in 1977, by court order, Richards was allowed to enter the women's draw of the tournament. Johnette Howard explained that:

> In August of 1977, she won a favorable decision in the New York State Supreme Court. She was then forty-three years old and, after years of hormone therapy, no threat to dominate the women's tour. Still, some players boycotted the first few pro tournaments Richards entered, and alarmists cried that allowing Richards to play would only encourage more men to have sex-change operations and stream into women's sports – an argument Navratilova, among many others, found patently ridiculous.
> (Howard, 2006, p. 182)

Susan Birrell and CL Cole capture the gendered ambiguity, as opposed to the previously described sexed ambiguity, of Renée Richards during this time period. As they describe:

> Diane Fromholtz' complaint captured the ambiguity most protesters could not work through: "People are laughing at us, at the way she walks on and acts like a female." ... With the very act of refuting Richards' claims to be female, Fromholtz genders Richards female. The most telling statement was Roz Reid's protest on behalf of his wife, Kerry Melville Reid: "We don't believe Renee is a woman. Kerry will never play her again."
> (Birrell & Cole, 1990, p. 8)

It was not just players who were confused by Richards' gender. For example, "early in the controversy W.E. Hester, vice-president of the USTA, stated, 'I don't know on what grounds we could admit her and on what grounds we can refuse to admit him'" (Birrell & Cole, 1990, p. 9).

Additionally, Birrell and Cole describe the media response to Richards as well as the player and tournament official responses. They note that:

The press followed their convention of mentioning details of physical appearance of women athletes they generally ignore in male athletes. By reporting on physical appearance, the press legitimates physicality as a valid means for assessing one's sex status, thus confusing the issue of the sex/gender relationship and obscuring the cultural production of such relationships.

(Birrell & Cole, 1990, p. 9)

According to Birrell and Cole, Richards accepted this and even expanded upon it because it "represented a casual and ready acceptance of her femaleness" (Birrell & Cole, p. 9). Furthermore, "because the media focused on men's 'natural' ability rather than the years of privileged access to sport that Richard Raskind had enjoyed, they foregrounded physical definitions of sex and gender and obscured cultural ones" (Birrell & Cole, 1990, p. 16). So, too, did Richards offer herself for this interpretation. Indeed, "Richards' inability to dominate women's tennis is offered as proof of his/her status as a woman" (Birrell & Cole, 1990, p. 16).

Renée Richards pushed the boundaries of womanhood in women's professional tennis. She risked public exposure but, politically, she was motivated for these changes to occur in tennis. Richards' actions paved the way for the relatively easy entry of Sarah Gronert from Germany into professional tennis in 2012. Gronert was born intersex; however, the WTA had policies in place that quickly and quietly cleared Gronert for competition as a woman. Gronert has Richards to thank for that.

The public outing of Billie Jean King and Martina Navratilova, 1981

In *Excitable Speech: A Politics of the Performative* (1997), Judith Butler makes the claim that identities do not exist until speech calls them forward.[4] Indeed, one "must utter the term in order to perform the circumscription of its usage" (Butler, 1997, p. 104). The example she uses is homosexuality in the US military. Since the origins of the US military, there has been homosexuality within the ranks; however, it was not homosexuality then, merely the act of having sex. Attempts to punish and contain homosexuality within the military did not exist until the issue of homosexuality in the military had been named, and therefore labeled. As Butler explains:

The regulations [against homosexuality] bring the term into public discourse, rhetorically enunciating the term, performing the circumscription by which – and through which – the term becomes speakable.... The regulation must conjure one who defines him or herself as a homosexual in order to make plain that no such self-definition is permissible within the military.

(1997, p. 104)

Prior to being named, homosexuality technically did not exist because it had not yet been called forth. The same can be said of lesbians in women's sports, especially women's tennis.

Once "lesbian" was in the discourse and, likely, the stereotypical images the term conjures, women's sports became the grounds where the hunt took place. Lesbian politics had an abrupt public meeting with women's professional tennis in 1981. Billie Jean King, who had been married to Larry King since 1965, was publicly outed as a lesbian in April 1981, when her former secretary and lover, Marilyn Barnett, sued her for "galimony." Soon after, in late July 1981, Martina Navratilova was publicly outed as a lesbian when a newspaper article in the *New York Daily News* confirmed that she and Rita Mae Brown, the novelist, had been lovers, and that she was currently having an affair with Nancy Lieberman, who, at the time, was a basketball player for the Dallas Diamonds of the Women's Pro Basketball League (predecessor to the Women's National Basketball League). The responses from both King and Navratilova, though attempts to protect themselves, set lesbian and LGBTQ politics back ten or more years.[5] This is ironic given their sainthood status in LGBTQ politics now. However, given the context of LGBTQ politics in 1981, this might have been the best that either of them could do at the time.

Billie Jean King attributes her delay in coming out as a lesbian to three things: 1) she was married to Larry King at the time; 2) her parents were homophobic; and, 3) it would be the end of women's professional tennis. In 2007, King said of her marriage to Larry, which ended in divorce in 1987:

> It was very hard on me because I was outed and I think you have to do it in your own time. Fifty percent of gay people know who they are by the age of 13, I was in the other 50%.[6] I would never have married Larry if I'd known. I would never have done that to him. I was totally in love with Larry when I was 21.
>
> (Walsh, 2007)

Furthermore, King elaborated on her family and the potential impact her outing could have had on women's tennis when she said:

> I wanted to tell the truth but my parents were homophobic and I was in the closet. As well as that, I had people tell me that if I talked about what I was going through, it would be the end of the women's tour. I couldn't get a closet deep enough. I've got a homophobic family, a tour that will die if I come out, the world is homophobic and, yeah, I was homophobic. If you speak with gays, bisexuals, lesbians and transgenders, you will find a lot of homophobia because of the way we all grew up. One of my big goals was always to be honest with my parents and I couldn't be for a long time. I tried to bring up the subject but felt I couldn't. My mother would say, "We're not talking about things like that," and I was pretty easily stopped because I was reluctant anyway. I ended up with an eating disorder that

came from trying to numb myself from my feelings. I needed to surrender far sooner than I did. At the age of 51, I was finally able to talk about it properly with my parents and no longer did I have to measure my words with them. That was a turning point for me as it meant I didn't have regrets any more.

(Walsh, 2007)

Thus, in an effort to protect women's tennis, as alluded to before, the Founders cohort remained focused on prize money equity, not allowing identity politics to derail that commitment. King maintained her silence so that the Founders cohort could reach and maintain its objectives.

In a potentially controversial position to take, it is the contention here that lesbian politics were set back a decade or more with the public outing of King and Navratilova due to their responses to the situations. King took the angle that her affair with Barnett was a mistake. Though she may have been claiming that her affair with Barnett specifically was a mistake, since Barnett was the type of person to publicly do her harm, since King was married and had a commitment to her husband. Instead, what is remembered is that King asserted that the lesbian relationship without any qualifiers was a mistake. In her second autobiography, rushed to publication in 1982 in order to get her side of the story added to the discourse as quickly as possible, King asserted that:

> What bothered me when I became aware that my privacy would be invaded and the affair would be publicly disclosed in the lawsuit was what people would think whenever my name came up. I feared that I always would be categorized by that, whatever else I have accomplished.... I worked hard and became famous for being a tennis champion, and then, because of the disclosure, I was put in the vulnerable position of being remembered and categorized because of this very private and inconsequential episode.
>
> (King & Deford, 1982, p. 10)

With this statement, King leaves very little wiggle room to claim that she is only dismissing Barnett, not homosexuality altogether. Indeed, Susan Birrell and Mary McDonald (2012) claim that this event is a "heteronarrative," a story of King that begins with a telling of her relationship with her husband. Barnett provides a "narrative disruption" to this narrative, and then the narrative is resolved by King and her husband's relationship not only remaining intact, but seemingly being strengthened.

Similarly, Navratilova's angle following her public outing was that she was bisexual and just happened to have these two relationships with women, but she usually was more attracted to men.[7] Though Lieberman simply disappeared, recrafting herself as a born-again Christian[8] and a heterosexual woman, Brown went on the offensive with the publication of her book *Sudden Death* in 1984, a soap opera novel about women's professional tennis and an ever so slightly veiled depiction of Navratilova. Navratilova's autobiography, *Martina*, published in 1985, was a direct response to Brown's *Sudden Death*, her attempt at adding her own account to the discourse. Not to be outdone, Brown became lovers with Judy Nelson, who had sued Navratilova for "galimony" in 1991 after their eight-year relationship ended.

Circling back to Butler's analysis of the term homosexuality, she asserts that "a homosexual is one whose definition is to be left to others, one who is denied the act of self-definition with respect to his or her sexuality, one whose self-denial is a prerequisite for military service" (1997, p. 105). Similarly, King and Navratilova did not have the opportunity for self-definition, though they each quickly attempted self-definition after being outed, with mixed success.

For all of the negative issues for lesbian politics brought up here, King and Navratilova did open the door for discourse on the topic of lesbians in sport. Given the 2016 World Cup championship kiss between Abby Wambach and her then-wife, Sarah Huffman, in a packed stadium and on national and international television, lesbians in sport seem like such a benign issue now, more than 30 years later. However, King and Navratilova started the conversation, even if awkwardly.

Margaret Court and the lesbian menace in women's tennis

Margaret Court dominated women's tennis from 1960 to 1970, and again in 1973. In total, Court won 24 Grand Slam singles titles which leads all players, male or female, in the history of tennis.[9] Billie Jean King wrote a vivid description of Margaret Court, the player, in 1974:

> She was tall, powerful, consistent, and moved beautifully for a person her size – and her game hasn't changed much since I first met her. Very predictable, very mechanical. No touch, no finesse, very little versatility. But she didn't need any of that because she was so damned big and so damned consistent. She just played the same way every day and got away with it because she was such a great, physically imposing athlete. Her personality hasn't changed much, either. In 1962 she was shy, almost diffident. She trained diligently, liked her tennis, and that was it – very Australian.
> (King & Chapin, 1974, p. 70)

Indeed, Rosie Casals nicknamed Court "the arm" because she had incredible reach. A player can get away with being predictable and mechanical if she can reach every ball that comes her way.

Billie Jean King was a solid contender in women's tennis, beginning in 1966 until 1974; however, King dominated women's tennis from 1971–1972, breaking into Court's reign, winning half of the available Grand Slam singles titles during those two years.

King and Court had vastly different worldviews off the court. In her autobiography (Court & McGann, 1976), Court continually mentioned the abortion that King had, which was announced in the inaugural issue of *Ms. Magazine* in

1972, with disdain. In fact, any mention of King seems to be made with disdain and dismissiveness. Court, on the other hand, had three children during her tennis career, taking a year or more off with the birth of each child, and only retiring after becoming pregnant with her fourth child.

Court likes to set up these dichotomies in her autobiography, *Court on Court: A Life in Tennis* – how she either has more tennis talent, or more of a moral standing than anyone else. For example, Court wrote that:

> Billie Jean has changed tremendously from the person I first met at Wimbledon in 1962. We got on very well then despite our intense rivalry. She has high moral standards and was a good person. She'd talk about her faith in God and reading the bible and having a family – that's a long way from the Billie Jean who told the whole world about her abortion, when she became an active women's libber.
>
> (Court & McGann, 1976, p. 164)

King, on the other hand, always spoke of Court with respect and admiration in her autobiography, *Billie Jean* (King & Chapin, 1974), even when describing their differences. For example, King describes the differences between her and Larry, her husband, and Court and Barry, her husband, in the following passage:

> Larry and I have been compared (most unfavorably) with Margaret Court and her husband, Barry. They were married in late 1967, and four years later she dropped off the circuit for eleven months to have her child, Danny. When she started playing again in mid-1972 the three of them were an inseparable fixture on the circuit. Which was great. Barry was a delightful Australian sportsman from Perth who really enjoyed traveling and taking care of Danny while Margaret played, and since it was pretty obvious they had a good thing going, more power to them. But it just wasn't the way that Larry and I could ever have lived – if for no other reason than that he goes bananas if he has to spend more than forty-eight hours in the same city. This time, the comparisons were really vicious, especially after my abortion became big news.
>
> (King & Chapin, 1974, p. 150)

King, though, spins this interest by the media in comparing the two women through a feminist lens when she states:

> It wasn't just the comparison that bothered me ... I felt it was another example of the old double standard. Nobody ever writes about the really intimate life of a male athlete. It's usually off limits, just like it is with male politicians and other male public figures. I don't think I should be treated any differently just because I was a woman.
>
> (King & Chapin, 1974, p. 150)

It seems as though King is able to easily separate the accomplishments of Court the tennis player from the less desirable attributes of Court the minister.

Court, indeed, distanced herself from women's liberation and feminism, which also meant that she was distancing herself from King. Court wrote that:

> Since I'm no women's libber I wasn't crazy for an exclusively female tour. Naturally I sympathized with the aim of increasing women's prize money, but I honestly didn't believe we were entitled to equal money with men until we could prove that the public wanted to see us play as much as they wanted to see the men.
> (Court & McGann, 1976, p. 157)

However, because she was the top female player in the most high-profile female sport, Court was, whether she liked it or not, a symbol for women's liberation. Court continues by stating that:

> [Billie Jean King] also won't let up on women's lib and me. "Margaret says she's not a women's libber, but she is," Billie Jean declared on a recent television sports show. "Look at Barry – he doesn't work, she's supporting the family." She says this everywhere she goes. In some stupid way she thinks I'm playing only because of the big money in the game. I'd probably still be playing if tennis were strictly amateur because I enjoy the game. Barry understands this. Despite what Billie Jean says, he has a full-time job.
> (Court & McGann, 1976, p. 165)

Indeed, Barry Court, Margaret's husband, did have a job, of sorts. He was his wife's manager while she was playing on the tour. Male players have wives who do these duties, but they are just called wives. Husbands of female tennis players are, apparently, managers. This would be the double standard that King is exposing.

On the need for feminism and women's liberation, King states that there are two reasons they are needed: 1) all women have faced sexism at one point or another; and, 2) all women have different desires and expectations for their own lives. King continues by asserting:

> Liberalized abortion laws? Yes. An end to job discrimination? Of course. Equal pay for equal work? No question. But those are details. What really counts is for us to be able to fulfill our potential in whatever way we choose. And the awareness of that possibility, that right, is only the beginning; the achievement is the end.
> (King & Chapin, 1974, p. 162)

Interestingly, Court's resurgence in 1973 helped fuel the artificial binary between King and Court, between feminists and those perceived to be anti-feminist, or at least not willing to push against the traditional (i.e., white, upper class and male) tennis establishment. This division was not lessened at all by Court's failed attempt at beating Bobby Riggs in the first Battle of the Sexes match. Played on Mother's Day in 1973, it has been dubbed "The Mother's Day Massacre." Court's failure to beat Riggs – and, in fact, Court was completely obliterated by Riggs 6–2, 6–1 – forced King to play Riggs whose requests she had otherwise been ignoring (King & Chapin, 1974). King won that five-set match in a very convincing manner, 6–4, 6–3, 6–3. Women's liberation was here to stay.

The first time Martina Navratilova played Margaret Court in the 1975 Australian Open quarter-final, Navratilova was 18 and Court was 32 years of age and well past her tennis prime. Of this match, Court wrote:

> For some reason my quarter-final match with 18-year-old Martina Navratilova was not put into the stadium but onto an outside court, with loudspeakers blaring and trains rattling by. I found the conditions extremely distracting and did not concentrate properly against Martina, who put me out in straight sets. Once again the press blared "*Upset*," but it was not all that surprising. Martina at 15 was champion of Czechoslovakia, a tremendously talented and fiercely competitive left-hander who plays the serve and volley game. She is capable of beating any player in the world. In a few years – or maybe even sooner – she could well be the world's number one player.
>
> (Court & McGann, 1976, p. 196)

Indeed, Navratilova clarified that, during this time period, only the women's semi-finals and finals were played in the stadium (Navratilova, May 15, 2014). All other matches were relegated to outside courts. A few months later, at the US Open, Navratilova defected from Czechoslovakia, seeking political asylum in the United States.

Navratilova did, indeed, reach the pinnacle of women's tennis as Court predicted. Court, however, did not approve of Navratilova's off-court lesbian life. A few months after King's outing, to put her own spin on a *New York Daily News* article that had been published, Navratilova publicly came out through Skip Bayless, a journalist for the *Dallas Morning News* (Bayless, 1981). Neither King nor Navratilova were allowed to come out as lesbians on their own terms during this time period; however, each did the best they could under difficult conditions. The notable difference between King and Navratilova in 1981 was that King was nearing the end of her career and Navratilova was just emerging into her most dominant years on tour.

In 1990, the week after Navratilova won her record ninth Wimbledon title, Court gave an interview in which she stated that Navratilova and other lesbians were ruining tennis and that Navratilova herself was a poor role model for children (Associated Press, 1990). More specifically:

> Wimbledon champion Martina Navratilova is a poor role model for aspiring professional tennis players because she is a homosexual, former Grand

Slam winner Margaret Court says. Court ... said in newspaper and radio interviews today that Navratilova's admitted homosexuality is a bad example for younger players. "She (Navratilova) is a great player, but I'd like to see somebody at the top to whom the younger players can look up to," said the 47-year-old Court, a born-again Christian who now lives in Perth. "It is very sad for children to be exposed to it (homosexuality)."

Court said some players had been led into homosexuality by other senior players, but did not identify them. She also said she believes Navratilova was influenced into a lesbian lifestyle during her early years on the pro tour. Court added that some players are accompanied to tournaments by their families to shield them from potential trouble. "If I had a daughter on the circuit, I'd want to be there," Court said. "There are now some players who don't even go to the tournament changing rooms because of the problem."

(Associated Press, 1990)

This turned out to be Court's first foray into merging her current occupation as a Christian minister with her former tennis career. This is significant later on when defenders of Court assert that to protest at the Australian Open is inappropriate because these two lives of Court are separate. They, indeed, are not separate; how could they be?

Martina Navratilova: Gender, aesthetic masculinity, and lesbian culture

During the Joiners cohort, nationality, sex, and sexuality emerged and have been discussed. The other component of the triad with sex and sexuality is gender. Gender, though seemingly innocuous, can imply to the onlooker a person's sex and sexuality (Tredway, 2014).

Martina Navratilova has been a symbol for lesbians worldwide for over four decades. We have seen her as a teenager, as a world champion, advertising Subaru cars (which have been called "the lesbian Volvo" in LGBTQ communities for decades), and as the poster child for AARP (formerly, the American Association of Retired Persons). Navratilova was the face of lesbian culture that everyone could see and know, at least through celebrity-mediated snippets.

Navratilova, now the aesthetic embodiment of female masculinity, was, when her tennis career began in the early 1970s, what would popularly be referred to as androgynous. Navratilova's own gendered embodiment follows the prescribed notions of gender held within the women's movement and lesbian culture. As the gendered aesthetic shifted within lesbian culture, so too did Navratilova's aesthetic. Though Navratilova is viewed as a trailblazer for lesbians, it is actually more likely the case that Navratilova was at the front door when society arrived to open the door just a crack, with Navratilova pushing it the rest of the way open. She was simply the most powerful woman with the luxury of being in the most high-profile women's sport.[10] In essence, when lesbian culture leaned towards androgyny in the 1970s with second-wave feminism, so did Navratilova.

When it leaned towards butch-femme aesthetics beginning in the mid-1980s, Navratilova was butch, or, what I will refer to as exhibiting female masculinity.

Martina Navratilova was the female tennis player who most epitomized masculinity within the dominant discourse. She rushed the net, she was from Eastern Europe, which brought with it negative stigmas that the US held about female athletes from the Soviet Bloc, and, most of all, after the mid-1980s, she was muscular; however, the ways in which she was feminine get muffled in the discourse. In 1980, Navratilova proclaimed, "I find it offensive and ridiculous that anyone should think that I am gay" (Gever, 2003, p. 159). The next year, just after Billie Jean King's public outing, Navratilova, though already known for almost a decade as bisexual, was publicly outed when an article was published in the *New York Daily News* linking her with Nancy Lieberman. In a self-assessment, Navratilova claimed that her "biggest image problem was not lesbianism per se. ... The major problem she described in her autobiography is femininity or, rather, her shortcomings in that department" (Gever, 2003, pp. 166–167). Navratilova seems to be asserting that sexuality is not as much of an issue in women's tennis and the media spotlight is actually on a lack of a feminine performance. It is possible that Navratilova was not so much lacking femininity, but that she had been marked as masculine through the public discourse, similar to Amélie Mauresmo.[11]

With every gain that women have made in sport, there has been a simultaneous reaction questioning the sexual orientation of women athletes as well as the actual sex/gender of women in sport. Simply stated, the assumption has been, as KL Broad asserts, "sports are masculine; therefore, women in sports are masculine; therefore, women in sports are lesbians" (2002, p. 182).

Indeed, homophobia is used in this way to police women and even thwart their athletic achievements. Martha Gever describes the closet of women's tennis which was, surprisingly, aided by journalists:

> Long before "don't ask; don't tell" became shorthand for official U.S. government policies ... the same principles governed a tacit bargain struck between the sports press and lesbian or gay athletes. Navratilova (and undoubtedly countless others) went along with the strategy, because it allowed them to keep in check nosy, scolding members of the press, or at least those who always treated homosexuality as a sensational topic.
> (2003, p. 161)

Journalists, at least before the current mass media age of televised press conferences, were the main conduit between athletes and the general public. During the 1970s–1990s, this tacit agreement was critically important for closeted lesbian players.

Lesbian culture, for better or for worse, has a history of strongly-prescribed gender norms. From the 1920s through the 1960s, lesbian culture was centered around bar culture, and lesbians were either butch or femme, with no middle ground available. With the emergence and strengthening of the women's movement in the late 1960s and 1970s, lesbians were androgynous and those who were butch or femme were viewed as outdated or, worse, perpetuating heterosexual normativity and patriarchy. Kath Weston claims that:

> One way to characterize the 1970s with respect to the gendering of relations among lesbians would be as an androgynous interlude between the first and second waves of butch/femme. During this period, the women's movement exerted considerable influence on the wider lesbian population.... They began to minimize gendered differentiation in appearance.
> (2002, pp. 78–79)

Of note, this "androgynous interlude" is among white lesbians. Black and Latina lesbian culture maintained the butch/femme social structures through this time period (see, for example, the classic lesbian text, *Boots of Leather, Slippers of Gold: The History of a Lesbian Community*, Kennedy & Davis, 1993). Elaborating further, Jack Halberstam asserts that:

> Some women rejected butch-femme and its forms of sexual role playing as a gross mimicry of heterosexuality. The rejection of the butch as a repulsive stereotype by some lesbian feminists also had the unfortunate effect of pathologizing the only visible signifier of queer dyke desire; the rejection of the femme produced limits for lesbian feminine expression and grounded middle-class white feminism within an androgynous aesthetic. The suppression of role playing, therefore, by lesbian feminists in the 1970s and 1980s further erased an elaborate and carefully scripted language of desire that butch and femme dykes had produced in response to dominant culture's attempts to wipe them out.
> (1998, p. 121)

This erasing of masculine and feminine gendered aesthetics among lesbians in the 1970s was enacted as a way to prevent the perceived gendered domination of one person over another in sexual relationships. To feminists of this era, a lesbian who was masculine was assuming male privilege and, thus, in a position to subjugate her more feminine partner. Likewise, during this time period, lesbians who took on a more feminine aesthetic were viewed as buying into the view that they were second-class citizens. Thus, androgyny, where everyone dressed in the same non-gendered "fashion" was the standard for lesbian aesthetics.

Martina Navratilova has been a celebrity and an icon for lesbian culture since the 1970s, traversing all three of the previously mentioned eras of lesbian culture. In 1972, Navratilova was 16 and played in her first tournament in the US. Navratilova had an androgynous aesthetic in the 1970s. Her style of play was to serve-and-volley, serving the ball and then rushing the net. This style was very common through the 1970s, because many of the major tennis tournaments were played on grass, along with three of the four Grand Slam events (Wimbledon – which still is, the US Open, and the Australian Open). Grass courts cause the ball to have a low, and sometimes erratic, bounce. Serve-and-volleyers have a huge advantage on grass because they hit the ball in the air, not off the bounce.

In the early 1980s, however, butch-femme aesthetics returned to lesbian culture. Weston explains that:

> Eighties butch-femme ... is a self-conscious aesthetic that plays with style and power, rather than an embrace of one's "true" nature against the constraints of straight society.
>
> (2002, p. 68)

Furthermore, Halberstam asserts, through Rita Laporte, that:

> The qualities, femininity and masculinity, are distributed in varying proportions in all Lesbians.... A butch is simply a Lesbian who finds herself attracted to and complemented by a Lesbian more feminine than she, whether this butch be very or only slightly more masculine than feminine.
>
> (1998, p. 122; quoting Laporte, 1971, p. 4)[12]

Rather than the highly-structured butch-femme expectations and norms in lesbian culture from the 1920s through the 1960s, the 1980s were marked by a more performance-based aesthetic that did not necessarily dictate all the facets of the lives of each butch and femme, merely the lesbian's outward appearance.

From my own history, this era was marked more as so-called butch lesbians being the protesters in the streets, facing the police who were all too willing to remind us of the status quo, and, especially, being the ones to draw everyone's fire, so that those lesbians younger than us could just exist and gather strength to then take our places on the front lines. Femmes in this era did not mark themselves as lesbians like butch lesbians did. In this way, femmes were sort of undercover in the world. As Kara Keeling asserts in her discussion of Black femmes, "the black femme is invisible within these common senses because the things that distinguish her as a black femme are not visible to those common senses until she is placed in relationship to the butch" (2007, pp. 144–145). This is true of white femmes as well.

In the 1980s, though, Navratilova crafted her body into an incredible physique for sport. And, with her new body, she became the dominant force in women's tennis. In Grand Slam tournaments alone, Navratilova won 18 singles titles, 31 women's doubles titles and 10 mixed doubles titles. At Wimbledon, she reached the final 12 times, including 9 consecutive years from 1982–1990, winning 9 times. Navratilova is one of only three women to have won the Grand Slam "boxed set": winning the singles, doubles, and mixed doubles titles at each Grand Slam event. She holds the record for the most singles titles (167) and the most doubles titles (177) on tour. Navratilova also holds three of the six longest winning streaks in singles, with the longest being 74 consecutive matches, which she reached in 1984.

By the 1980s, with the emergence of "teen phenoms" and the moving of two of the three grass court Grand Slam events to hard courts, leaving Wimbledon as the only grass court event, the serve-and-volley style of play began to wane, especially for women.[13] At this time, the serve-and-volley game was deemed overly aggressive (i.e., masculine) with increased numbers of baseline players from the Chris Evert mold, exhibiting societal ideals of femininity: patience, counter-punching, hitting consistently but not with power, keeping the ball in play until the other player makes a mistake, etc. Navratilova's winning streak through the 1980s fed into this change, too. Navratilova, being a serve-and-volleyer, who is also a lesbian, did not impede the linking of the serve-and-volley game with masculinity among female players.

Though there are still pockets of lesbians espousing butch-femme aesthetics, in the mid- to late-1990s, lesbian culture began moving towards a blending of masculine and feminine aesthetics – what is popularly referred to as "gender fuck" fashion. Weston claims that gender fuck "represent[s] a deliberate attempt to disconcert viewers by denaturalizing gender" (2002, p. 76). One can remember Navratilova's wedding suit, tailored and masculine, that she wore with a delicate pair of heels of the same color when she married Julia Lemigova in December 2014. This era marks the beginning of queer culture. For instance, a person did not have to be a lesbian to mark herself as masculine, though, in doing so, this person would be considered "queer." Heterosexual men wore skirts, as did butch lesbians. Gay men grew facial hair and straight women stopped shaving their legs. Anything is possible with gender fuck fashion.

In her important work, *Female Masculinity*, Halberstam, in referring to and extending Susan Cahn's argument about women's sports, states that:

> She [Susan Cahn] insists: "Women's athletic freedom requires that certain attributes long defined as masculine – skill, strength, speed, physical dominance, uninhibited use of space and motion – become human qualities and not those of a particular gender." The only way to extend such attributes to women, I argue, is not simply to make them "human" but to allow them to extend to women as masculinity.
>
> (1998, p. 272; quoting Cahn, 1994, p. 279)

Indeed, particular features of masculinity for women will always be stigmatized unless the entire gender form is allowed to be used freely by women. Women's sports are where female masculinity will be appropriated and normalized first. This friction – what Anna Tsing refers to as "the awkward, unequal, unstable, and creative qualities of interconnection across difference" ... "can lead to new arrangements of culture and power" (2005, pp. 4–5). The friction of female masculinity and sport is power both in sports and in society in general. Women, by not allowing themselves to be subjugated, demand power from the status quo and, often, it is given.

In tennis, maybe instead of having the docile femme playing at the baseline against her counterpart, the imaginary aggressive butch, serving and volleying, we should move away from the imaginary. Allow women to play the game they have. Stop the ever-increasing technical specifications of rackets which only serve baseline players who need power, not serve-and-volleyers who need finesse. And, along those lines, why is a style of play that requires finesse considered masculine?

Navratilova, then, kept lesbian aesthetics and lesbian culture in the public discourse simply by her visibility in the public arena. In regards to gender expression, Navratilova has shown social activism against the status quo for four decades.

The curious case of the absence of race-based identity politics in the Joiners cohort

The Joiners cohort can be identified as the era of identity politics in women's professional tennis with nationality, lesbianism, and what constitutes womanhood, taking center stage. Race, however, took a different path and will not emerge as a fixture of identity politics until the Sustainers cohort, with the emergence of Venus and Serena Williams.

This is not to say that there were not dominant Black women in women's professional tennis at the time. We saw Zina Garrison, a continual top-ten player throughout her career, become a Wimbledon finalist in 1990. Other top-ranked Black women included Katrina Adams, the former president of the USTA, Lori McNeil, and Chanda Rubin.

This literal white-washing of race during the Joiners cohort was not simply an issue with Blackness. GiGi Fernandez and Mary Jo Fernandez (who are not related) were not explicitly identified as Latinas or Hispanic in the US discourse. GiGi Fernandez is from Puerto Rico and Mary Jo Fernandez is of Dominican descent, but born and raised in Miami, Florida. However, with the dominance of players from Spain and Latin America, their *Hispanidad* might have seemed less prominent in women's tennis.[14]

Black tennis players in the Joiners cohort worked to position themselves as seamlessly as possible into the white, upper-class world of women's tennis, unlike the Williams sisters of the Sustainers cohort. These two competing ways of being for Black tennis players highlight the longevity of the debates between Booker T. Washington and W. E. B. Du Bois from the late-1800s to the mid-1900s. Washington would have approved of Zina Garrison's comportment on and off the court. To him, Black people could elevate themselves through hard work and economic independence, while simply accepting that discrimination would happen, showing that they were productive members of society. On the contrary, Du Bois advocated for education, political action, and civil rights in the face of racial discrimination. The primary differences between Washington and Du Bois were based on accommodation and gradualism, fully accommodating and very gradual change versus not accommodating and very rapid change, respectively. In women's tennis, the Black women of the Joiners cohort would appear to be submissive to white people and the white establishment in order to have a place at the table, expecting that change would occur gradually over time. Venus and Serena Williams, of the Sustainers cohort, resort to political demands to get that place at the table. They want the change to occur in the present, boycotting, for example, the Indian Wells tournament, until they are assured that it will be a racially-just venue in which to play.

Conclusion

The Joiners cohort, then, carried on the social activism work for economic justice through equal prize money that the Founders cohort had begun. This cohort also ushered in various types of identity politics, including those based on nationality, sex, sexuality, and gender. Martina Navratilova's success forced people to look at the construct of nationality in the Cold War context, lesbianism, and female masculinity. Billie Jean King also played a part in the reconfiguring of the discourse to account for (and allow) lesbians in tennis. Furthermore, Renée Richards, by suing the USTA for entry into the 1976 US Open, opened the door for a reinterpretation of what constitutes a woman. All of these examples we now see as social activism, but, at the time, especially with the outing of King and Navratilova, they were just trying to survive in a very tumultuous and homophobic world outside of women's tennis.

Interestingly, race was not a prominent theme during the Joiners cohort. Race would emerge as a force for social activism in the Sustainers cohort with the entry of Venus and Serena Williams into women's professional tennis. Indeed, given their appearance and class backgrounds, the Williams sisters could not "pass" for respectable Black, or "Black ladies." Thus, they could not be whitewashed into homogeneity as Black players in the past had been.

Notes

1 When I asked Martina via Twitter whether she was purposefully avoiding the area before she received her US citizenship, she replied, "no – played world team tennis instead – the French and Australian opens were not that big a deal then. Different now." (Navratilova, tweet, 2016). WTT is based in the US.
2 This is the exam that was conducted on me before I was allowed to play professional women's tennis events.
3 There has never been a suspicion that a female has impersonated a man in the Olympics.
4 This is exactly the opposite of JL Austin (1975) who asserts that when it is discovered that something exists, it is then that a word is created to bring it forth.
5 And it's not like the devolution of Rita Mae Brown into a novelist, whose main characters are cats, didn't also set lesbian politics back a decade or more.
6 I am not sure where these numbers come from. They are new to me.
7 Interestingly, in 1988, at the start of my tennis career, this is the angle that I was advised to take. My mom even believed that I was bisexual because that is what she read in the *San Francisco Chronicle*. This is when I had to explain to my mom the use of media spin in order to maintain one's public persona and potentially lucrative endorsements.

8 And Lieberman was raised Jewish, so becoming a born-again Christian must have taken a lot of work!
9 Court leads all players through 2019. Serena Williams is still actively playing and holds 23 Grand Slam singles titles, so Court's record is under threat.
10 Golf is the other historically high-profile women's sport; however, it has never been the site for political protest or social movements the way tennis has been.
11 For a detailed account of what occurred when Amélie Mauresmo came out as a lesbian, see Tredway, 2014.
12 It is interesting to note that this piece was written in 1971. It was meant as a defense against the wave of feminist "mandates" for androgyny.
13 The US Open moved from Forest Hills Tennis Club in 1977, where it was played on grass courts, to its current hard court location at Flushing Meadows. The Australian Open moved from Kooyang Lawn Tennis Club to its current location at Melbourne Park in 1988 where it is now played on a rubberized court surface akin to hard courts.
14 Additionally, my American Indian background was never discussed, not that it was taboo, but, rather, it was just not a topic of interest. Looking back, it seems like it should have been profound that a pro player who was half American Indian was coached by a Salvadoran from a previous generation, yet it wasn't.

4 The Sustainers
The corporatization of women's tennis, 1987–present

Following the gains for various identity-based social movements during the era of the Joiners cohort, corporatization was becoming entrenched across society during the Sustainers cohort, causing individualization through competitiveness for supposedly limited resources. Politically, it seems, the Sustainers cohort is a generation of malaise. Women's professional tennis had, by this time, steadily increasing prize money and an increasing number of available tournaments, so the Founders cohort's primary issue had been realized. Also, at this point, women's tennis had recovered and incorporated different understandings of the identity politics from the Joiners cohort. A rolling back of feminist advances were taking place as feminism moved from a complex theoretical framework to popular culture, such as magazine articles. The concept of "girl power" emerged, linked with third-wave feminism, which offered faux empowerment, precisely because it was an apolitical form of feminism. In popular culture, feminism became understood as an aesthetic and, as such, was commodified, thereby increasing the power of the status quo. On the surface, feminism seemed political, which worked to quell the masses, but underneath, it was an empty shell of what it once was, thereby offering no threat to those in power.

The Sustainers cohort is marked by heightened individualism and a disavowal of the history and struggles in women's tennis.[1] The primary issues that I look at in this chapter are the corporatization and restructuring of the WTA and the creation and enforcement of feminine ideals for female players. As the WTA crafted itself more and more into a corporate model, players jockeyed for position within this hierarchical structure, disregarding community and collective action. Within this context, women do things that are not actually good for them. For example, female athletes may pose for the *Sports Illustrated* bathing suit issue, and think that it is their own personal empowerment that allowed it to happen, but their actions support the status quo which, in turn, harms women.

The Sustainers cohort references the current era, where many of the issues that the Founders cohort were working towards have been realized – and the movement has been mainstreamed to some extent. Indeed, the struggles for creating a viable women's tennis tour were over by this period. As the WTA becomes more and more corporate, however, women respond in differing ways. Nancy Whittier asserts that, "in sharp contrast to joiners, sustainers were largely pessimistic about the prospects for sweeping social change" (1995, p. 70). Indeed, Michael Messner, Max Greenberg and Tal Peretz mention that, with this cohort, "All of the rage is gone" (2015, p. 180), compared to the Founders and Joiners cohorts. Again, the movement seemed to be already in place. The goal, then, is to keep it on course moving forward, but there are no greater political goals to work towards. As such, the Sustainers cohort seems to be almost apolitical, with very little social activism occurring.

The Sustainers cohort began with Steffi Graf's first Grand Slam singles title, the French Open of 1987. This cohort is identified with the continued domination of Steffi Graf and the emergence of a new crop of young players, most of whom were born after the actions of the Original 9, and either dismissed the actions and importance of the Original 9, or had not even heard of them. We are still in this generational cohort.

The Sustainers cohort is marked by the corporatization that pervades women's tennis during this era. With it, the individualism of the players and the corporatization of the WTA emerged. Corporatization, and the broader framework of neoliberalism, often imposes a flattening of identities; that is, identities within this system become irrelevant within the framework of individualism. To clarify, individualism is encouraged and promoted, but within prescribed constraints.

One such battle for individualism within prescribed constraints occurred with the entry of Venus and Serena Williams into women's professional tennis. There had been Black players before – most notably Zina Garrison, Katrina Adams, Lori McNeil, and Chanda Rubin from the Joiners cohort – however, they ensured that their performances meshed with the cultural milieu of women's professional tennis. Prior to the Williams sisters, there had not been Black players who performed Blackness as overtly, with seemingly little regard for the cultural milieu of women's professional tennis, as they did.

The effects of corporatization on women's professional tennis

Corporatization has been riding the coat-tails of neoliberalism which, in a nutshell, refers to the economic policies that transfer public goods to the private domain at the institutional and governmental level. The private domain is the corporate sector of society. Wendy Brown, the noted feminist political scientist, offers the following definition:

> Neoliberalism is most commonly understood as enacting an ensemble of economic policies in accord with its root principle of affirming free markets. These include deregulation of industries and capital flows; radical reduction in welfare state provisions and protections for the vulnerable; privatized and outsourced public goods, ranging from education, parks, postal services, roads, and social welfare to prisons and militaries; replacement of progressive with regressive tax and tariff schemes; the end of wealth redistribution as an economic or social-political policy; the conversion of every human need or desire into a profitable enterprise, from college admissions

preparation to human organ transplants, from baby adoptions to pollution rights, from avoiding lines to securing legroom on an airplane; and, most recently, the financialization of everything and the increasing dominance of finance capital over productive capital in the dynamics of the economy and everyday life.

(Brown, 2015, p. 28)

If all of these changes in society were to happen at once, members of a given society would oppose them. These changes, however, are rolled out slowly with constant distancing by those in power to the interconnections between these issues. Thus, the move to the private domain is done with popular support, due to the belief that it will benefit their own individual rights and freedoms. However, individual rights and freedoms are not protected per se. Instead, individuals are responsible for their own successes and failures. The noted theorist of neoliberalism, David Harvey, explains further:

> While personal and individual freedom in the marketplace is guaranteed, each individual is held responsible and accountable for his or her own actions and well-being.... Individual success or failure are interpreted in terms of entrepreneurial virtues or personal failings ... rather than being attributed to any systemic property.
>
> (2005, pp. 65–66)

Thus, under the guise of individualism and freedom, the public domain is transferred to the private domain. With the public domain, everyone could use it, however institutional and governmental rules could impede on freedoms. Within the private domain, everything has a value or a price tag. Based on what one could afford economically, one could have endless individual freedoms. The inverse, though, is that those with limited economic means have fewer freedoms.

Adding to this discussion on corporatization in society, specific to sport, since it is a mirror of society, sport also reflects corporatization. David Andrews explains:

> The populist dictates of the contemporary culture industries–preoccupied with the desire to produce texts that resonate with, as opposed to controvert, mainstream views and values–generate popular representations of the sporting world that incorporate and covertly normalize various armatures of the neoliberal agenda. Hence, through their composite and conjunctural constitution, both the sport spectacle *in toto*, and its composite sub-strands (the performative, embodied, promotional, pernicious, delivery, spatial, ceremonial, and social spectacles) are efficient propagators of the prevailing neoliberal consensus.... The economic logics and rationalities underpinning these neoliberal processes are core component parts of a truly transnational model of corporate sport, the ubiquity of which normalizes the neoliberal order.
>
> (Andrews, 2016, p. 10)

Sport is not a separate entity from the society in which it is played. Thus, sport rarely counters the neoliberal ideals that permeate society.

With this emergence of corporatization is the introduction of the tenets of third-wave feminism, or postfeminism, as Angela McRobbie would claim. Third-wave feminism is marked by an increase in individualism among women, yet it is predominantly isolated to the performances that one displays, especially attire, not any substantive features of the individual. Furthermore, the focus of third-wave feminism, with this catapulting of individuals, is on individual gains and not on any sustained politics that will benefit all women. This apolitical bend is what leads McRobbie to contend that feminism is a politics that has ended. Thus, we have postfeminism. In describing the feminist politics of pop superstar Beyoncé, bell hooks asserts:

> In the world of art-making, a black female creator as powerfully placed as Beyoncé can both create images and present viewers with her own interpretation of what those images mean. However, her interpretation cannot stand as truth. For example, Beyoncé uses her non-fictional voice and persona to claim feminism, even to claim, as she does in a recent issue of *Elle* magazine, "to give clarity to the true meaning" of the term, but her construction of feminism cannot be trusted. Her vision of feminism does not call for an end to patriarchal domination. It's all about insisting on equal rights for men and women. In the world of fantasy feminism, there are no class, sex, and race hierarchies that breakdown simplified categories of women and men, no call to challenge and change systems of domination, no emphasis on intersectionality. In such a simplified worldview, women gaining the freedom to be like men can be seen as powerful. But it is a false construction of power as so many men, especially black men, do not possess actual power.
>
> (hooks, 2016)

Indeed, on the surface, the feminism espoused seems politically charged. Lift the veil, and one sees that the politics have been extracted, leaving an empty shell of what feminism once was.

The events that show the emergence and prominence of corporatization in women's professional tennis are the focus on celebrity individualism, the corporatization of the WTA, and imposing structures and media advertising to create the approved individual who is a professional tennis player. Interestingly, there is overlap across these categories. The events that occurred which showed that neoliberalism was being ushered in, and could be considered celebrity individualism, are Steffi Graf's disavowal of previous activism in women's tennis and the reaction to the stabbing of Monica Seles. The depoliticization of the Original 9 with the repoliticization of Billie Jean King as the lone individual who ushered in women's professional tennis is both celebrity individualism and corporatization. The corporatization and globalization of the WTA can be identified with the coup and reorganization of the WTA and the emergence of Li Na, which facilitated the entry of the WTA into Chinese markets. Lastly, the efforts to curb grunting in women's tennis and the "strong is beautiful" advertising campaign point to the creation of the approved type of woman who is a professional tennis player.

Rewriting the origin story of women's professional tennis and the mainstream repoliticization of Billie Jean King

The most glaring example of the influx of corporatization on women's tennis is the sudden shift of Billie Jean King from poster child, through the efforts of second-wave feminism's social activism, to being the face of neoliberal feminism. Billie Jean King is a formidable figure in the history of women's tennis. At the same time that she is viewed as a revolutionary figure, she was also invited by President Obama to be his delegate to the Sochi Olympics in 2014. Clearly, King has arrived in the mainstream.

David Andrews, in discussing a similar transformation of Muhammad Ali, points to "historical amnesia" (2006, p. 124). Much like King now, Ali was an outsider, one of society's problems that needed correcting. On Ali's transformation from rogue to hero, Andrews wrote:

> Ali corroborated his status as a cultural icon of historical proportions, while simultaneously erasing his threatening political stridency. Vague allusions to his controversial and outspoken past, coupled with the public sympathy derived from his apparent physical decline due to the ravages of Parkinson's Disease, gave Ali an aura of authentic individuality: a prized commodity in the culturally and politically myopic 1990s. As a result, Ali became a culturally resonant exemplar of postmodern American individualism and was thereby symbolically severed from his role as torchbearer for a collective struggle against various forms of American oppression.
>
> (2006, pp. 124–125)

Similarly, there are allusions to King's activist past, however, the rhetoric more often points to the ways in which she is very much a mainstream celebrity; for example, the US Open is played at the Billie Jean King National Tennis Center (which, interestingly, houses Arthur Ashe Stadium), and, as mentioned previously, King was selected as President Obama's delegate to the 2014 Sochi Olympics. Granted, after her selection, the discourse was on how King was "Obama's middle finger," pointing (no pun intended) to King's radical past, and conjuring up images of her as a crusader for LGBTQ rights, but only those people who are very much mainstream are selected to represent the President of the United States at international events.

Interestingly, as we get further and further from the events of the early 1970s and the accomplishments of the Founders cohort, Billie Jean King comes to symbolize all of the social movement that took place, with an erasure of the other eight women of the Original 9. For example, in all of the WTA timelines that they publish, "1973 – King founded the Women's Tennis Association" appears (WTA, 2013). The WTA, of anyone, knows their own history, so it lets me know that there is some greater force at work here – neoliberalism. Corporations are identified as having a founder, co-founders of two people at most. For the WTA to move forward as a corporation, coupled with the celebrity individualism of neoliberalism, King gets moved upwards in the imaginary of the origin story, while all the others get demoted.

Celebrity individualism in women's professional tennis

Corporatization through the advancement of celebrity individualism has shown itself in two ways in women's tennis. The first is Steffi Graf's disavowal of women's tennis history and the activism that created women's professional tennis. The second was the response to the tragic on-court stabbing of Monica Seles.

The emergence of Steffi Graf and the disavowal of women's tennis history and activism

For the most part, the breaking up of women's tennis history into cohorts is subjective. Others may, in fact, use different events as the beginning or end points of certain cohorts, or argue that a specific cohort never existed.

During an interview with Pam Shriver, I described to her the historical framework that I was using: The Founders cohort, the Joiners cohort, and the Sustainers cohort (Messner, Greenberg & Peretz, 2015). She immediately grasped the distinctions between the cohorts and agreed that they fit women's tennis well. Shriver also pointed to Steffi Graf as the person who caused the split between the Joiners cohort and the Sustainers cohort. To her, Graf's distancing of herself from the Original 9 and women's tennis history was cause for concern (Shriver, private interview, 2015). She gave this example so quickly, and tied it in so nicely with the beginning of the Sustainers cohort, that it seems that it must have seemed like an obvious break at the time, though unnameable. This disavowal of the struggles and accomplishments of her predecessors, and the fact that she became a tennis champion who was emulated by others, led to Graf ushering in a new era for women's tennis, the Sustainers cohort.

Graf burst onto the women's tour with a power game that had not been seen among women before. In 1987, at the age of 18, she won the French Open, her first Grand Slam singles title. That year she was also a finalist at Wimbledon and the US Open. The following year, 1988, Graf won the Grand Slam, winning all four Grand Slam singles titles during a calendar year. She would go on to win a total of 22 Grand Slam singles titles before her career was over.

Prior to the emergence of Graf and other youngsters from her era, players lived in the locker room, playing cards, arranging practice sessions, chatting with players, reading books – anything to pass the time until their matches began. With Graf's era, there is an increase in the separation between players.

The locker room was simply where you changed clothes before and after matches. In the meantime, a player would just stay in their hotel room until their scheduled match was nearing. This is where the breakdown in the transference of knowledge from the previous cohorts occurred. Individual careers became more important than being one in a lineage of remarkable women working together for the strength of women's tennis.

The stabbing of Monica Seles, 1993

Monica Seles became the youngest Grand Slam singles champion in history when she won the French Open in 1990 at the age of 16. Technically a left-hander since she served left-handed, Seles hit with two hands on both her backhand and forehand sides. Seles' first tournament win was the Virginia Slims of Houston in 1989, where she defeated the soon-to-retire Chris Evert in the final with (and I remember this well) non-stop moon balls. Evert, who used the pace on the ball from her opponents and then guided the ball with pinpoint accuracy in return, had no answer for moon balls.

Having won eight Grand Slam singles titles between 1990 and 1993, Steffi Graf was her chief rival. On April 30, 1993, Günter Parche, a man obsessed with Steffi Graf, stabbed Seles in the back, between the shoulder bones to a depth of about 0.6 inches, during a changeover in her match against Magdalena Maleeva in Hamburg, Germany. The psychological toll of the injury was immense. Although she was healed within a few weeks, Seles did not return to competition for two years. When she did return, Seles had a redesigned serve in which she began with her racket already in the "back scratch" position, rather than the traditional way with the racket in front, followed by a smooth motion to bring the racket to the "back scratch" position.

Parche was charged with the crime but never jailed because he was considered psychologically unfit. Instead, Parche was given two years of probation in which time he was mandated to receive psychological treatment.

Parche admitted to having stabbed Seles so that Graf would win more often. Indeed, Graf benefited greatly from Parche's actions, winning four Grand Slams in a row immediately following the incident. Graf, having won 11 Grand Slam singles titles prior to Seles' stabbing, won 10 of the next 13 Grand Slam singles titles (excluding the 1995 and 1996 Australian Open in which she did not play) following the stabbing. Graf won the 1999 French Open title as her last, and 22nd total, Grand Slam singles title.

Seles, on the other hand, had won 8 of the 11 Grand Slam events that preceded her stabbing (excluding the 1991 Wimbledon event in which she did not play). Following the stabbing, Seles was not the same player. She won the 1996 Australian Open singles title, defeating Graf in the final, in the second Grand Slam event of her return. Other than this win, Seles was a finalist three times, a semi-finalist four times, and a quarter-finalist 12 times in the 26 Grand Slam events that she played before her retirement in 2003. She was definitely a changed player.

On-court security at tournaments went through a variety of changes following the stabbing of Seles. First, seats were turned so that players faced the crowd nearest them during the changeover. This was quickly overruled by the players because, although you can quickly see a person approaching, it is too distracting to watch spectators who are that close. The current arrangement seems to be the addition of six security officers whose only job is to protect the players and on-court officials. During changeovers, there is one security officer at each corner of the stadium and two security officers standing between each of the player's chairs and the spectators. During play, these security officers are usually seated in the first rows so they are still present.

What followed the stabbing of Monica Seles was almost two decades of distance between tennis players and fans. Players became further distanced from the audience. Fans could see the players and buy their latest tennis outfits or sneakers, but they could not interact with the players. This, in turn, fed into the celebritization of these athletes.

The corporatization and globalization of the Women's Tennis Association

Corporatization and globalization go hand in hand. The impetus to establish a corporation is to make gains in the marketplace. Once a marketplace is saturated, new marketplaces need to be created and cultivated in order to ensure the economic viability of the corporation. The WTA was not immune to this. Through restructuring, the WTA moved from being more of a player's association to being a corporation. This also had the effect of moving the WTA further away from its social activism origins. Then, after saturating the markets in the US and Europe, the WTA expanded into the Middle East and, as will be explained here, China.

The restructuring of the WTA, 1997–1998

David Harvey, in his analysis of neoliberalism, warns against the unraveling of democracy and the movement of resources to the elites of a group or society. He explains:

> Neoliberal theorists are ... profoundly suspicious of democracy. Governance by majority rule is seen as a potential threat to individual rights and constitutional liberties. Democracy is viewed as a luxury, only possible under conditions of relative affluence coupled with a strong middle-class presence to guarantee political stability. Neoliberals therefore tend to favour governance by experts and elites. A strong preference exists for government by executive order and by judicial decision rather than democratic and parliamentary decision-making. Neoliberals prefer to insulate key institutions, such as the central bank, from democratic pressures. Given that neoliberal theory centres on the rule of law and a strict interpretation of

constitutionality, it follows that conflict and opposition must be mediated through the courts. Solutions and remedies to any problems have to be sought by individuals through the legal system.

(2005, pp. 66–67)

This is what occurred within the WTA. An organization that had been created for the benefit of all women who play tennis professionally was now pressured by the top players, the elites, to ensure that resources and decisions benefited them.

For years prior to 1997, there had been a steadily increasing scaling back of the Tier II and Tier III tournaments, where mid-level players could do their best in terms of gaining ranking points and prize money. Furthermore, the structure of the WTA itself included the position of president, which was always held by an influential current player, elected by a vote of all the players, and there was a vibrant player's association. During my own playing career from 1988–1992, the position of president was held by Chris Evert (1975–1976, 1983–1991) and Pam Shriver (1991–1994). The commitment to the players, no matter what the ranking or level of play, was primary. Of course, players were expected to move up the tournament tiers as their level of play increased. There was not the sense that there were the stars of tennis in one level, and all of the others in the lower levels.

On November 2, 1997, Patricia Hy-Boulais, a Canadian player ranked #64 at the time, was the president of the WTA Players Association. Hy-Boulais' presidency followed the presidency of the American Marianne Werdel-Witmeyer (1995–1997), whose highest ranking had been #45 three years earlier, so one can already see that the power of this position is diminishing. She, along with six other players – Nathalie Tauziat of France (ranked #11), Dominique Van Roost of Belgium (ranked #18), Johnnette Kruger of South Africa (ranked #27), Florencia Labat of Argentina (ranked #39), Karin Kschwendt of Austria (ranked #169) and Linda Wild of the US (ranked #222)[2] – accused the WTA of spending far more energy and money on the top players and neglecting the mid-level players. Of course, prize money was higher for Tier I tournaments. What the Players Association objected to was all of the WTA resources – staffing, marketing, amenities, etc. – being primarily devoted to the top-level tournaments and not spread more evenly across all the different tournaments. Hy-Boulais was advocating for the dismissal of Sara Fornaciari, executive director of the WTA. It was she, Hy-Boulais contended, who was causing the greater and greater disparity with player compensation. Indeed, "In that Nov. 2 coup, Patricia Hy-Boulais, the player/president of the association, led a move to restructure the group's board of directors with a series of appointments and demotions that were unilaterally condemned by the top players" (Finn, 1998).

Hy-Boulais' actions, as expected, were met with huge resistance from the top players at the time, especially world #1, Martina Hingis. The plaintiffs for the case who joined Hingis were Jana Novotna of the Czech Republic (ranked #2), Lindsay Davenport of the US (ranked #3), Amanda Coetzer of South Africa (ranked #4), Monica Seles of the US (ranked #5), Arantxa Sanchez Vicario of Spain (ranked #9), Mary Joe Fernandez of the US (ranked #10), and Steffi Graf of Germany (ranked #28, though #1 the previous year). Notably absent from this list of plaintiffs were Iva Majoli of Croatia (ranked #6), Mary Pierce of France (ranked #7), and Irina Spirlea of Romania (ranked #8),[3] who did not take sides on this issue.

On February 9, 1998, litigation and mediation was settled between the two warring parties of the WTA, with the judge ordering the agreed upon restructuring of the WTA to begin. Before the restructuring, the WTA Players Association was led by a president who was voted into the position by the players. Apart from the president, the Players Association could have an unlimited number of people on the board. Typically, as might be expected, the board was stacked with representatives who supported the president. After the restructuring, the position of president was eliminated, as was that of the executive director, thus removing Hy-Boulais and Fornaciari from the WTA leadership (Finn, 1998). In place of the executive director, the position of CEO was created. The Players' Association was also disbanded and replaced with the Players Council, which is still in existence today.

The Council includes four players who are ranked between #1–20, one player ranked #21 or lower, one player ranked between #21–50, one player ranked between #51–100, and one player ranked #100 or lower. The players on the Players Council in 2015 were: Serena Williams, Venus Williams, Lucie Safarova, Samantha Stosur (the four ranked between #1–20), Marina Erakovic (ranked #21 or lower), Francesca Schiavone (ranked between #21–50), Akgul Amanmuradova (ranked #51–100), and Irina Falconi (ranked #100 or lower). Indeed, this is an excellent group of players to represent the other players. There is no elected president. The Council of eight players does not have regularly scheduled meetings, but meets when issues arise. In addition, there are two "nonplayer representatives" who sit on the WTA board, one selected by the players in the top-20 and the other selected by "the remaining players" (Finn, 1998).

The restructuring of the WTA was unfortunate. David Harvey asserts that, "the main substantive achievement of neoliberalization ... has been to redistribute, rather than to generate, wealth and income" (2005, p. 159). Indeed, the redistribution was upwards, taken from the mid-level players and given to the top-ranked players. The previously player-centered WTA was fashioned into a corporate entity. Of course, now, the focus is on the stars of the game, without much concern for the rest of the players, regardless of ranking or social status.

In 1997, top players felt that they were being ruled by lower-ranking players; however, as corporations go, the top players now play at the whim of the corporations. And now those few are the CEO and other executives of the WTA, not the players. Beginning in 2009, rather than having the tournament structure of Tier I, Tier II, Tier III, and Tier IV for the various levels of tournaments, the WTA shifted to premier events. These premier tournaments include "premier mandatory" events which, as could be guessed, are mandatory for every player whose ranking would place them in the main draw, "premier 5" events which are top-level tournaments with prize money offerings less than that of premier mandatory events, and "premier" events which are also important events. In addition to the premier events, there are "international" tournaments. These tournaments offer less prize money and fewer ranking points than any of the premier events. In 2015, there were four premier mandatory events – Indian Wells, Key Biscayne, Madrid, and Beijing, with prize money topping $4.5 million at each event; five premier 5 events, as could have been guessed – Dubai, Rome, Cincinnati, Toronto/Montreal (the tournament flip-flops with the Association of Tennis Professionals (ATP) tournament each year), and Wuhan, with prize money of $2 million at each event. There are also 12 premier events with prize money ranging from $600,000 to $1 million.

In addition to this shift in tournament structure is an attempted diminishing on the part of the WTA of the Grand Slam events. During the Joiners cohort, Martina Navratilova and Chris Evert arranged their schedules so that they did not play the same WTA events during the year. This spread the star-power around to the various tournaments during this time. It also boosted the Grand Slam events, because that is where they were both in the draws and likely to meet in the finals. Grand Slam events are still the highest standard in professional tennis.

Li Na and the opening up of Asian markets within globalization

In a corporation looking to expand globally to create more markets, Li Na was a gift for the WTA. Li offered a fetishization of China while also opening the floodgates for the entry of the WTA into Asian markets.

Li was born and raised in Wuhan, China. There is a state-run tennis academy there, so Li was able to remain close to her family while also being trained, unlike many other athletes who come through the state-run athletic system in China who have to live far away from their families. When Li won the French Open in 2011, she became the first Asian player, male or female, to win a Grand Slam singles title. She added another Grand Slam singles title when she won the 2014 Australian Open, after having been a finalist there twice before in 2011 and 2013.

David Harvey explains the economic history of China and how it came to be a center for capitalism despite it being a closed communist country. He says:

> In December 1978, faced with the dual difficulties of political uncertainty in the wake of Mao's death in 1976 and several years of economic stagnation, the Chinese leadership under Deng Xiaoping announced a programme of economic reform. We may never know for sure whether Deng was all along a secret "capitalist roader" (as Mao had claimed during the Cultural Revolution) or whether the reforms were simply a desperate move to ensure China's economic security and bolster its prestige in the face of the rising

tide of capitalist development in the rest of East and South-East Asia. The reforms just happened to coincide – and it is very hard to consider this as anything other than a conjunctural accident of world-historical significance – with the turn to neoliberal solutions in Britain and the United States. The outcome in China has been the construction of a particular kind of market economy that increasingly incorporates neoliberal elements interdigitated with authoritarian centralized control.

(2005, p. 120)

Further elaborating, Harvey explains the apparent surprise that China emerged as a global market:

These reforms would not have assumed the significance we now accord to them, nor would China's extraordinary subsequent economic evolution have taken the path and registered the achievements it did, had there not been significant and seemingly unrelated parallel shifts in the advanced capitalist world with respect to how the world market worked. The gathering strength of neoliberal policies on international trade during the 1980s opened up the whole world to transformative market and financial forces. In so doing it opened up a space for China's tumultuous entry and incorporation into the world market.... The spectacular emergence of China as a global economic power after 1980 was in part an unintended consequence of the neoliberal turn in the advanced capitalist world.

(2005, p. 121)

Women's tennis, with the popularity and success of Li Na, capitalized on the growing markets in China.

As mentioned previously, the WTA has two major tournaments in China, the premier mandatory tournament in Beijing, and the premier 5 tournament in Li's hometown of Wuhan. The China Open in Beijing, played at the National Tennis Center which was built for the 2008 Olympics, began as a Tier II tournament in 2004, and was upgraded to a premier tournament in 2009. The Dongfeng Motor Wuhan Open was first played in 2014, and, given that it is played in her hometown and that she is a prominent figure at the tournament, it is considered to be Li's personal tournament.

The creation (and enforcement) of the ideal woman for professional tennis

Corporatization, via mass individualization, ushers in governance, especially self-governance, in an effort to control society. At the same time, corporatization offers images of who a person should be, or who a person should aspire to be. These twin pillars of self-governance and aspiration have been codified in women's tennis. The first issue is the imposing of policies within the WTA that are meant to curb the grunting that players do on court. The second issue is the "strong is beautiful" advertising campaign that the WTA continues to use, which offers aspirational images of the women.

Anti-grunting policies

Grunting while hitting the ball has caused a contentious debate on the women's tour. First noticeable with Monica Seles (who actually had a double-grunt, one for taking the racket back, along with the typical grunt for swinging through the ball), the grunt is now standard in women's tennis, with each player having their own sound. Maria Sharapova and Victoria Azarenka are known for having the loudest grunts in women's tennis, based on decibels. Of her grunting, Sharapova stated that "you've watched me grow up, you've watched me play tennis. I've been the same over the course of my career. No one important enough has told me to change or do something different" (Rothenberg, 2012).

Grunting in tennis can be seen as a positive or a negative. The underlying reason to grunt while hitting the ball is to ensure that one's body is relaxed and, more specifically, that one is breathing properly instead of holding one's breath, which is what happens when a person gets tight or nervous. Also, exhaling upon impact with the ball increases power. As such, the grunt itself is an auditory reminder to the player doing the grunting that a certain level of relaxation is being maintained. So, too, does grunting add flavor to women's tennis. Nick Bollettieri, the renowned coach of many of the loudest grunters, said: "I think tennis is a little dull.... We need a little charisma, we need a little shouting, we need a little disagreement. You've got to have a little pizzazz" (Perrotta, 2015).

On the other side, players who grunt have been accused of cheating, either by grunting to block one's opponent from hearing what spin, if any, has been put on the ball, or, simply, in an effort to cause a hindrance for one's opponent. Indeed, obnoxiously loud grunting can actually lead to penalties from the chair umpire using the "hindrance rule." The hindrance rule sets guidelines that "[if] a player is hindered in playing the point by a deliberate act of the opponent(s), the player shall win the point."

But what is at the heart of this call to arms to ban women from grunting while they play tennis? According to Katy Waldman at *Slate*:

> It seems to be mostly fans, former or waning stars, and officials who are complaining about the grunting anyway. If female players sounding their barbaric yawps on the Wimbledon green prove sooo distracting, perhaps the better question is: Why? Because of sex. A woman grunting on the tennis court sounds like she's having a baby or having sex. And not very ladylike sex – primal, bestial, no-holds-barred sex, the kind that stodgy Wimbledon-goers are loathe to imagine in their country club. With that specter of nooky comes empowerment and a possible inversion of gender norms: What else can these Amazonian women pull off without male assistance?
>
> (Waldman, 2012)

Could that really be the answer?

Beginning in 2012, the WTA has implemented a series of ways in which it hopes that grunting will be eliminated for future generations of players. The plan was agreed to by all four Grand Slam tournaments, the International Tennis Federation, the WTA Players Council, and, of course, the WTA. According to Andrew Walker, Chief Marketing Officer for the WTA at the time, the effort to diminish grunting from women's tennis

> stemmed from an increase in negative fan reaction to excessive grunting and an increase in media coverage, and we made a determination that the landscape had changed, and we owed it to the fans to take a look at it.
>
> (Belson, 2012)

The three ways that grunting was to be curbed in 2012 was by:

1. Chair umpires using hand-held devices that gage grunt levels;
2. A new rule that lays out exactly what is too loud and what is not; and
3. Education of junior players at large tennis academies and national tennis centers.

Rather than enforcing changes among top-level players, the WTA is beginning with enforcement among junior players. Thus, in 20 years, there will be no grunting in women's tennis. This is the plan that the WTA has put in place. Walker noted that "if junior players start getting docked points for excessive grunting, they won't care what their role models do," meaning they may model their game on Sharapova's or Azarenka's, but not necessarily their grunting styles. "If we get the proper education and enforcement, it will resolve itself" (Belson, 2012).

The leaders of men's tennis have not moved towards banning loud grunting. When Stacey Allaster, the former CEO of the WTA, was asked about the differences between male and female grunting in tennis, she noted that "our female DNA transmits it in a different way" (Belson, 2012). And this is the woman who was in the most senior position at the organization which governs the most high-profile women's sport in the world.

Three years later, the WTA has yet to provide chair umpires with the hand-held device to determine the egregiousness of a player's grunts. Mary Carillo, a former professional player and now a television analyst, said: "They're not tackling it, to my mind – they're hoping that it all dies down…. It's not going to change. That's been made very clear – loud and clear! 'Loud and Clear' should be the name of your story" (Perrotta, 2015).

The "Strong is Beautiful" advertising campaign

The advertising campaigns for the WTA seem like ad campaigns for a postfeminist movement. We know the women as world-class athletes; however, these two campaigns only feature tour players in sequins, flowing dresses, and other very feminine attire. Furthermore, the campaigns focus primarily on love and beauty, markedly feminine traits.

In the "Strong is Beautiful" WTA campaign ads, players are wearing anything but athletic wear, nor are they playing tennis. In the images, "the sport's stars are often dressed in frilly (and skimpy) skirts, with full make-up, looking glamorous, and in settings full of provocative imagery" (Fink, 2012, p. 52). Added to the imagery is glitter that explodes off the ball upon impact. Frilly clothes, makeup, glitter – the main components of the feminine code. Indeed, Nicole LaVoi claims that, "Yes, these women are beautiful, but we see lots of cleavage and legs, and it's set to music that is reminiscent of soft-core porn" (Adams, 2011).

This projection of femininity is used in a specific way, and for a specific reason. As Mary Jo Kane explains, "This approach, or so the argument goes, reassures (especially male) fans, corporate sponsors, and TV audiences that females can engage in highly competitive sports while retaining non-threatening femininity" (Kane, 2011). Janet Fink elaborates by stating that, "This tactic reassures the public that not all female athletes are lesbian, that women can be athletically talented and sexy, and the typical gender order is not threatened by women in sport" (2012, p. 54). Indeed, it is not that sex sells women's sports, but that sex sells sex. Kane states "that what males are interested in consuming is not a women's athletic event but sportswomen's bodies as objects of sexual desire" (Kane, 2011).

This projection of (hyper-) femininity also operates to keep homophobia at a distance. The idea is that women who are *that* feminine could not possibly be lesbians.

What is most interesting to me is the appropriation of an art installation which, when it gets a corporate overlay, suddenly becomes imbued with hyper-femininity and sexual imagery. I first saw the film clip in a museum space during an exhibit on women and sport. The Arlington (Virginia) Arts Center housed the exhibit "She Got Game" (Arlington Arts Center, 2012) in the early months of 2012.[4] I was moved by the imagery in the film, the gracefulness of the players and the juxtaposition of colors. The darkness in the room allowed the colors to be even more prominent. The only light in the room was coming from this continually looping film. The film was created by Dewey Nicks, the famed fashion and advertising photographer (Nowness, 2011). In the art installation, there were no WTA corporate logos in the film or in the museum space where the film was played.

Now, after the corporate appropriation of the short film, and being aware of the critiques waged against it by feminist sport sociologists, I cannot unsee the hyper-femininity and sex, and return to viewing the film as an art piece.

The depoliticization of women's tennis and players has been distinct since around 2010. In ways, as previously described, Serena Williams has pushed against the homogenization of players in the media and advertising; however, she, too, had a part in the "Strong is Beautiful" advertising campaign that the

WTA rolled out in December 2012. This only adds to the complexity of this advertising campaign.

Within neoliberalism as it has been incorporated into women's tennis, there has been a celebritization of female tennis players, even Billie Jean King, a former player who belonged to the Founders cohort, a corporatization of the WTA, and the imposition on individuals of self-governance (in terms of grunting), and aspirational images. Thus, the WTA, as a corporation, is invested in the market values of its commodities and is hoping for a strong return on that investment. These commodities are actual women, though. Additionally, as in society, women seem to be meant to be seen, not heard.

Unapologetic Blackness and individualism: Can they coexist?

Countering the imposition of corporatization, with its flattening of identities, is the emergence of Venus and Serena Williams who wilfully display an unapologetic Blackness, with pride in who they are and where they have come from. As with Billie Jean King spanning two areas, Li Na could be used as an analysis of the commodification and consumption of race in women's tennis; however, she is a better fit in explaining how the WTA as a corporation used Li in order to infiltrate and conquer the economic markets of China. Race and neoliberalism occurred in two distinct, yet similar ways, during the Sustainers cohort. Venus and Serena Williams emerged and offered unapologetic Blackness as an identity within women's professional tennis. There had been Black players before, but none elicited the fear and excitement of unapologetic Blackness before. The fetishization of their otherness, their race, offered the WTA broader global appeal.

The Williams sisters offer something new to women's tennis in the era of the Sustainers cohort. In the choice between individualism or social justice, they chose social justice. David Harvey explains: "Left movements failed to recognize or confront, let alone transcend, the inherent tension between the quest for individual freedoms and social justice" (2005, p. 43). Harvey goes on to assert that social activism that allows for individualism will be absorbed into our neoliberal society. Activism aimed at social justice, on the other hand, will continue to be a thorn in the craw of the neoliberal powers that be.

Venus and Serena Williams are sisters, with Venus being the elder by 15 months. Venus played in her first Grand Slam events in 1997. Serena joined her in playing Grand Slam events in 1998. Through 2019, Venus holds 7 Grand Slam singles titles (5 Wimbledon titles and 2 US Open titles), and Serena holds 23 Grand Slam singles titles (7 Australian Open titles, 3 French Open titles, 7 Wimbledon titles, and 6 US Open titles). Serena is second in tennis history for most Grand Slam singles titles, amongst both men and women, only behind Margaret Court, who has 24 titles. Additionally, the Williams sisters have combined to win 14 Grand Slam doubles titles (4 Australian Open titles, 2 French Open titles, 6 Wimbledon titles, and 2 US Open titles), and they have each won two Grand Slam mixed doubles titles. Though Venus has an enviable record, we, quite possibly, might never again see a player dominate women's tennis as Serena has.

Though Venus and Serena are similarly situated in US culture and women's tennis, this section focuses a bit more on Serena, whose displays of unapologetic Blackness have been more dominant. Traveling down a slippery slope here, as I am neither Black, nor from an urban setting, let me explain what I mean by unapologetic Blackness.

Venus and Serena are positioned within tennis differently than Black tennis players in the past. In writing about them, and their positioning within the white, upper-class world of women's tennis, Patricia Hill Collins asserts:

> Unlike Althea Gibson, Zina Garrison, and other African American female tennis stars whose demeanor and style of play resembled the White women dominating the sport, the Williams sisters basically reject tennis norms. They are exceptionally strong and play power games like men. They rebuff tennis "whites" in favor of form-fitting, flashy outfits in all sorts of colors. They play with their hair fixed in beaded, African-influenced cornrows that are occasionally dyed blond. The tennis world cannot remove them because the Williams sisters win. Their working-class origins mean that they don't fit into the traditional tennis world and they express little desire to mimic their White counterparts. Yet their achievements force issues of excellence and diversity to the forefront of American politics.
>
> (2005, p. 135)

Collins is the first to claim that Serena and Venus not only operate differently than their white counterparts in women's tennis, but that they operate differently than their Black predecessors. Gibson and Garrison attempted "to mimic their White counterparts" (2005, p. 135) in order to find success in tennis and to ensure that their environments were less hostile. It is unclear, really, what makes the tennis world uneasy about the Williams sisters. Is it that the Williams sisters win and do so while they "reject tennis norms," as Collins asserts (2005), or is it based on a collection of unspoken feelings that are tied up in color-blind racism? Most likely, these are linked, and a perceived rejection of tennis norms is responded to with color-blind racism.

More interesting might be the question of what it is about tennis that compelled Gibson and Garrison "to mimic their White counterparts" (2005, p. 135) that is not as prevalent now. Venus and Serena display a style, indeed, that is their own "conspicuous flair" (Jackson Jr., 2001, p. 173) in the white world of tennis. John L Jackson, Jr. asserts that "when black people lack flavor, they are dangerously close to a pejorative behavioral territory often termed 'acting white'" (2001, p. 173). Clearly, Serena does not aspire to "act white." She seems to aspire for tennis greatness (which I think she has already achieved) while maintaining a strong Black aesthetic and style, which, as can be seen by the up-and-coming Black women in US tennis – Madison Keys, Sloane Stephens, and Taylor Townsend – has opened the door for Black women to enter the world of tennis with less of a need to "mimic their White counterparts." This unapologetic Blackness displayed by Venus and Serena is what sets them apart from others in women's professional tennis.

Nervous to be interviewing Serena during a press conference, I began my question, "As a celebrity athlete …" Before answering my question, Serena corrected me: "I think that there is a lot of, I guess, quote/unquote celebrity athletes" (S. Williams, 2015c). It was clear that she did not want to be identified as a celebrity, with its focus on individualism. Being a celebrity, and thus viewed as an individual and not a member of a group of people, would run counter to the social justice work that she hopes to accomplish, such as her work on policing, prisoner rights, and prison reform in the US which adversely affects Black communities to a greater extent than other communities, for example.

The individualism afforded through neoliberalism offered the Williams sisters space for the performance of their own style of Blackness. However, individualism within the logic of neoliberalism has constraints. Those constraints have been most blatantly foisted upon Serena, so she will be the focus here.

Venus and Serena Williams have been racially constructed within women's tennis

The Williams sisters have been racially constructed within women's tennis through their clothing, their hair, and their mannerisms, essentially through their identity performances (Douglas, 2002, 2005, 2012; Schultz, 2005; Spencer, 2001, 2004). Jaime Schultz asserts that there is color-blind racism in the rhetoric around Serena, and that Serena must navigate the intersectionality of both gender and race (2005). In regards to color-blind racism, Schultz states that:

> The success and visibility of Serena and [her sister] Venus Williams, in tennis and consumer culture, obscures their radicalized exceptionality, extending the myths of color blindness and equal opportunity in US sport and society. Specifically, their accomplishments conceal the social and economic factors that hinder other African Americans' participation in tennis.
>
> (2005, p. 340)

Indeed, Serena can be used as an example of successfully pulling oneself up by one's bootstraps. However, by allowing Americans to focus on the success of the Williams sisters, Tiger Woods, and even President Obama, the struggles that African Americans face every day are made invisible.

Looking through the lens of intersectionality, Venus' and Serena's race cannot be separated from their gender, and their gender cannot be separated from their race. When spectators see Venus and Serena, they see both their race and their gender as one whole.

Janell Hobson discusses the media attention to Serena's outfit during the 2002 US Open, which was described as the catsuit, an outfit that seemed to accentuate her buttocks. Interestingly, Serena recently named this outfit along with her jean skirt outfit (from the 2004 US Open) as her favorites so far (Williams, 2014a). In describing the catsuit, Hobson asserts that:

> When tennis champion Serena Williams, days before winning the 2002 US Open, appeared on the courts in a black spandex suit, media frenzy ensued. Her black female body, adorned in all its "ghetto" glamour – bleached-blonde braids and a tight-fitting suit that outlined the contours of her posterior, among other things – managed to disrupt (literally and figuratively) the elitist game of tennis. Williams, who defended herself by stating that she wanted to wear something "comfortable" as she moved around the tennis court, was nonetheless attacked in the press for her "tackiness" and "inappropriate" display of sexuality. This seemingly exaggerated response to Williams's choice of sportswear reveals an anxiety that is best understood within a larger historical context of attitudes toward the exhibition of the black female body. This history – a history of enslavement, colonial conquest and ethnographic exhibition – variously labeled the black female body "grotesque," "strange," "unfeminine," "lascivious," and "obscene." This negative attitude toward the black female body targets one aspect of the body in particular: the buttocks.
>
> (2003, p. 87)

According to Schultz, "it is this association of Williams's buttocks with the grotesque that particularly differentiates her from discussions of white female tennis stars" (2005, p. 350). Furthermore, by discussing Serena's buttocks, people can talk about Serena's race without discussing race directly. This speaking about racialized events, objects or body parts, without speaking of race, is a primary component of color-blind racism.

This is just one example of the racialization of Serena in women's tennis. Many more, we can be assured, occur in Serena's day-to-day life.

Venus and Serena Williams have experienced racism in women's professional tennis

Venus and Serena have experienced racism in women's tennis. Most notably, this occurred at the 2001 Indian Wells tennis tournament, a tournament that, since 2001, neither Williams sister had played until 2015 for Serena and 2016 for Venus, despite the tournament being a mandatory event.

Nancy Spencer's account of the 2001 Indian Wells tournament (2004) is the most useful for an understanding of what occurred. The agreed-upon facts from both sides of the debacle are that: 1) Serena was slated to play against her sister, Venus, in a semi-final match; and, 2) Venus withdrew from the semi-final match citing an injury. The Williams camp asserts that Venus told WTA staff the day before the scheduled match with Serena that she was too injured to play, but they did not take Venus seriously (Williams & Paisner, 2009, pp. 62–84). What occurred is that a few minutes before the scheduled Williams vs. Williams match, WTA staff announced to the spectators that the match was canceled, with Venus withdrawing due to injury. During the final the next day, Serena played against Kim Clijsters. As Serena walked onto the court, she met a sea of boos and racist abuse. Many of the fans believed that Venus forfeited the match, just so Serena would get through to the final (Spencer, 2004). Indeed, as Ben Carrington so eloquently paraphrases Frantz Fanon:

> the ability to consume the Other while practicing racism, to hold stereotypical beliefs about blacks while claiming to not see race, to idolize black representations while not being able to treat actual black people as equal human beings, has long been recognized as a central component of how racism is reproduced in putatively "non-racial" spaces.
>
> (2010, p. 175)

Both Williams sisters had vowed never to return to Indian Wells until Serena, through negotiations with the tournament owner, tournament director, and the CEO of the WTA, decided to play the event in 2015. Indian Wells is a mandatory event on the WTA schedule, meaning that, if a player's ranking is high enough to qualify for the main draw, it is mandatory that the player plays the tournament. By refusing to play the Indian Wells tournament, Serena and Venus faced either: a) a $75,000 fine and a two-tournament suspension; or, b) charity or community work within 125 miles of Indian Wells, meetings with potential tournament advertisers and sponsors, or – and this is an interesting "punishment" in this area of late-capitalist corporations – must help promote one of the WTA's marketing campaigns (Oberjuerge, 2009; Robson, 2009). Of course, every player would choose the latter rather than paying a fine and being suspended. In addition to choosing one of these options, Serena and Venus forfeit part of the bonus pool which is split between the players who play all of the mandatory events (which, along with Indian Wells also include Miami, Madrid, and Beijing) and the tournament is calculated into their rankings as zero points earned. Opting for these sanctions rather than playing the tournament paint the picture of the extent of racist vitriol that the Williams family endured there.

Serena's return to Indian Wells was not without a political current. She wrote a piece for *Time* magazine describing her experiences at Indian Wells and her reasons for returning. In it, Serena wrote, "We [she and Venus] were outsiders.... As a black tennis player, I looked different. I sounded different. I dressed differently. I served differently. But when I stepped onto the court, I could compete with anyone" (Williams, 2015). Furthermore, she describes what occurred at Indian Wells in 2001:

> When I arrived at Indian Wells in 2001, I was looking to take another title. I was ready. But however ready I was, nothing could have prepared me for what happened in the final. As I walked out onto the court, the crowd immediately started jeering and booing. In my last match, the semifinals, I was set to play my sister, but Venus had tendinitis and had to pull out. Apparently that angered many fans. Throughout my whole career, integrity has been everything to me. It is also everything and more to Venus. The false allegations that our matches were fixed hurt, cut and ripped into

us deeply. The under-current of racism was painful, confusing and unfair. In a game I loved with all my heart, at one of my most cherished tournaments, I suddenly felt unwelcome, alone and afraid.... This haunted me for a long time. It haunted Venus and our family as well. But most of all, it angered and saddened my father. He dedicated his whole life to prepping us for this incredible journey, and there he had to sit and watch his daughter being taunted, sparking cold memories of his experiences growing up in the South.

(Williams, 2015)

Ultimately, Serena decided to return because, as she says, people and societies change and grow. Given her 19 Grand Slam titles, too, Serena clearly sits on top of women's tennis and, thus, has far more power in women's tennis than she did in 2001 when she held only one Grand Slam title, the 1999 US Open.

I'm fortunate to be at a point in my career where I have nothing to prove. I'm still as driven as ever, but the ride is a little easier. I play for the love of the game. And it is with that love in mind, and a new understanding of the true meaning of forgiveness, that I will proudly return to Indian Wells in 2015. I was raised by my mom to love and forgive freely.... I have faith that fans at Indian Wells have grown with the game and know me better than they did in 2001. Indian Wells was a pivotal moment of my story, and I am a part of the tournament's story as well. Together we have a chance to write a different ending.

(Williams, 2015)

After observing Serena's successful return to Indian Wells, Venus returned in 2016.

Along with naming the 2001 Indian Wells tournament as racist, the other political move that Serena has made is to join forces with Equal Justice Initiative for a fundraising effort related to the Indian Wells tournament (Equal Justice Initiative, 2015). Based in Montgomery, Alabama, the Equal Justice Initiative provides legal representation to defendants and incarcerated individuals who have been denied fair and just treatment in the US legal system. With Serena's efforts, not only can fans win courtside seats for Serena's matches at Indian Wells, this fundraising effort also ensures that Serena has an even larger support network at the tournament while she plays. Dotted throughout the stadium will be people that she knows understand the racism against her and Venus that occurred there. Ben Carrington has claimed that:

The black athletic body (male and female) has become a powerful signifier within contemporary media culture. This signifier has increasingly served to redefine and in some sense reduce the agency of embodied freedom into a narrow set of "power" and "performance" motifs that are radically decontextualized from broader political movements, thus separating the black body from any connection to social change and hence to a depoliticization of the black athlete itself.

(2010, p. 104)

Indeed, by shining a light on the inequality present in the US legal system, and how Black people are disproportionately incarcerated, Serena is (re)claiming a critical consciousness in regards to race in the arena of professional tennis, and her position within that matrix.

The Black female athletic body in women's tennis

In 1952, Frantz Fanon wrote that "there is one expression that with time has become particularly eroticized: the black athlete" (1952/2008, p. 136). Fanon was writing about the male Black athlete; however, the same holds true for female Black athletes, possibly to an even greater extent. Ben Carrington explains further:

> The black athlete is ... positioned as a site for voyeuristic admiration – the black athlete is idolized for its sheer super-human physicality – but also controlled by a complex process of objectification and sexualization that once again renders the threat of negritude controllable to white patriarchy.... The fear of the black athlete as a commodity-sign is thus appropriated, its political symbolic potential neutered, and finally "domesticated" by its exploitation within contemporary consumer society and its attendant media culture.
>
> (2010, p. 88)

Fanon acknowledges the objectification and sexualization of the Black male body; however, for the Black female body, this objectification and sexualization is far greater because the Black female body is objectified and sexualized both for being female and for being Black.

Similarly, David Leonard asserts that "the simultaneous adoration of Black athletes and entertainers further legitimizes claims of colorblindness" (2004, p. 286). Color-blind racism in sport functions in that "Black athletes not only elucidate the fulfillment of the American Dream but also America's imagined racial progress" (Leonard, 2004, p. 288). For instance, as Kevin Hylton asserts:

> the discourse that follows Serena and Venus Williams is one of novelty and awe, but ostensibly a raced, classed and gendered one underpinned by their working-class roots and African American heritage which often trivializes their achievements when they are described as 'natural athletes' and therefore "physical" rather than "cerebral" beings.
>
> (2009, p. 8)

Being white and saying something like, "I'm not racist. I love Serena Williams!" doesn't mean that you are open for understanding the complexities of racism in the United States. It is necessary to know how one is complicit in certain forms of racism and how one has unfair advantages based on race. Serena is *both* a naturally gifted athlete *and* incredibly intelligent at crafting points, besides having worked very hard to hone her skills. These attributes, taken together, have allowed her to become the champion that she is.

In regards to sport, the power and physicality, perceived or real, of Black women, create a landscape that requires navigation between the "voyeuristic admiration" and lesbian accusations. Collins asserts that:

> for all female athletes and for Black women athletes in particular, the danger lies in being identified as lesbians. The stereotype of women athletes as "manly" and as being lesbians and for Black women as being more "masculine" than White women converge to provide a very different interpretive context for Black female athletes.
>
> (2005, p. 135)

Put another way, white women are considered masculine if they play sports. Black women are simply considered masculine, a stereotype residual from slavery, meaning that Black female athletes are doubly stigmatized. Female Black athletes, then, must contend with sexist and racist stereotypes while striving for greatness on the court, as is the case for Venus and Serena.

The constraining of Serena Williams' individualism[5]

At the US Open tennis championships in 2004, 2009, 2011, and again in 2018, Serena had public disagreements with on-court officials that were understood by some spectators as aggressive, hostile, and even violent (Spencer, 2012). Serena's on-court outbursts trigger a heightened perception of violence as compared to similar outbursts by White tennis players because Serena is not viewed as the greatest tennis player to have ever played the sport, but as a Black woman, and Black women are perceived to be violent (Muhammad, 2010; Gross, 2006). The responses to Serena's outbursts are where the constraint of Serena by the tennis establishment occurs.

2004 US Open. Serena's first major outburst at the US Open occurred in 2004 in a quarter-final match against Jennifer Capriati. At 4–6, 6–4, deuce, Serena hit a seeming winner down the far side line; however, Mariana Alves, the chair umpire, overruled the linesperson's call, declaring that the ball was out. Replays of the shot show that the ball was clearly inside the line. Indeed, Serena did not even know the point went against her until she was standing to serve and the umpire said "advantage Capriati" (USA Channel, 2004). The entire match was riddled with bad line calls, most, if not all, going against Serena.[6] This match was the first time that Serena had a major outburst at a tennis event. Though, in hindsight, this outburst is seen as a non-issue, Serena was viewed as barely in control of her emotions at the time.

116 *The Sustainers*

2009 US Open. During the 2009 US Open, Serena played Kim Clijsters in the semi-finals. Serving at 4–6, 5–6, and 15–30, two points away from losing the match, Shino Tsurubuchi, a linesperson, called a foot fault on Serena's second serve giving Clijsters two match points at 15–40. A foot fault means that one of Serena's feet touched the service line, or she landed inside the court, before she made contact with the ball during her serve. This was the first foot fault called during the entire match and it came at a crucial time. After the foot fault, Serena approached Tsurubuchi and shouted: "I swear to God I'll fucking take this ball and shove it down your fucking throat! Do you hear me!? I swear to God. You better be glad, you better be fucking glad that I'm not, I swear" (Australia 9, 2009). Then Tsurubuchi scampered to Louise Engzell, the chair umpire, and, after Serena seemed calmer, resumed her position as linesperson. For some reason, Serena approached Tsurubuchi again and yelled at her a second time. Tsurubuchi ran to Engzell and, after a discussion, Brian Early, the tournament referee, was called to the court. Serena listened to the discussion of the three officials – Early, Engzell, and Tsurubuchi – from a distance. Then, when the discussion included Serena, she shouted at Tsurubuchi: "I didn't say that I would kill you! Are you serious!?" (Australia 9, 2009). Serena, who had already been given a warning early in the match for racket abuse, was penalized one point for her outburst, and, because Clijsters had double match point, the penalty point ended the match. Serena was out of the US Open and Clijsters was through to the final.

Following this match, Serena was fined $10,000 on site and, after further investigation, the Grand Slam committee levied a fine of $175,000 against Serena, a tennis record, for her tirade. This fine was levied with the potential of its being reduced to $82,500 if Serena successfully refrained from verbal abuse of officials during a two-year probationary period, which she did. The paternalism inherent with reducing the fine for "good behavior" is distasteful. It would be hard to imagine that kind of paternalism levied against anyone from the men's tour or one of the white women from the women's tour.

2011 US Open. During the 2011 US Open final between Serena and Samantha Stosur, controversy erupted once again for Serena. Serving at 2–6, 30–40, Serena hit what seemed to be a winning shot and shouted "Come on!", her trademark shout for pumping herself up. Though Stosur was able to reach the ball with the frame of her racket, and in no way could have returned the shot, Serena's shout was declared by Eva Asderaki, the chair umpire, to have disrupted Stosur's play. Instead of playing the point over, which was recommended by both John McEnroe and Mary Carillo, the CBS analysts for the match (CBS Sports, 2011), the point went directly to Stosur under the "intentional hindrance" rule. While arguing with Asderaki, Serena suddenly said: "Aren't you the one who screwed me over last time?" followed quickly by, "Yeah, you are." However, Asderaki was not the chair umpire during either the 2004 match against Jennifer Capriati nor the 2009 match with Kim Clijsters. That was Mariana Alves and Louise Engzell, respectively. At the changeover at 2–6, 2–1, Serena told Asderaki:

If you ever see me walking down the hall, look the other way, because you're out of control. You're totally out of control. You're a hater, and you are unattractive inside. Who would do such a thing? And I never complain. Wow. I get a code violation for expressing who I am. We're in America last I checked. Can I get a water or am I gonna get a violation for a water? Really, don't even look at me! I promise you, don't look at me, 'cause I am not the one. Don't look my way.

(CBS Sports, 2011)

Again, though, Serena processes her feelings on court through a "code of street" (Anderson, 1999), a display that shows that she is angry and that she has a lack of faith in the fairness of the officiating – the policing if you will, but in no way is a predecessor to outright physical violence.

Following this match, Serena was fined $2,000. Also, because Serena was still in her two-year probationary period, the Grand Slam committee had to investigate this incident as well. It was deemed, however, not to be egregious enough to ban Serena from future tournaments. The committee noted that, "Williams's conduct, while verbally abusive, [did] not rise to the level of a major offence under the grand slam code of conduct" (Busfield, 2011).

2018 US Open. During the final against Naomi Osaka at the 2018 US Open, Serena again had verbal disagreements with Carlos Ramos, the chair umpire. The chain of events began with a warning from Ramos for having received coaching from the stands. She immediately exclaimed that she would "rather lose than have to cheat to win." Then, after having come back in the second set for 3-1, Serena lost the next game, smashing her racket to the ground in disgust with her play. She was docked a point penalty, the next step in the process of penalties after an official warning.

Having thought that the coaching warning was an unofficial warning – what is called a "soft warning" – Serena did not know that she had a point penalty until the start of the next game which began with Osaka up 15-0. In an escalating round of discussions between Serena and Ramos, she exclaimed, "I have never cheated in my life! You owe me an apology," which he never granted. In her continual discussion with Ramos, Serena stated, "You stole a point from me. You're a thief, too!" To this, Ramos issued a game penalty, the third penalty, making the score in the second set 5-3, Osaka serving for the match. When Ramos called both players over to explain the ruling, Serena burst out laughing and asked, "Are you kidding me?" Serena asked to speak to tournament referee Brian Earley, whom she told,

This is not fair. This has happened to me too many times.... To lose a game for saying that is not fair. There's a lot of men out here that have said a lot of things, and because they are men, that doesn't happen.

After the match, Serena was fined $17,000 for having called Ramos a "liar" and a "thief."

Following this match, public perceptions of Serena again centered on her being violent, out of control and hostile. Serena, on the other hand, in thinking of her history at the US Open, responded to a question in the press conference following the match:

Question: You mentioned how at this tournament something always seems to come up. When that was happening out there, were you flashing back to 2009? Does it bring up more things, piling on?

Serena: I think, yeah, that's hard for me. You know, I think it's just instantly, just like, Oh, gosh, I don't want to go back to 2004. Forget 2009, you know. It started way back then. So it's always something. But that's also kind of, like, this game mentally that you have to play with. You know, sometimes it might seem like things always happen, but I don't know the word I'm looking for. You just kind of have to, like, try to realize that it's coincidence. Maybe it's coincidence, so....

In both the 2009 and 2011 US Open, Serena did break rules of tennis. The problem, however, is in the gray area between the rules of tennis, their interpretation, and the imposition of sanctions based on those interpretations. The problem with the 2009 US Open is that foot faults are simply not called, except in the most egregious of cases, in the final rounds of major tournaments and never in the late stages of a match. Indeed,

> [John] McEnroe and fellow [CBS Sports] broadcaster Dick Enberg criticized the official whom Williams berated, disagreeing Williams was guilty of a foot fault, then saying the official should never have enforced the rule at this point in the match. In other words, they justified Williams' actions.
>
> (Peele, 2009)

However, whether or not Serena foot faulted is not the question we should be pursuing. Since we cannot see a foot fault from the replays, I would claim that Serena's foot fault was not egregious. The real question, then, is: How is Serena treated differently on court than other (white) players? Again, foot faults are rarely called in later rounds of major tournaments, and are never called during critical points of a match unless, of course, the foot fault is egregious.

During the 2011 US Open, Serena shouted "Come on!" when she hit a winning shot. From replays, it appears that Stosur had no chance to return the shot. Points in which a disruption like this occur are almost always ruled by the chair umpires to be played over. Also, in many cases, players will give the point to the other player if they know that they had no chance to return the shot. Considering that Stosur was in a very formidable lead, this would have been a commendable move on her part. However, Stosur did not and, with the strict interpretation of the rules by the chair umpire, the point went directly to Stosur.

In both of these instances, Serena did break rules of tennis as they are written. The rules, however, have not been regularly interpreted for other players in the ways that they were interpreted for Serena, if ever. In this sense, Serena is forced to play competitive tennis by different rules (because the rules are interpreted differently for her) than others in women's tennis. What, then, is different about Serena in the world of women's tennis? It seems too obvious to state that it is her race; however, that is the primary difference between Serena and the other players.

Serena is always surprised, seemingly caught off-guard, when rulings come down from the chair umpire. Indeed, after more than a decade of playing tennis professionally, she knows what the norms are and she knows when she is being subjected to a ruling that is not the norm and, hence, is not fair. The quick turn by spectators to arguments that Serena is too aggressive, too powerful, etc., only serve to deflect everyone from seeing the different ways the rules are interpreted for Serena versus her opponents. This deflection is a method of color-blind racism.

Carrington analyzed the heavyweight boxer Jack Johnson who emerged in the early 20th century. Using Carrington's description of the contradictions of Johnson at the time for the Black middle class could also be used to describe Serena, as a Black female athlete, for white spectators. Carrington writes:

> [Serena] embodied a series of contradictions. [Her] sheer physicality, confidence and strength both impress and unsettle [white people]. [She] represented a version of negritude that was neither afraid of nor intimidated by whiteness. There were few, if any, public figures of the time that were so strident in their public disregard for white attempts at reducing blacks to the status of social inferior. In fact, it was not so much that [Serena] refused to accept [her] subordinate position to whites but that [she] actively and willfully suggested [*her*] *superiority.*
>
> (2010, p. 89; italics in original)

Serena has shown her superiority by having won 21 Grand Slam singles titles thus far, which is a feat that will likely not be accomplished again. Furthermore, she is still competing! And in willfully suggesting her superiority, even with the constraints on her individualism, Serena inserts an unapologetic Blackness into the whiteness of tennis.

Conclusion

The Sustainers cohort, then, shows a change in social activism following the Founders cohort and the Joiners cohort. This change occurred as players negotiated how to exist and have an impact within the confines of corporatization and individualism. Some events that occurred during the Sustainers cohort include Steffi Graf's disavowal of the social activism of the previous generations of women's tennis, the depoliticization of the Original 9 with the simultaneous repoliticization of Billie Jean King as the individual who created women's tennis. Additionally, the coup and subsequent restructuring of the WTA set it on course to become a corporate entity rather than a player's association. Likewise, too, anti-grunting policies and the "strong is beautiful" advertising campaign ushered in an overlay of postfeminism; that women's tennis had arrived and there was no more need for social activism.

Interestingly, unapologetic Blackness entered women's tennis via the individualizing structures that were taking shape. The Williams sisters were allowed to offer unapologetic Blackness as their own style of individualism, however, in the case of Serena, this individualism is constantly monitored and constrained. Countering the individualism of neoliberalism, the Williams sisters maintained an agenda of social justice. Their work on social justice issues, as well as the efforts of other players, led to the creation of the Throwbacks cohort that will be the focus of the next chapter.

Notes

1 This is the cohort where I likely should have belonged; however, having Rosie Casals from the Founders cohort as my coach seemed to have pulled me to the Joiners cohort, which I identify with.
2 These rankings are the end-of-year rankings for 1997 (WTA Tour Rankings).
3 Again, these rankings are the end-of-year rankings for 1997 (WTA Tour Rankings).
4 The exhibit also included Tara Mateik's "Putting the Balls Away" (www.taramateik.com/putting-the-balls-away/), a re-enactment of the Battle of the Sexes tennis match in which Mateik plays both parts, that of Billie Jean King and Bobby Riggs, with the original commentary by Howard Cosell and Rosie Casals in the background. Hilarious!
5 Some of this section appears in *Ethnic and Racial Studies*, in my article titled, "Serena Williams and (the perception of) violence: Intersectionality, the performance of Blackness, and women's professional tennis," published in 2019.
6 This match was the one most often cited by proponents of the Hawkeye computer system for line-calling.

5 The Throwbacks

Individual players fighting for broader social justice issues

Women's professional tennis has had four generational cohorts so far. First, the Founders cohort was focused on equal prize money and a comparable offering of tournaments for the women as the men. Second, the Joiners cohort kept the work of the Founders cohort alive, ensuring that equal prize money was continually sought; however, identity politics entered women's tennis during the cohort. Third, the Sustainers cohort shows us when the corporatization of women's tennis occurred, including individualism, albeit within constraints.

The Throwbacks cohort marks a move away from the individualism that marked the Sustainers cohort.[1] It also includes a return to both strands of social activism that have occurred in women's professional tennis: equality and representation. The contextual moment that this cohort emerges through can be explained through the weakening of the category of sex – most notably via the strengthening of the gay marriage debates, but also the parallel trans movement and anti-sexism efforts. With the marriage equality debates, the issue was that two people, regardless of sex, could become legally married, which had the effect of loosening the rigidity for which the category of sex was known. In addition, the past decade has also seen an increasing adoption of social media outlets for players to express their thoughts on disparate matters, so much more is known about players than in prior eras. Interestingly, the Founders cohort was begun because of sex, and the discrimination that women players faced. The Throwbacks cohort emerges as sex, as a categorical determinant, is unraveling.

What does social activism for equality and representation in women's tennis look like with an unraveling of the category of sex? Within tennis, there have been four major ways this has played out: exposure of LGBTQ issues, continued pressure for equal prize money, men supporting women in their fight for equality, and Serena Williams, an enigmatic activist athlete who, because of the loosening of the rigidity of sex as a category, has had her accomplishments valued more highly than women in the past within the dominant culture, which has opened up avenues for social activism for her.

I have documented a new cohort emerging, one which Pam Shriver of the Joiners cohort referred to as "Throwbacks" (Shriver, private interview, 2015). The Throwbacks cohort is operating alongside the Sustainers cohort. Within the Throwbacks cohort, women are merging social activism with their accomplishments in tennis. These players operate successfully within the Sustainers cohort with its focus on corporatization and marketing; however, they are inspired by the efforts of the Founders cohort and the Joiners cohort to create change, and make society at large better.

To be clear, the Sustainers cohort and the Throwbacks cohort are operating at the same time. All of the current players belong to the Sustainers cohort; however, only a few belong to the Throwbacks cohort. These few players belong to both the Sustainers and the Throwbacks cohorts. As such, they are operating within the confines of the corporatization and mass-marketing of the Sustainers cohort while also working towards social justice via various projects.

The players of the Throwbacks cohort use the power they have gained from successfully operating within the Sustainers cohort to work on social justice issues. When I asked Venus Williams, after briefly explaining the generational cohorts of social activism within women's tennis, if a Throwbacks cohort that was focused on social justice was emerging, she simply said: "High hopes" (V. Williams, 2015). The Throwbacks cohort is far from being the end of the Sustainers cohort and the beginning of the new, but there are "high hopes" for its growth.

Indeed, during the Throwbacks cohort is the period when intersectionality is most dominant in its truest, most ideal, form. Intersectionality explains the experiences of people with particular and multiple subjectivities and how those subjectivities operate within various domains of power. Furthermore, there is an embedded component of social activism within intersectionality allowing for, and encouraging, the push against these various domains of power. It is this form of intersectionality that appears most prominently in the Throwbacks cohort.

David Harvey, in discussing neoliberalism, asserts that social change and social activism struggle between individualism and social justice. He wrote: "Left movements failed to recognize or confront, let alone transcend, the inherent tension between the quest for individual freedoms and social justice." (2005, p. 43). When I mistakenly referred to Serena Williams as a "celebrity athlete" as I began my question at the press conference interview, she corrected that part – "I think that there is a lot of, I guess, quote/unquote celebrity athletes" (S. Williams, 2015c) – before addressing the rest of what I had asked. It was clear that she was rejecting the status of celebrity with its hyper-focus on the individual. Her work was more than that, and it was more than just hers.

The Throwbacks cohort has been marked by a return to identity politics. In 1999, the first push against the constraints of neoliberalism in the Sustainers cohort came from Amélie Mauresmo. "Coming out" as a lesbian was her opposition to the silencing – the individualism within prescribed constraints – that marked the Sustainers cohort and it strengthened broader social justice movements working on LGBTQ issues. Venus Williams fought for equal prize money at the Grand Slam events from 2005 until it was enacted in 2007. Though this was an issue specific to women's professional tennis, Venus had to draw the attention of British Parliament and get the ministers on her side in order for this battle to be successful. In 2012, in response to the homophobic remarks from the now evangelical minister Margaret Court, who, as a player, was a member of the Founders cohort, Martina Navratilova and Laura Robson visibly and vocally threw their support behind the Rainbow Flags Over Margaret Court Arena social movement that emerged at the Australian Open. The activism of this group was unique in that it was fan-based and focused against a former player at a Grand Slam event. This, of course, had influence on the marriage equality discussions in Australia. Finally, Serena Williams has worked tirelessly on racial equity in tennis, as well as in society at large. She is the activist athlete of the modern era.

Amélie Mauresmo "coming out" as a lesbian, 1999[2]

In many ways, Mauresmo took the reins as a social activist when she proclaimed that she came out, "not because she wanted to become a symbol or the focus of attention, but because she did not want to dance around the subject throughout her career" (Forman & Plymire, 2005, p. 120), as Martina Navratilova did for a decade with the social fears prevalent during the Joiners cohort. Indeed, Mauresmo asserted that closeted players on the women's tennis tour "had a hard time dealing with their situation … I feel sorry for them" (Miller, McKay, & Martin, 2001, p. 106). Mauresmo, then, had seen that she could not exist within the confines of the closet while being in a public arena. She is a reluctant social activist in ways; however, she was quickly made the lesbian icon of tennis by LGBTQ social movements outside of tennis.

Two analyses of the media attention Amélie Mauresmo received before and after coming out as a lesbian were carried out by Toby Miller, Jim McKay, and Randy Martin (2001) and Pamela Forman and Darcy Plymire (2005). Both studies highlight the difference in focus and attention that Mauresmo received. Forman and Plymire point to the shift in focus from Mauresmo's ranking to her body:

> Prior to the news conference at the Australian Open semifinals [in which she came out], the adjective most often used to describe Mauresmo was "unseeded".... After the semifinal match with [Lindsay] Davenport and the subsequent comments from Davenport and [Martina] Hingis, correspondents quickly focused their attention on Mauresmo's body.
>
> (2005, p. 121)

Additionally, Miller, McKay, and Martin note that "Mauresmo's musculature is unexceptional next to that of such players as Mary Pierce and Venus and Serena Williams [when she first joined the tour]. This suggests that sexuality animated the controversy" (2001, p. 104). Indeed, Mauresmo's body structure is indistinguishable from most female professional tennis players of her time. This, then, raises the question of what people were actually seeing when they looked at Mauresmo after she came out as a lesbian.

Eve Kosofsky Sedgwick asserts that "the closet is the defining structure for gay oppression in this century" (1993, p. 48). In the public discourse, a person is either in or out of the closet, establishing yet another binary system, and this structure is only used to describe gay people, or those who have non-normative gender performances. Furthermore, Sedgwick states that:

> "Closetedness" itself is a performance initiated as such by the speech act of a silence – not a particular silence, but a silence that accrues particularity by fits and starts, in relation to the discourse that surrounds and differentially constitutes it. The speech acts that coming out, in turn, can comprise are as strangely specific.
>
> (2008, p. 3)

This closet is a site of speculation. If a person is in the closet, that person is understood as gay. If the closet is not even an applicable site, the person is understood as heterosexual. Furthermore, as opposed to Judith Butler's speech act which can name and, therefore, empower female masculinity, Sedgwick's closet is a speech act which is silent. That is, by choosing the closet, the person is choosing silence.

In women's tennis, the closet is always a site of speculation. Female athletes are always under the gaze of feminine and heterosexual critique. As KL Broad explains:

> With every gain that women have made in sport, there has been a simultaneous reaction questioning the sexual orientation of women athletes as well as the actual sex/gender of women in sport. Simply stated, the assumption has been, "sports are masculine; therefore, women in sports are masculine; therefore, women in sports are lesbians."
>
> (2002, p. 182)

Indeed, homophobia is used in this way to police women and even thwart their athletic achievements. Martha Gever describes the closet of women's tennis which was, surprisingly, aided by journalists:

> Long before "don't ask; don't tell" became shorthand for official US government policies ... the same principles governed a tacit bargain struck between the sports press and lesbian or gay athletes. Navratilova (and undoubtedly countless others) went along with the strategy, because it allowed them to keep in check nosy, scolding members of the press, or at least those who always treated homosexuality as a sensational topic.
>
> (2003, p. 161)

Journalists, at least before the current mass media age of televised press conferences, were the main conduit between athletes and the general public. During the 1970s–1990s, this tacit agreement was critically important for closeted lesbian players.

There have been only three women in the history of women's tennis who have come out publicly during their careers: Billie Jean King, Martina Navratilova and Amélie Mauresmo. Countless others may have come out after their tennis careers were over, or came out to family and friends, but not to the scrutiny of the public. That there have only been three athletes come out publicly during their careers points to a deeply-rooted homophobic climate in women's tennis.

Billie Jean King and Martina Navratilova both came out publicly in the early 1980s. It was not until 1999 that a third lesbian came out publicly in women's tennis while still an active player. Amélie Mauresmo was a very successful player on the professional tennis circuit from 1994 until her retirement in 2009. During that time, she was ranked #1 in the world in 2004 and again in 2006. She won two Grand Slam singles titles, the Australian Open, and Wimbledon in 2006. She also represented France during Federation Cup play.

Mauresmo came out as a lesbian at the 1999 Australian Open, in which she was unseeded, after beating Lindsay Davenport, then the #1 ranked player in the world, in the semi-finals to the surprise of everyone. Mauresmo lost to Martina Hingis, then the #2 ranked player in the world, in the finals.

In an article published in the now-defunct *Stanford Humanities Review*, Judith Butler, while writing about Navratilova's accomplishments, wrote:

> What are we charting when we note that Martina was once outside the [gender] ideal – because outside of recognizable gender, too strong, too muscular, too aggressive – and that she ended her career by exemplifying that very ideal? Such a move could not be possible if gender ideals were not capable of transformation, of becoming more capacious, of responding to the challenge of what is excluded from their terms by expanding the very terms of gender themselves.
>
> (1998)

Butler, however, could not have foreseen what would take place during the following year, 1999, when Mauresmo came out. Prior to coming out, Mauresmo was most often described as "unseeded" (Forman & Plymire, 2005, p. 121) – meaning that she was not ranked high enough to be "seeded" or placed in a more protected spot in a tournament's draw. The dominant discourse immediately changed after her coming out. After the homophobic and genderphobic comments by Davenport and Hingis which immediately followed Mauresmo's coming out, the dominant discourse switched to descriptions of Mauresmo's muscularity (Forman & Plymire, 2005, p. 121). Indeed, the authors seem to be claiming that Davenport and Hingis created the discourse that the media, then, ran with. If being a lesbian is a shunning of male access, what was so threatening about Mauresmo to Davenport and Hingis? It might be impossible to know what they were threatened by, and why Mauresmo's coming out was more threatening to them than, seemingly, to men.

Davenport, though 6'2½" and 174 pounds compared to Mauresmo's 5'9" and 141 pound frame, asserted that Mauresmo's "power and physique were

126 *The Throwbacks*

overwhelming, that playing her was like playing 'a guy'" (Forman & Plymire, 2005, p. 120) and that her muscles "looked huge to me. I think they must have grown; maybe because she is wearing a tank top" (Miller, McKay, & Martin, 2001, p. 104). Davenport further elaborated:

> A couple of times, I mean, I thought I was playing a guy, the girl was hitting so hard, so strong.... She is so strong in those shoulders and she just hits the ball very well.... I mean, she hits the ball not like any other girl. She hits it so hard and with so much topspin.... Women's tennis isn't usually played like that.
>
> (Miller, McKay, & Martin, 2001, p. 104)

Considering their size differential, it seems inconceivable that Davenport felt physically threatened on the court. However, in the dominant discourse that proclaims that lesbians are masculine, Davenport may have suddenly been made to focus upon Mauresmo's muscularity. In response to Davenport, Mauresmo said: "The fact that I'm strong physically is maybe impressing her. It means that I'm a very solid player, so I take it as a compliment" (Miller, McKay, & Martin, 2001, p. 104).

Before the final was played, Martina Hingis announced to journalists, Mauresmo "came to Melbourne with her girlfriend; I think she's half a man" (Miller, McKay, & Martin, 2001, p. 104; Forman & Plymire, 2005, p. 120). To this, Mauresmo stated, "On top of wanting to beat her, now I'm enraged!" (Miller, McKay, & Martin, 2001, p. 104). In response to Hingis's statement, Billie Jean King requested that Chris Evert, Hingis's tour mentor, counsel her protégé on homophobia. Hingis, ironically, is named after Martina Navratilova. Though, it is possible, that this made Hingis want to differentiate herself from lesbians even more.

Journalists from around the world bounced onto this site of sensational-ism created by Davenport, Hingis, and the Australian press. As noted previously, players and the press had a "don't ask, don't tell" policy; however, if a player came out, he or she was fair game. Comments made by journalists after Mauresmo came out include:

- "Mauresmo's thickly muscled shoulders bulge from her dark blue tank top, and she struts cockily around the court like a weightlifter in the gym" (Forman and Plymire, 2005, p. 121), wrote one *Associated Press* reporter.
- "Oh, Man, She's Good" (Miller, McKay, & Martin, 2001, p. 105), from the *Herald Sun*.
- "Women normally only play tennis against men in mixed doubles. But that all changed yesterday if you believe the world's number one player Lindsay Davenport" (Miller, McKay, & Martin, 2001, p. 105), from the *Daily Telegraph*.
- "Shoulders like Lou Ferrigno – she is the French 'incroyable hulk'" (Miller, McKay, & Martin, 2001, p. 105) from the *Daily Telegraph*.

- "Where is women's tennis headed? Mind boggles at the muscle monsters" (Miller, McKay, & Martin, 2001, p. 105), from the *Daily Telegraph*.
- "Huge linebacker shoulders" (Miller, McKay, and Martin 2001, p. 105).

It is most likely a fact that Mauresmo's muscles did not grow between the time she was closeted playing Davenport in the semi-finals and out as a lesbian playing Hingis in the final.

As noted previously, Miller, McKay, and Martin claimed that "Mauresmo's musculature is unexceptional next to that of such players as Mary Pierce and Venus and Serena Williams. This suggests that sexuality animated the controversy" (2001, p. 104). Indeed, Mauresmo's musculature was not more pronounced than others on the tour. However, Mauresmo was marked as masculine when she came out as a lesbian. Susan Cahn asserts that:

> The lesbian athlete, with her reputation for masculine style, body type, and desire, represents a refusal to issue this reassurance [of being a "normal" woman]. Her sexual autonomy and her rejection of conventional femininity – as defined through heterosexuality – make her the locus for enduring fears that women in sport transgress gender lines and disrupt the social order.
>
> (1994, p. 265)

Mauresmo, then, was socially constructed as masculine in the discourse because, by rejecting heterosexuality, she, essentially, was understood as rejecting femininity.

Pamela Forman and Darcy Plymire, in describing the media's attention on Mauresmo, state that:

> By coming out as a lesbian and fitting certain stereotypical notions of masculine lesbianism [by being an accomplished athlete], Mauresmo allows the press, advertisers, and women's tennis symbolically to demonstrate their sympathy with women's issues while differentiating the real lesbian from other strong women on tour. In addition, embracing Mauresmo allows those same entities to portray themselves as tolerant and progressive without identifying themselves or their products too closely with lesbians. Interestingly, the press compliments itself further by castigating Martina Hingis for her homophobia. This move reinforces the assumption that homophobia and heterosexist oppression are problems of individual ignorance rather than of the socioeconomic or political system.
>
> (Forman & Plymire, 2005, p. 125)

Mauresmo was simply coded as masculine in the dominant discourse after she came out; however, she was embraced by some. Indeed, the "press, advertisers, and women's tennis" could feel comfortable being sympathetic to Mauresmo precisely because she was not masculine.

To reiterate, Martha Gever asserts that: "If there is to be a lesbian celebrity then she must represent triumphant female masculinity" (2003, p. 186). Indeed, as Susan Cahn notes: "Women's athletic freedom requires that certain attributes long defined as masculine – skill, strength, speed, physical dominance, uninhibited use of space and motion – become human qualities and not those of a particular gender" (1994, p. 279).

Sedgwick asserts that: "Knowledge, after all, is not itself power, although it is the magnetic field of power. Ignorance and opacity collude or compete with knowledge in mobilizing the flows of energy, desire, goods, meanings, persons" (2008, p. 4). That can be seen with understandings of gender and sexuality in women's tennis. Features, like muscles, are accentuated in the public discourse. With Amélie Mauresmo, her muscles became the focal point. Lindsay Davenport, apparently, "think[s] they must have grown" (Miller, McKay, & Martin, 2001, p. 104) in the process of turning the knob, opening the door, and leaving the closet.

Part of this section is excerpted from my previously published 2014 article, "Judith Butler Redux – The Heterosexual Matrix and the Out Lesbian Athlete: Amélie Mauresmo, Gender Performance, and Women's Professional Tennis," published in the *Journal of the Philosophy of Sport*.

Venus Williams' fight for equal prize money, 2005–2007

Given that the WTA Tour is a separate tennis tour from the ATP Tour, it is understandable how prize money at those events are not equal. The tours operate with different sponsors and different tournament classifications. The Grand Slam events, however, are a different story. They are governed by the ITF, not the separate tennis tours.

Leading the way, the US Open has offered equal prize money to men and women since 1973. This remarkable milestone is greatly due to the influence of the Original 9 and their refusal to play the US Open in 1973 if they did not equalize the prize money.

The Australian Open began offering equal prize money to men and women in 1984, but then stopped in 1995, citing the higher ratings for men's matches. In 2001, the Australian Open quietly began offering equal prize money again. The French Open and Wimbledon, however, maintained different prize money structures. They did so until Venus Williams stepped in to agitate for equal prize money at Wimbledon. Literally the day after Wimbledon agreed to offer equal prize money, the French Open made a statement that they would do the same.

What was occurring in women's tennis between 1973 and 2007 and why did Wimbledon and the French Open not follow the US Open's lead sooner? Of this, Selena Roberts asserts that:

> I think that for the women, there were probably some decades there where there weren't a lot of strong powerful voices fighting for the women.

Sometimes you got the feeling that the women were just happy with what they were getting.

(DuVernay, 2013)

Indeed, Billie Jean King supported this statement when she said:

> Venus is the only one since, probably, my generation that's had this drive to want to change this equal prize money. I think that it was really a blessing, believe me. I was thrilled because she is so wonderful. I think the world of her as a person and I was really thrilled that she stepped up.
>
> (DuVernay, 2013)

The US Open

The year of 1973 was a huge year for women's professional tennis. In between the formation of the WTA in June and the Battle of the Sexes match between Billie Jean King and Bobby Riggs in September, discussions were being had between King and Bill Talbert, the tournament chairman for the US Open. On July 19, 1973, Ban deodorants, a subsidiary of Bristol-Myers, stated that it would offer the US Open a "sports grant" for $55,000 to close the gap between men's and women's prize money (Keese, 1973). Thus, when the US Open of 1973 began a month later, men and women, in each round of play, were given the same prize money. In supporting women's tennis, Joseph G. Kelnberger, vice president of Bristol-Myers Product Division, stated: "We feel that the women's game is equally as exciting and entertaining as the men's, and we hope that our direct involvement with the 1973 US Open clearly indicates our positive position on behalf of women in sports" (Keese, 1973).

During the 1972 US Open, the men's champion, Ilie Năstase, earned $25,000 and the women's champion, Billie Jean King, earned $10,000 (Keese, 1973). In 1973, the men's prize money remained the same, whereas the women's champion would earn $25,000 as well. When asked if men would protest, Talbert said, "I don't know…. If there is, I'll just tell the men to go out and sell their product better" (Keese, 1973).

The Australian Open

Between 1984 and 1995, the Australian Open offered equal prize money to men and women.[3] Then, between 1995 and 2000, men were paid more. In 2001, the Australian Open again offered equal prize money to men and women. Bart McGuire, the CEO of the WTA Tour at the time, stated that:

> Equalizing prize money at the Grand Slams is a major goal…. It is a goal that we have preferred to approach through persuasion and diplomacy rather than through more aggressive means…. Tennis Australia has responded very positively to our approach, and to the fact that women's tennis has

generated record attendance and extraordinary worldwide publicity, as well as dramatically increased television coverage and television ratings.

(The Independent, 2000)

Thus, by 2001, half of the Grand Slam events were offering equal prize money. It would take another six years for all of the Grand Slams to achieve equality in their pay structures.

Wimbledon and the French Open

At the first Wimbledon championships of the "open" era in 1968, Rod Laver, the men's singles champion made £2,000. Billie Jean King, the women's singles champion made £750. From 1975 until 2000, the women's prize money was exactly 90 percent of the men's prize money, except for 1992 when it reached 91 percent. From 2001 until 2004, the women's prize money was pegged at 93 percent of the men's prize money. Then, for 2005 and 2006, the women's prize money was 95 percent that of the men's prize money. It seemed to many observers that Wimbledon was simply being obligatorily sexist by not equalizing the pay structure. For example, in 2006, the men's champion, Roger Federer, received £655,000 and the women's champion, Amélie Mauresmo, received £625,000. The small difference appeared to show that Wimbledon simply would not offer equal prize money on principle. Indeed, Chris Gorringe, the All England Lawn Tennis Club secretary, even stated on BBC radio, "If we paid the women more, we wouldn't have so much to spend on petunias" (DuVernay, 2013).

Venus Williams first made a public statement about the need for equal prize money in 1998, after a first-round match at Wimbledon. In 2005, the day before her final against Lindsay Davenport, Williams spoke at the board meeting of the All England Lawn Tennis and Croquet Club, the first player in history to do so. She began by asking those present to close their eyes and imagine being a little girl who, once you "get to this stage … you're told you're not the same as a boy" (Sreedhar, 2015).

In 2006, despite increasing criticism of the unequal pay structure at Wimbledon, Tim Phillips, the club chairman, stated that:

> This issue is one of a judgment on fairness…. We believe that what we do at the moment is actually fair to the men as well as to the women. … It just doesn't seem right to us that the lady players could play in three events and could take away significantly more than the men's champion who battles away through these best-of-five matches…. We also would point [out] that the top 10 ladies last year earned more from Wimbledon that the top 10 men did…. We don't see it as an equal rights issue.
>
> (BBC Sport, 2006)

In fact, the way that women at the 2006 Wimbledon championships supposedly earned more money, as Phillips would see it, was through juggling the demands of playing three events (women's singles, women's doubles, and mixed doubles) instead of one event (men's singles).

Accusing Wimbledon of using a "Victorian-era view," Larry Scott, then the CEO of the WTA, countered by saying that "in the 21st century, it is morally indefensible that women competitors in a Grand Slam tournament should be receiving considerably less prize money than their male counterparts" (BBC Sport, 2006). Venus Williams took yet another angle, threatening to boycott, if the prize money issue was not rectified. She asserted:

> We want to be treated equally as the men. This is not just about women's tennis but about women all over the world.... At Wimbledon we would like to have equal prize money to prove that we are equal on all fronts.... We will keep lobbying on the matter. We don't want to deprive fans from seeing women's tennis but we are willing to be extremely proactive in our stance.
>
> (BBC Sport, 2006)

This issue continued to grow in fervor. The WTA began creating precise marketing angles that would deflate any arguments in support of men making more money than women. Their primary arguments were:

- Women are ready and willing to play five-set matches, equal to the men. Entertainment value is not based on the length of a match, however, but on quality.
- To the argument that tickets to the men's final cost more than the tickets to the women's final, the WTA questioned who was setting the price. Of course, Wimbledon was setting the price. Since both events were selling out, Wimbledon's stance did not hold any weight.

During the 2005 Wimbledon, Larry Scott held a meeting with all ten of the top-10 players. In the meeting, he explained the issue of equal prize money and that there was a meeting with the leaders of each of the four Grand Slams – the Australian Open, the French Open, Wimbledon, and the US Open – the Friday before the women's final held on Saturday. No player had ever attended this meeting. He told the ten players that it would be a great coup if the two who were playing in the final attended that meeting. All of the players agreed that they would do it (DuVernay, 2013). For the meeting, Venus was in attendance; Lindsay Davenport was not. What transpired, however, had a deep impact on those who were there. According to Larry Scott and Venus, this is what happened:

> VENUS: You could definitely feel the awkwardness. People were wondering what was going to happen.
> LARRY: We had not talked a lot about what she would say. I just told her to be herself and I thought that it would be very powerful.

VENUS: I am not going to express how I feel but I didn't have any script. So I got in there and said, "Everyone close your eyes." I was like, "no peeking."

LARRY: Everyone's reaction around the table, they weren't sure they heard what they thought they heard. She said: "Now I would like you to imagine that you are a young girl growing up who has dreams and aspirations for being an athlete, or a scientist, an artist, or president of the United States. And then, one day, someone tells you that you can't be the same, you can't reach that same level as a boy who has worked equally as hard as you, done as well as you, that there is a limit to what you can achieve because of your gender."

VENUS: And when your eyes are closed you actually do have to visualize what the person is talking about because you lose that sense of sight that we rely on so much.

LARRY: She completely changed the whole dynamic of the conversation by making it personal. Not just personal for her, but personal for every single person in the room that day.

VENUS: People really had to look inside themselves and say, "Is this really what we want to keep doing?"

LARRY: And that was it. Everyone opened their eyes, and there were some questions, some talk about where we are, where we were. And then we left.

(DuVernay, 2013)

In 2006, compelled by Venus' statements and feeling mounting pressure to offer equal prize money, the French Open made their pay structure equal. The All England Lawn Tennis Club announces its prize money each year in February preceding the start of Wimbledon in late June. In February of 2006, Scott heard from tournament officials that Wimbledon would not be offering equal prize money that year, despite the seeming success of Venus' appeal to the entire Grand Slam committee. As previously stated, women made 95 percent of the prize money that the men made at Wimbledon. Scott explained, "There is no science to it. You are trying to make a statement" (DuVernay, 2013). Venus stepped up her activism even more:

> For me, I felt like this can't go on. Someone has to speak up.... It fuels your fire more. You just feel like, ok that's fine, I'm ready to fight some more. Let's get another game plan. What are we going to do next?
>
> (DuVernay, 2013)

The change in game plan was to make the issue of equal prize money a public issue, instead of one discussed in the private meetings that had been occurring between the WTA and the various tennis officials.

In the middle of the 2006 Wimbledon, on June 26, Williams issued an open letter to Wimbledon and to the public in which she laid out her claim for equal prize money. Williams' letter was so evocative that it compelled Janet Anderson, then a member of Parliament and a Labour Party politician, to bring up the issue of equal prize money during an open session of questions and answers in Parliament with Tony Blair, then the Prime Minister of Britain on June 28, 2006. This part of the parliamentary session was as follows:

SPEAKER OF PARLIAMENT: Janet Anderson.
ANDERSON: Is my right honourable friend aware that 30 years on from the introduction of the Equal Pay Act by a Labour Government, the winner of the women's singles at Wimbledon will receive £30,000 less in prize money than the winner of the men's singles? Wimbledon is the only Grand Slam competition in which that occurs. Will my right honourable friend support his right honourable friend, the Secretary of State for Culture, Media and Sport, in her efforts to persuade the Lawn Tennis Association to put this inequality right?
BLAIR: Well, I was somewhat coy on that yesterday, as I did not realize that my right honourable friend the Secretary for Culture, Media and Sport had pronounced on the matter already. Therefore, I am very happy to be bolder today, to welcome what she said, and to endorse it fully.
(Parliament, 2006)

With Blair's support, the old guard of the All England Lawn and Cricket Club board of directors had no defense.

Before the 2007 Wimbledon championships began, the board of directors announced that there would be equal prize money that year. In a gross understatement, Tim Phillips claimed during his announcement of the new prize money structure that "we believe this positive step will be widely welcomed" (Clarey, 2007). Venus Williams stated that:

The greatest tennis tournament in the world has reached an even greater height today. I applaud today's decision by Wimbledon, which recognizes the value of women's tennis. The 2007 championships will have even greater meaning and significance to me and my fellow players.
(Clarey, 2007)

Indeed, 2007 was a memorable Wimbledon for Williams as she collected her fourth Wimbledon singles title that year. Of the win, Billie Jean King wrote:

In 2007, I was there in the royal box at Wimbledon to watch Venus Williams accept the first-place trophy and a check for the same amount that the men's champion, Roger Federer, was paid the next day: about $1.4 million. It was the first time Wimbledon had offered equal prize money to both the men's and women's champion.... I waved to Venus, who was no more than 50 feet from me. She waved back. I could not help but smile on behalf of all my friends who signed that contract for $1 a decade before Venus was born. All those years of fighting for equal prize money, and when it finally happened at the most famous tennis club in the world, the woman who earned it truly understood why. And now she is one of the new leaders in the ongoing effort to achieve true equality in tennis and in other aspects of our culture.

(King and Brennan, 2008, p. 184)

Venus had previously won the Wimbledon singles title in 2000, 2001, and 2005, and she won her fifth singles title at Wimbledon the following year, in 2008.

Prior to advocating for equal prize money, Venus was already a cultural icon. She had feelings that the equal prize money issue was unfair, but she did not yet have her voice. Venus stated that:

> I wasn't out there looking to make these huge changes, but I felt like I don't like this, I don't think that it is fair, I feel that tennis is a premier sport for women so we have to set an example here.
>
> (DuVernay, 2013)

Speaking of activism among athletes, Billie Jean King stated that:

> Venus Williams wanted to take this on, was willing to take whatever came back at her because of it. Most players don't want to step up that much anymore, they don't want to get in trouble, it's their branding. They want to make sure that everyone wants to buy their products. So, for Venus to step up, it took a lot of courage.
>
> (DuVernay, 2013)

Jelani Cobb, director of the Institute of African American Studies at the University of Connecticut, points to Venus' outsider status in tennis in understanding her social activism:

> Sometimes it maybe takes an outsider to do [social activism]. That period when [Venus and Serena] were outside, when they were fighting to get inside, when they were wearing beads, when they were being criticized for their style, I think in some way, that lent itself to being able to step outside the sport and say this is wrong and needs to change.
>
> (DuVernay, 2013)

Men supporting women

The effort that men in professional tennis have put forth in support of women has come in two ways. The first is in indirect negotiations regarding prize money at Grand Slam events, and, in other cases, direct public condemnation of those who do not support women's equal prize money. The second manner in which men have supported women is through the hiring of women as coaches.

Men's efforts for equal prize money

Three of the top male players took different angles in support of equal prize money: Roger Federer, Rafael Nadal, and Andy Murray. These three men are using the debates from within women's tennis, rather than imposing their own politics, which shows the respect they have for women's tennis.

Roger Federer, Overall Increases in Prize Money. Roger Federer has to speak only on behalf of the ATP, but is proud that his efforts at increasing the overall prize money at Grand Slams also benefits women. Indeed, he said,

> I mean, I'm all for equal prize money. When I was fighting for prize money increases, especially at the slam level, I was always very aware of the fact that it was always going to impact the women's game, which I was very happy about. Both at the same time were growing.
> (Federer, March 24, 2016; press conference at Miami Open)

As the president of the ATP Players Council for many years, Federer helped negotiate prize money at tournaments.

Rafael Nadal, Wider Distribution of Prize Money. Rafael Nadal, similar to Federer, can only technically work on behalf of ATP efforts, but he consistently works to have increases in prize money distributed more equitably across all of the rounds, instead of just tacked onto the already huge amount the champions will make. Prior to his efforts to equalize the prize money, many players could not afford to attend the Grand Slam events due to the costs of travel. Now, players who lose in the first round earn enough prize money to cover their costs for the few days, and more, depending on how far they have traveled. Since Grand Slam events have the same prize money structures for men and women, Nadal's efforts to work on making the prize money distribution fairer in the men's game also facilitated the same for the women.

Andy Murray, Patrolling the Interwebs. Last, but definitely not least, Andy Murray recently did a complete Twitter takedown of another player, Sergiy Stakhovsky, a member of the ATP Players Council and a staunch opponent to women's equal prize money, leading to Stakhovsky's resignation from his position two days later.

The Twitter takedown was preceded earlier in the day when, during an interview, Murray said:

> One of the things Novak [Djokovic] said was that if women are selling more seats and tickets they should make more but at a tournament like this, for example, if Serena is playing on centre court and you have a men's match with Stakhovsky playing, people are coming to watch Serena.
> (ESPN News, 2016)

The tweet of the article that this quote comes from, and which led to the Murray-Stakhovsky debate, was posted by Donnie Sackey, Assistant Professor of English at Wayne State University (Sackey, 2016). The debate proceeded as follows:

STAKHOVSKY: @donniejsackey so you agree that a law student coming of Ivy League should earn same as lawyer coming out of any other University ??

MURRAY: @Stako_tennis @donniejsackey stako my man! How's things? What does the university someone goes to have to do with this?

STAKHOVSKY: @andy_murray long story. Thanks for mentioning me with tday☺ need some attention.. Although ur argument fails the moment we leave UK territory

MURRAY: @Stako_tennis as soon as we leave uk territory more people are watching you than Laura [Robson]? Really?

STAKHOVSKY: @andy_murray the venue in Kiev is ready, all you need to do is convince Laura to come .

SAM DAVIS [JOURNALIST]: I'm imagining @laurarobson5 rn like, "HOW DID I GET INVOLVED IN THIS ARGUMENT GET ME OUT BUT GO ANDY."

LAURA: @Around_ThePost lol I'm a bit confused by how I became involved but I'd rather not go to Kiev.

MURRAY: @Stako_tennis I played you in a Davis cup match in Ukraine and there must have been a thousand people there max!

STAKHOVSKY: @andy_murray you saw any empty seats??

MURRAY: @Stako_tennis how many empty seats were there serge? I wasn't counting was focusing on getting the W☺

MURRAY: @Stako_tennis but seriously explain about the university please.. Didn't quite understand where you were goin with that

STAKHOVSKY: @andy_murray have plenty of time tmrw)

STAKHOVSKY: @andy_murray if you go to the article it started from, u will understand .

MURRAY: @Stako_tennis I've read the article and still don't get it! I thought you were suggesting that someone who goes to a better university

MURRAY: @Stako_tennis should get a better job than someone who goes to a less prestigious university but then realised that would be ridiculous! ☺

STAKHOVSKY: @andy_murray ridiculous right ?? [with a post for salaries of law school graduates from various universities]

MURRAY: @Stako and which ivy league school did you go to? or you saying men's tennis is ivy league and women's tennis is average school?

STAKHOVSKY: @andy_murray you just stated that it is "ridiculous" that people would get a better job based on Uni they attend. Correct?

At this point, various people are responding negatively to Stakhovsky via this same Twitter post by Donnie Sackey, which Stakhovsky attempts to persuade to his side, and Murray has finished his part of the debate.

Two days later, Stakhovsky stepped down from his position on the ATP Players Council, no doubt from his Twitter debate loss to Murray and the many people who sided with Murray.

Women coaching men: The tide is turning

Women's labor is also being seen as important and valuable, and this has been shown through male players hiring women as coaches. The first to do this was Tim Mayotte hiring Billie Jean King. More recently, Andy Murray hired Amélie Mauresmo in 2014, and Conchita Martínez became the coach of the Spanish Davis Cup team, which consisted of Nadal, David Ferrer, and other top male players. This should not even be a story, yet it is a profound one in tennis.

Billie Jean King, Tim Mayotte's Coach. In 1990, Tim Mayotte asked Billie Jean King to be his coach. Unfortunately for Mayotte, King was working with Martina Navratilova in her efforts to earn her ninth Wimbledon singles title, which she did that July, so King put him on hold. Later in the year, however, King did begin working with Mayotte, juggling coaching Navratilova and Mayotte at the same time, often playing them against each other. Navratilova seemed to enjoy the company, stating that "it takes the heat off.... I'm not the only one doing something wrong" (Jenkins, 1991).

King did not coach just anybody who asked. Indeed, King says, "I'll only work with the smart ones" (Jenkins, 1991). Of their partnership, Mayotte asserted that "I don't think it's that big a deal.... It's just Billie continuing to break barriers" (Jenkins, 1991). King's teaching was a mix of love and direct feedback. While Mayotte sent an errant ball over the baseline, King shouted, "Oh, Timothy Spencer Mayotte, I love you, you're absolutely precious.... You're falling on your face" (Jenkins, 1991). Yet, like many great teachers, "sometimes King will talk for 45 minutes without a ball being struck. 'It can be pretty intellectual stuff,' Navratilova says. 'Your body is fine; it's your brain that's on fire'" (Jenkins, 1991). The deeper meaning of King's teaching can be understood as tennis is life, life is tennis. Sally Jenkins explains that:

> All of this is in keeping with King's conviction that tennis is not merely a game but a blueprint for constructive living. In her symbiotic, ordered view of the world, tennis is about fortitude – facing up to things – and the value of a good effort for its own sake. To her mind, the sport should be properly executed, pleasing to the eye and emotionally and intellectually gratifying. "It's about learning your craft," she says. "That's a wonderful thing – especially with today's consumerism and instant gratification. You can't buy that. It's about making decisions, corrections, choices. I don't think it's so much about becoming a tennis player. It's about becoming a person." ... She cannot stand to see tennis played badly or, worse, joylessly. "You have to see this to understand how she made me love the game again," Navratilova says.
>
> (Jenkins, 1991)

Of course, the partnership between Mayotte and King made news. It is not often that a woman coaches a man at the highest level of sport. However, "that their partnership was greeted with skepticism by the press and the tennis world amused both King and Mayotte ... Alexander Volkov saw King at a recent tournament. 'I have woman coach, too,' he said proudly" (Jenkins, 1991). King, though, faces the criticism directly: "Look, I don't think gender should enter into it.... But if you're going to argue, why shouldn't women make good coaches? We were brought up to listen, to nurture, to observe" (Jenkins, 1991).

Amélie Mauresmo, Andy Murray's Coach. Andy Murray has started a trend in the past in regards to coaching, and hopefully hiring Amélie Mauresmo as his coach will start another trend. Murray hired Ivan Lendl, the winner of eight Grand Slam singles titles, as his coach in 2011. Following this, Roger Federer and Novak Djokovic hired Stefan Edberg and Boris Becker, respectively, former Grand Slam champions as their coaches.

During the grass court season in 2010, Amélie Mauresmo coached fellow Frenchman Michael Llodra. The partnership was a success, with Llodra earning his fifth ATP singles title at Eastbourne that year. Thus, Mauresmo not only has the experience of being a winner of two Grand Slam singles titles, but also of having coached an ATP player.

On June 8, 2014, just prior to the start of the grass court season, Andy Murray announced that he had hired Amélie Mauresmo as his coach. Murray, describing his long-time coaching from his mother, said of the coaching appointment:

> It doesn't feel so different because I had my mum working with me until I was 17 years old.... She came to a few tournaments with me when I didn't have a coach on the futures tour, US Open juniors and stuff so I've always had a female influence in my career.... I've started to listen to my body a lot more because over time you start to pick up some things and I think that it's important that the people you work with respect that and understand that and listen to how you're feeling because it can just be pushed very hard every single day. It didn't feel like a strange thing to do.
>
> (Howson, 2014)

Though this was a shock to some, both Murray and Mauresmo downplayed the significance of a woman coaching a man as an issue of fit, and not a political stunt. Indeed, Mauresmo asserted that:

> I think he's maybe looking for something different, about emotions and sensitive things.... It's not really interesting for me, this part of the story, to be honest. All I'm interested in is to be able to help him in his goals.
>
> (Perrotta, 2014)

Reiterating this point, Mauresmo again said, "I guess it will maybe start to change things around in terms of this particular subject. But, to be honest, it is not my main concern today. I am here to help Andy the best I can" (BBC Sport, 2014).

Murray, on the other hand, with a veiled nod to Mauresmo's strength in being a champion while facing vitriolic scrutiny after she came out as a lesbian, stated, "Amélie is someone I have always looked up to and admired.... She's faced adversity plenty of times in her career, but was an amazing player" (Perrotta, 2014).

Despite Murray and Mauresmo downplaying the significance of this partnership, the news swept through press rooms like a wildfire. Though it was clear that Murray did not have much to say about the politics of their partnership, journalists continued to ask him about her more than a year later.

Conchita Martínez, Coach of Spain's Davis Cup Team. On July 5, 2015, Conchita Martínez was named the Davis Cup captain for Spain while already holding the post of Federation Cup captain. Davis Cup is a competition in men's tennis that pits countries against countries; Federation Cup is the same, but for women. Though it was a surprise that Martínez was named the captain, she actually replaced Gala León, a former player on the women's tour, who was fired due to poor performances by the team. Martínez, however, has playing credentials, including being the 1994 Wimbledon champion (and she is still the only female Wimbledon champion from Spain), that León could have only dreamed of. León struggled as a player, rarely making it past the first rounds in Grand Slam events, and did not have the gravitas to command the Spanish men – including Rafael Nadal and David Ferrer – who are each champions in their own right.

The naming of León as Davis Cup captain on September 21, 2014, sparked outrage in Spanish tennis. Her highest ranking had been #27, and she followed Carlos Moyá, the beloved Spaniard who had won the French Open and been ranked #1 in the world. Toni Nadal, a former pro and the uncle and coach of Rafael Nadal, went on the offensive:

> It is preferable that [the captain] is someone with a background in the world of men's tennis.... I have nothing against her. I don't know what her capabilities are, and I hope she does her job well, but in theory she is a person that doesn't know men's tennis, because men's tennis isn't the same as women's tennis.
>
> (Briggs, 2014)

Toni Nadal continued by asserting that, "it would seem to be more normal if the captain had been someone like Juan Carlos Ferrero [the 2003 French Open champion], or some ex-player of a certain level, which is what has happened recently" (Press Association, 2014). This is a valid concern given León's lack of experience in top-level tennis, whether women's or men's. However, Toni Nadal may have shown his true colors when he waged a concern that León's hiring could cause problems "at dressing-room level" (Briggs, 2014). This statement took the argument out of the realm of tennis credentials and made the argument about her being a woman. Asked about the locker room issue, León asserted that "that's not going to be problem. You just knock" (Associated Press, 2014). Feliciano Lopez, consistently a top-ranked player for Spain, attempted to buffer Toni Nadal's comments when he said,

> What Toni wanted to say is that it would be strange having a woman in the changing room, but that won't be a problem since it will only mean getting used to it, just like when men coach women's teams.
>
> (Associated Press, 2014)

Indeed, Lopez can see the bigger picture.

José Luis Escañuela, then the president of the Spanish Tennis Federation, staunchly supported the appointment of León. The day that Fernando Fernández-Ladreda replaced Escañuela, León was fired. Martínez was quickly hired within a week and now holds two positions for the Spanish Tennis Federation, Davis Cup captain, and Federation Cup captain. She is coaching the national team for both the men and the women. Indeed, the Spanish Tennis Federation

> sought the best solution for the difficult task our nation faces ... and established that it already had within its ranks a professional who enjoys the respect and esteem of the players and whose sporting career demonstrated her suitability for this undertaking.
>
> (Rogers, 2015)

As may have been suspected, Toni Nadal has made no public comment on the hiring of Martínez as Davis Cup captain.

Conclusion. What is interesting about Billie Jean King, Amélie Mauresmo, and Conchita Martínez breaking through to coach men is that they are each lesbians. This could just be coincidence, or it could be that dominant stereotypes about lesbians – for example, that lesbians are basically men already – helped them open the door, or something else entirely.

Sally Munt, in *Heroic Desire: Lesbian Identity and Cultural Space* (1998), analyzes the lesbian body. In her work, she identifies three types of lesbians. First, the hero. As Munt describes, the hero is the one that other lesbians want to be and, quite simply, want. Second is the flaneur. This lesbian is present at Pride marches, but rarely anything else. Third is the butch. Munt describes the butch as being on the front lines of lesbian liberation because she is the most obvious of the lesbians and, because of this, she is the most respected. Because of this "outlaw" performance, Munt acknowledges that the butch is the model for groups post-1970s.

In this formulation, Billie Jean King, Amélie Mauresmo, and Conchita Martínez are lesbian heroes. The lesbian hero is powerful in a world that says that she should not be. Indeed, "the butch hero is a stereotype that represented the 'inbetweeness' of lesbian identity that subverts the boundaries marked by the sex, gender, and sexuality system" (Forman & Plymire, 2005, p. 125). What can be gleaned from the histories of King and Mauresmo is that "the butch carries the shame of social ostracism and turns it inside out as heroic pride" (Munt, 1998, p. 55). Indeed, as Munt explains further:

> "In-betweenies" often invert and reject the boundaries set up to restrain them.... What starts as a stereotype can be read as a social type, bleeding

into the boundaries of dominant heterosexuality. The heroic form appropriated by lesbian culture is able to embody and manipulate this complex function, where ... the lesbian heroic moves between individuation and incorporation, inhabiting an "in-between" space where these stereotype and social type categorizations become indeterminate (in the latter case because heroic narratives close with a utopian social membership). The spatial manoeuvering of the lesbian hero allows the creation of an aspirational figure.

(1998, p. 8)

The lesbian hero, then, becomes the "aspirational figure" who gains access to a "utopian social membership." What I assert here is that King, Mauresmo, and Martínez are the women who gain access to men's tennis [the utopian social membership], and thereby become aspirational figures to other women.

Rainbow Flags Over Margaret Court Arena

At the 2012 Australian Open, fans created a small social movement that affected and influenced the players participating there, alongside public policy in Australia. "Rainbow Flags Over Margaret Court Arena" was a loosely-formed collective of people who used their Facebook page to organize. They formed in response to Margaret Court's homophobia-laden interview regarding the Australian Parliament's upcoming vote on allowing gay marriage at the national level. The movement was galvanized further, midway through the Australian Open, when Court was nominated as a "national living treasure" by the National Trust of Australia. Court, who is the most decorated player in the history of tennis, male or female, is now a conservative Christian minister following the Christian fundamentalist taglines. As such, she has likened homosexuality with sin and everlasting damnation.

The actions of the Rainbow Flags Over Margaret Court Arena group primarily involved being spectators at the Australian Open, in Margaret Court Arena, while waving rainbow flags and being adorned in various rainbow-themed clothing. The actions from this group compelled Laura Robson and Martina Navratilova to wear rainbow-themed clothing during their matches, and also compelled Court and Navratilova to post full-page responses directed to each other in the leading Melbourne newspaper, the *Herald Sun*. This friction between Court and Navratilova, in addition to Billie Jean King, actually has its origins in the 1960s.

Fans participating as social movement actors against a specific athlete at a venue named after the particular athlete is new. The Rainbow Flags Over Margaret Court Arena group was a very small grassroots movement that specifically used Margaret Court Arena at the Australian Open to draw attention to Margaret Court's anti-LGBTQ rhetoric. Some of the participants may not have even been tennis fans. It was the focus on Margaret Court Arena that made this movement unique.

142   The Throwbacks

Margaret Court The Minister: The 1980s through the 2010s

In retirement, Margaret Court was unsatisfied. She had "feelings of uselessness, inferiority, unworthiness" after retiring from tennis (Maloney, 2009). In 1972, Court converted from Roman Catholicism to Pentecostalism. In 1983, Court gained the theological qualifications to become a minister; however, she didn't become a practicing minister until 1991. In 1995, Court founded the Victory Life Centre in Perth and, in true mega-church fashion, her evangelical television show, "A Life of Victory," began airing on the Australian Christian Channel in 2007 and continues to be aired today.

By 1994, if Court's religious conservatism was not already known to Australians, it certainly became so after she proclaimed in a speech to Parliament that *"Homosexuality is an abomination to the Lord!"* (Bradshaw, 2011). Court unsuccessfully campaigned against the *Acts Amendment (Lesbian and Gay Law Reform) Act of 2002*. When this act was passed, it added a new definition of "de facto partner" into 62 Parliamentary Acts which worked to remove all remaining legislative discrimination of sexual orientation in legislative law.

Court asserts that she dislikes politics and even claimed that politics were the reason that she didn't join the Original 9 in pushing for equality for women's tennis (Court & McGann, 1976, p. 157); however, she cannot seem to see that gay rights issues are political issues and how her statements become political statements, not religious statements.

Prior to a 2012 Parliamentary vote on two bills (the *Marriage Equality Amendment Bill* and the *Marriage Amendment Bill*, which were both essentially the same), Court again went on the offensive. The public supported the bills 2:1; however, Parliament ultimately struck down both bills. In an interview conducted in December 2011, Margaret Court claimed that:

> Politically correct education has masterfully escorted homosexuality out from behind closed doors, into the community openly and now is aggressively demanding marriage rights that are not theirs to take.... No amount of legislation or political point-scoring can ever take out of the human heart the knowledge that in the beginning God created them male and female and provided each with a unique sexual function to bring forth new life.... To dismantle this sole definition of marriage and try to legitimise what God calls abominable sexual practices that include sodomy, reveals our ignorance as to the ills that come when society is forced to accept law that violates their very own God-given nature of what is right and what is wrong.
>
> (Lacy, 2011)

Court further asserted that:

> The fact that the homosexual cry is, "We can't help it as we were born this way", as the cause behind their own personal choice is cause for concern.... Every action begins with a thought. There is a choice to be made.
>
> (Lacy, 2011)

After three decades of continual backlash from Margaret Court, LGBTQ advocates in Australia reacted. With the 2012 Australian Open only weeks away from Court's December 2011 public ridicule of LGBTQ people, Rainbow Flags Over Margaret Court Arena was born. Doug Pollard, one of the group's organizers wrote that:

> Enough is enough, Margaret. For 20 years we have quietly tolerated your attacks on us and your predation on our young. But we've had enough. It is time for you to read something else besides the Bible and get acquainted with reality.
>
> (Pollard, 2012)

As a social movement, Rainbow Flags Over Margaret Court Arena was quick to act, finding an opportunity with the Australian Open taking place in mid- to late-January, establishing the group on Facebook, and creating, and, most importantly, maintaining, a clear and concise mission. Rainbow Flags Over Margaret Court Arena's mission, as stated on their Facebook page is "to support the gay community by inundating MCA [Margaret Court Arena] with rainbow flags during the Australian Open" (Rainbow Flags Over Margaret Court Arena, 2012). Their motivation was stated as being:

> In response to Ms. Court's dehumanizing rant about the gay community: Don't give in to hatred or be silenced by apathy or fear. We ask that you unfurl your rainbow flag in pride to support the gay community. Let's ensure that this is the last generation of gay youth to be isolated by silence in the face of bigotry. Be the change you want to see. Straight or gay – be a role model.
>
> (Rainbow Flags Over Margaret Court Arena, 2012)

Most directed their attention to Margaret Court herself. Others were demanding that the Australian Open change the name of the arena, possibly back to its original name of Show Court 1 which it held prior to 2003. Pollard asserted that, in creating their message:

> The risk lay in attacking someone who was considered something of an Australian icon. I neutralised this by making it clear that I was not calling into question her achievements in tennis (although, by modern standards, they're not that wonderful) but her fitness to pronounce on gay issues. Other people not involved with the organising of the protest did not make this distinction.
>
> (Pollard, 2014)

Upon hearing of the proposed demonstrations at the arena that bears her name, Court emphatically stated:

> Are they not wanting me to come to the Australian Open? Is that what they are trying to do? I don't run from anything.... I have always been a

champion and always loved what I do and love tennis. I think it is very sad they can bring it into [the Australian Open]. It is hard that they can voice their opinions but I am not allowed to voice my opinion. There is something wrong somewhere.

(LeGrand, 2012)

Court clearly has no idea that LGBTQ people view her as voicing her opinion all of the time without restraint. Indeed, Rennae Stubbs, a former Australian tennis player and out lesbian, said that:

Margaret has said her feelings and it's public, and it has leverage.... So I think this is the only way the people feel that they can be heard, through a sign of solidarity. As long as it [a protest] is done tastefully, that's the most important thing for me.

(CBSsports.com, 2012)

The demands of Rainbow Flags Over Margaret Court Arena originally included demanding a name change for the arena. A petition for this reached its goal of 1,500 signatures on the Change.org website and the petition was delivered to Tennis Australia (Newburrie, 2012). However, by January 16, 2012, the organizers, responding to those who had voiced concern about the name change – Court has won more Grand Slam singles titles than any other champion in the history of tennis after all – listed three demands:

- On the last day of the Australian Open 2012, replace all "Tennis Australia" flags with rainbow flags;
- Join the "Fair Go, Sport!" program run by the Victorian Anti-Discrimination Commissioner; and;
- Help Australian Open players make "It gets better" videos.

In the end, Tennis Australia joined the "Fair Go, Sport!" program. The other demands were not met.

In addition to Court's public admonition of homosexuality, midway through the Australian Open, Court was nominated as a "national living treasure" by the National Trust of Australia. The National Trust of Australia's CEO, Brian Scarsbrick, stated that, "the title National Living Treasure is conferred when someone accomplishes an outstanding achievement, swelling the country's consciousness with admiration, pride and acknowledgement" (Australian Christian Lobby, 2012). Very briefly, the "national living treasure" registry began in 1997 and includes 100 people who were selected through a vote of the Australian public. In 2004, replacements were voted upon for those who had died since the 1997 list was made. In 2012, replacements were again voted upon to replace those who had died since the updated 2004 list was made. Court was nominated at this time, but was not selected. Incidentally, the list does include five tennis players – Evonne Goolagong, Rod Laver, John Newcombe, Ken Rosewall, and Pat Rafter.

Following Court's statements against gay marriage, Billie Jean King responded by saying:

> I totally respect her opinion, but I don't agree with her at all. We have a rising problem with homophobia globally.... This is about civil rights. It's about equality, having equal opportunities and rights. Everyone gets too wigged out on it. I guess because it's sexual, people get funny. But it's just about equal rights. That's all it is. And I don't know what they're trying to make it into. It's just equal rights.... Talk about it, get it out in the open. Just because you find something in the Bible? Well, I can find something else in the Bible. Judge not that ye be judged, so stop judging. Get your own act together, everyone deserves the same rights and that's it.... To me, it should be a non-issue. Someday it will be, but we have to fight like crazy until it is. It goes along with bullying. The bullying and homophobia go hand in hand.
>
> (Ginn, 2012)

Court responded to King and others who found her original statement offensive, in what she called an apology, through an op-ed piece for Melbourne's leading local newspaper, the *Herald Sun*, in order to clarify her position. In it, she wrote:

> We live in a blessed nation but Australia is on a steep moral decline. Everywhere you look we are making excuses for a sliding lifestyle and more people are blind to it than ever before.... As a society we are losing touch with fundamental Christian values, as our leaders lean towards an agenda of political correctness to keep the minorities happy.... Minorities are now making it harder for the majority. They are increasingly taking everything that is good in society and pushing it to the side. Looking back, you can see that there has been a steep decline, especially when it comes to the issue of sexuality. Let me be clear. I believe that a person's sexuality is a choice. In the Bible it said that homosexuality is among sins that are works of the flesh. It is not something you are born with. My concern is that we are advocating to young people that it is OK to have these feelings. But I truly believe if you are told you are gay from a young age, soon enough it will start to impact your life and you will live it. If somebody is told they are gay they often start to believe it.... I can't understand, if we are a blessed nation under a biblical Constitution, why there is such a push to change it? We will only start to tear away at the rich fabric and sustained values. Then God will take his hand off our nation and the lights will go out....
>
> (Court, 2012)

First, this is not an apology. Second, there has never been a sanctioned study on people who continuously call children gay and how that influences their later sexuality. Third, Court is digging in her heels that being LGBTQ is a choice that one consciously makes, which it is, indeed, in some cases, but certainly not in all cases.

Court's statement in December 2011, and her so-called apology above, did not go unnoticed in tennis circles. Navratilova and King quickly responded to Court. Navratilova responded using Melbourne's *Herald Sun*, the same venue Court had used. Navratilova wrote:

Dear Margaret,
Do you remember the first time we were on the same court? I sure do. It was at Wimbledon. I was about 17. You went to hit some serves on the clay court out back, and I helped you pick up your balls. I remember looking up to you. You were one of my role models, and I felt so privileged to be on the same court with you, even as your ball girl. I think that is why it truly pains me now that we can't see eye to eye. And while I still admire all your accomplishments on the court, I'm disappointed by your inability to acknowledge me as your equal off the court.... Giving gays and lesbians the right to marry isn't just a gay rights issue; it is a human rights issue. It is about equal rights and protection under the law for all human beings. Quite simply, it is the right thing to do. It most certainly is a secular issue and not a religious one. One does not need to be a Christian in order to fall in love and want to marry, straight or gay, otherwise atheists would not be allowed to marry, right? Marriage can be and often is a religious celebration but legally speaking, it is a contract between two people who promise to love each other.... You frame the whole gay issue in religious terms and quote the Bible. While I am not a theologian, I do know these same Bibles have been used in the past to justify slavery, to deny men of colour the right to vote, to deny women the right to vote and to try to deny inter-racial couples the right to marry. As we all now know, the Bible was wrong on these issues and perhaps more importantly, fundamentalists have been on the wrong side of history over and over again; it seems to me they are on the wrong side when it comes to equal rights for gays and lesbians. You say it is a choice to be gay; do you mean to say you had feelings for women as well as men and chose men? That might explain your certainty on the issue. The feelings one has for either gender are most certainly not a choice, they simply are; the butterflies that hit you in the gut are not a choice, they are just there. The choice is whether or not one acts on such feelings.... Perhaps of the many things you said in your opposition to granting same-sex marriage rights was your statement that Australia is in moral decline and giving us equal rights would further this decline, basically labelling us immoral. That one really hurts. I am trying to figure out which period in Australia's history you would like to go back to. Maybe it was when the convicts first were shipped here or perhaps it was when wealthy landowners had as many as four votes each, or when women couldn't vote at all, or when women couldn't be pastors. I really have a hard time seeing how two people who love each other and want to affirm that love by certifying their commitment to each other by getting

married are acting immorally. Loving another human being is immoral? Really? ...

(Navratilova, 2012b)

During the press conference after Navratilova's legends doubles match on Margaret Court Arena, she was asked about playing on that court. Navratilova responded by saying:

> Playing on Margaret Court Arena, it's an honor, as always, to be on that court. You know, it's not a personal issue. Clearly Margaret Court's views that she has expressed on same-sex marriage, same-gender marriage, I think are outdated. But it's not about any one person. It's not about religious rights, it's about human rights. It's a secular view, not a religious view. She's only seeing it from one viewpoint. The biggest concern I have there is opponents of same-sex marriage keep saying, Well, children should have a father and a mother. Well, they don't. What are you going to do about the kids?
>
> (Navratilova, 2012a)

When asked whether she had spoken to Court recently, Navratilova said:

> I have not seen her. I have spoken to her years ago, but, you know, she was all about Adam and Eve, not Adam and Steve. She repeated that about four or five times, so I just felt I couldn't get through to her. Maybe she thought she could get through to me.
>
> (Navratilova, 2012a)

On January 13, 2012, prior to the start of the Australian Open, Rennae Stubbs posted a warning on the Rainbow Flags Over Margaret Court Arena Facebook page. Stubbs is an Australian player who won 60 doubles titles with various partners before her retirement in 2011. Stubbs is also an out lesbian. She wrote:

> Remember, this is not about one person, this is about human rights for all. Wear your rainbow colors, but just know, any major flags or signs will NOT be accepted and peaceful will be a bigger statement. This is still a place for a tennis tournament and there are players to consider. Do the right thing and support with honor and respect. Let's change the world a little but let's do it with honor.
>
> (Rainbow Flags Over Margaret Court Arena, 2012)

Stubbs guided demonstrators to an excellent middle ground between protesting and tennis, so that neither were interrupted. Indeed, this tactic proved to be the best course of action given that Tennis Australia, when asked by Court supporters when they were going to start confiscating the rainbow items, firmly stated that they had no intention of confiscating items or ejecting people given how the demonstrations had been unfolding thus far.

In speaking about the fans in the arena, Stubbs noted that:

> I didn't really notice anything that different, other than some interesting outfits of people wearing rainbow colors. Australians like their sport too much to disrupt anything but they also always want the world to know, we won't stand for intolerance, ignorance or inequality.
>
> (Stubbs, 2014)

Indeed, Svetlana Kuznetsova, who played five matches on Margaret Court Arena in 2012 between singles and doubles matches, was surprised to hear that there had been a social movement in the stands while she played (Kuznetsova, 2014). Despite signs not being allowed, Stubbs claimed that "I think in the end, it's a sporting event and the message was loud and clear in the press and how people thought" (Stubbs, 2014).

Laura Robson seemingly inadvertently stepped into the LGBTQ limelight when she wore a rainbow headband during her first-round match on Margaret Court Arena again Jelena Jankovic on January 16, 2012. When asked about it, Robson said, "It was just a rainbow-coloured hairband.... I didn't see anything about a protest today. I wore it because I believe in equal rights for everyone. That's it" (Mitchell, 2012). Robson did know that there was a storm brewing in regards to Court. As she stated:

> I did [know about the comments] ... but it was through newspapers and things. I never saw a direct quote from her. So I don't want to comment when I actually haven't spoken to her. I believe in equal rights for everyone – that is why I wore it.
>
> (Mitchell, 2012)

Upon hearing about Robson's rainbow hairband, Billie Jean King said, "No way, she did? Laura? I would have never believed that.... She said it was about equality. Bingo that's exactly what it is" (Ginn, 2012). When asked about the risks that Robson faced, Rennae Stubbs noted that there were "none at all. It was a very sweet and heartfelt tribute by a young player to let the world know, she wouldn't stand for inequality. It was very well received" (Stubbs, 2014).

Interestingly, two days before Robson's match, Tyler Green posted on the Rainbow Flags Over Margaret Court Arena page that "Laura Robson is looking for a rainbow ribbon (apparently to wear onto MCA). Someone please point her toward one!" (Rainbow Flags Over Margaret Court Arena, 2012). And, the day before Robson's match, the following was posted on the Facebook page: "My new favorite tennis player, Laura Robson, will be wearing a rainbow ribbon for her match at MCA against Jankovic. Go Laura!!!!" (Rainbow Flags Over Margaret Court Arena, 2012). Clearly, this was no random accident on Robson's part. She had planned beforehand to make a statement regarding LGBTQ rights.

Martina Navratilova wore rainbow ribbons sewn around the sleeves and waistband of her polo shirt while playing on Margaret Court Arena. Her match on January 22, 2012, stirred controversy when there were no official photos or video of Navratilova and her doubles partner, Nicole Bradtke. The only photo of the match on the Australian Open website was one of Martina Hingis and Iva Majoli who lost the match to Navratilova and Bradtke. The Rainbow Flags Over Margaret Court Arena group was quick to point this out. Tennis Australia offered no explanation.

As is traditional, Court is invited to the Australian Open each year as an honored guest by the tournament director, Craig Tiley. Tiley acknowledged that Tennis Australia, the governing body for tennis in Australia, and the WTA, did not agree with Court's views (LeGrand, 2012). Indeed, on January 12, 2012, before the Australian Open began, Tennis Australia, following the lead of the WTA, gave a respectfully damning statement in regards to Margaret Court. Tennis Australia stated that:

> Margaret Court has won more grand slam titles than any other player and has been honoured for her achievements in tennis and she is a legend of the sport. We respect her playing record, it is second to none. But her personal views are her own, and are definitely not shared by Tennis Australia. Like the WTA, we believe that everyone should be treated equally and fairly. We concur wholeheartedly with the WTA who stated that "all human beings, regardless of gender, race, ethnicity, sexual orientation or otherwise, should be treated equally. This is a fundamental right and principle, including within the world of sport. Anyone advocating otherwise is advocating against fundamental and essential rights." TA does not support any view that contravenes these basic human rights.
>
> (Tennis Australia, 2012)

As mentioned previously, some demonstrators supported that idea of renaming Margaret Court Arena. Some have proposed Evonne Goolagong Arena, since she did so much beyond tennis to help Aboriginal Australians. Others have proposed Rennae Stubbs Arena, since she was so successful on the tour as a doubles specialist while being an out lesbian. King, however, countered the idea of renaming Margaret Court Arena. She said:

> No, no, no, get rid of her for that? Because you don't agree with her? Are you kidding? Just because you don't agree with someone? Please. She deserves it. She's a great player.... I thought the center court should be Laver and her name together. They're the two greatest champions in our game, and she had more Slams.... For her to have Court 3 is terrible. I was furious. I went to the heads of Australia, I told them I don't agree with this. You can't do this, you can't give her court 3, she deserves much better than this. That's a disgrace to women. She won 63 Grand Slam titles, how could you ever give her court 3. It was diabolical.
>
> (Ginn, 2012)

As a player, it is clear that King has the utmost respect for Court. Furthermore, it is interesting to think of this as a question of sexism against Court – having a smaller arena named after her – than it is about removing her name from an arena because of her non-tennis activities.

The irony of the controversy surrounding Court is that she was a part of the women's liberation movement. Whether she willingly chose the mantle or not does not matter. Court was one of the leading champions in women's tennis when women's tennis, the highest profile sport for women, was symbiotically linked to the women's liberation movement. To now denounce King and Navratilova, two pioneering women whom Court competed alongside, along with all LGBTQ people, is a smack in the face to the women's liberation movement and the LGBTQ rights movement.

Doug Pollard, the organizer of Rainbow Flags Over Margaret Court Arena, claims that the movement was a success. He asserted that:

> I would say that overall the action was successful. Although we were unable to flood the arena with flags, largely due to problems with supply – there was no supplier of rainbow merchandise in Melbourne, and there were stories of party shops claiming to have run out of rainbow flags when they were approached, which was also my personal experience – the issue gained wide TV, radio and newspaper coverage across Australia, and two players, including Martina Navratilova, wore rainbow symbols and made public comments.
>
> (Pollard, 2014)

Indeed, the movement was successful in two ways. First, it opened up a space for dialogue around gay marriage in Australia, especially the limitations of the Church in being the arbiter of the sanctity of marriage. To this end, their demonstrations seem to have been the catalyst that kept Court from gaining enough votes to be listed as a "national living treasure" in 2012.

Second, the civility which guided their demonstrations carved a space of legitimacy which others can follow for demonstrations at tennis tournaments or other sporting events in the future. Indeed, Tennis Australia supported the peaceful protests of the Rainbow Flags Over Margaret Court Arena demonstrators when detractors called for their removal from the grounds or, at minimum, a confiscation of their rainbow flag items.

Rennae Stubbs claimed that:

> I think that most Australians support gay marriage and equality. I don't think it's a Margaret Court or Billie Jean King issue, it's a right and wrong issue of equality for Australians and their people and the majority now support that measure.
>
> (Stubbs, 2014)

Indeed, gay marriage is a much larger issue than these few athletes. However, that does not mean that covering Margaret Court Arena with rainbow flags was a waste of time. Indeed, it shone a light on Margaret Court and helped people move to an understanding of the separation between Margaret Court the player and Margaret Court the minister. The majority of Australians decided they could do without Margaret Court the minister, even while they fully respect her accomplishments on the tennis court.

Though Rainbow Flags Over Margaret Court Arena was a fan-based social movement, its importance as an example of the post-Sustainers cohort is in how Martina Navratilova, (which was predictable), and Laura Robson (which was a surprise), supported the movement through their on-court attire and their words. This is also an example of a moving away from the isolated celebrity tennis players who were disengaged with fans that typified the Sustainers cohort. The fans and these two players were in it together.

Serena Williams, an activist athlete

Serena Williams has never shied away from controversy when it involves social justice issues, especially in regards to race. Serena Williams' social activism has kept her differences from other players on tour at the forefront. Her activism always seems focused only on race-based social issues. This, however, is what is seen when only viewing the surface. Serena's race-based social activism is inflected with intersectionality – she does not waver in pulling in her sex and class background to paint a fuller picture. This point will be explained more fully further in this chapter.

Race

Protest of the Confederate Flag, 2000. In 2000, as an 18-year-old, Williams withdrew from the Family Circle Cup in Charleston, South Carolina, heeding the call by the National Association for the Advancement of Colored People (NAACP) to boycott South Carolina for its refusal to remove the confederate flag from the state house. Williams asserted: "I wouldn't go to Charleston until the flag was removed. Once it was, I went there, and only after the Confederate flag was removed" (Williams, June 29, 2015). By the following year, the confederate flag had been removed from atop the state house; however, it was still flying on the grounds of the state house, at a monument built for it. The flag was not completely removed from the grounds until July 10, 2015.

Indian Wells Tournament, 2001. The most prominent display of antiracist activism by Williams was her 14-year boycott of the tournament in Indian Wells. It is widely documented what occurred there in 2001 (see, for example, Spencer, 2004). On March 15, 2001, the Williams sisters were set to play a semi-final match against each other in Indian Wells. Venus contends that she told the WTA the day before that she injured her knee during her quarter-final match and was doubtful that she could play, but, Venus claims, the WTA did not take her seriously. The WTA, as Venus asserts, told her to wait until the next day to know for sure whether her injury was bad enough to keep her from being able to play (Williams & Paisner, 2009, pp. 62–84). As a caveat, there is no reason to not believe Venus' account of her interaction with the WTA. The following day, just minutes before the match between the Williams sisters was set to begin, it was announced that Venus had withdrawn due to an injury.

Serena was through to the final where she faced Kim Clijsters. As the players walked on court, Serena was met with a sea of boos from the spectators. During a changeover after the match had begun, Venus and Richard Williams, Venus and Serena's father, arrived in the player's box. Again, the sea of boos came over the stadium and both Venus and Richard recall hearing racially-based hate speech directed at them and Serena, who was on court. Richard described what happened:

> When Venus and I were walking down the stairs to our seats, people kept calling me nigger.... One guy said, "I wish it was '75; we'd skin you alive." That's when I stopped and walked toward that way. Then I realized that (my) best bet was to handle the situation non-violently. I had trouble holding back tears. I think Indian Wells disgraced America.
>
> (Smith, 2001)

Serena won this match, referring to it as the worst match she had ever won, and, subsequently, she refused to play Indian Wells again until this past year, 2015. Of the boycott, Serena said:

> I'm not going to be playing at Indian Wells.... I've had some extremely life-altering things that happened to me there. So I told Larry Scott [then the CEO of the WTA] there are things that happened there that he understands shouldn't happen, especially me being African-American.... We've been struggling for so long.... I try to stand up for what I believe in.
>
> (Clarey, 2008)

In response to Indian Wells being a mandatory tournament for players, meaning that when Serena and Venus did not play the event, they had to conduct promotions for it, Serena said: "I won't be able to say anything positive about Indian Wells.... If they really want me to promote it, then honestly, I don't know what to say" (Clarey, 2008). Venus, on the other hand, has continued her boycott of Indian Wells, having not played this year. She is not expected to play next year.[4]

Serena's return to Indian Wells in 2015 was not without its politics, which shows her ever-growing nuanced understanding of racial politics within the world of tennis, when she joined forces with the Equal Justice Initiative (EJI). EJI is a legal organization that works towards eradicating the proliferation of children incarcerated as adults, abolishing the death penalty, and working towards sentencing reform, all with the background knowledge that these incarceration issues are heavily influenced by race and poverty. The political statement that Serena made by joining forces with EJI for her return to Indian Wells, without ever verbalizing it, is that she and her family were falsely accused (it was widely assumed that Richard told Venus to throw the match for Serena) and there were policies in place (for example, the mandatory tournaments of which Indian Wells is one) that were an attempt to force her to play Indian Wells despite the rampant racism that she and her family were subjected to, making the tournament an unsafe space. Her refusal to play the event for 14 years and her subsequent return as a collaborative effort with EJI speaks volumes.

Race and class

The Williams sisters are continually described as being from Compton, California, which is where they were raised. However, this city conjures up the definitive images of poverty and Blackness. Richard Williams even described his daughters as "Cinderellas of the ghetto," noting as well "that they are not fearful of opponents since they are from the ghetto" (Spencer, 2001, p. 87). Describing their hometown more directly, Nancy Spencer notes that:

> By 1991, Compton had become perhaps the most familiar signifier of "racially-coded urban America" and all that entailed. Between 1987 and 1990, especially during [President Ronald] Reagan's so-called war on drugs, Compton had been made the premiere national referent for racially-coded poverty, gangs, drugs, and threat. During 1987, African American gang activity in Compton was routinely featured in the news to explain causes of urban deterioration, community decline, escalating violence, and the need for increased policing. Moreover, as rap became an increasingly pervasive form of popular culture, albeit a racially-coded form associated with violence, the articulation of Compton and black youth was reinforced.
> (Spencer, 2001, pp. 91–92)

Furthermore, on April 29, 1992, Compton became the epicenter of rioting in Los Angeles which began in response to the acquittal of four police officers for the brutal beating of a Black man, Rodney King. At the close of 2015, we have been offered a few more cities to use as signifiers for racial unrest: Ferguson, Baltimore, Charleston, and Chicago.

Often when Serena and Venus are discussed, their hometown is mentioned and in a tone that implies that it is a miracle that they were able to escape. The media creates a "ghetto-to-US Open final narrative" for the Williams sisters, as Nancy Spencer described (2001, p. 98), that is juxtaposed against players from more affluent backgrounds. In this way, the Williams sisters continue to be marked by Compton, even after having lived elsewhere for more than two decades.

There are now two other prominent African-American female tennis players: Madison Keys from Rock Island, Illinois, and Sloane Stephens from Plantation, Florida. The hometowns of these two women are never discussed by the media. These places simply do not invoke the racial anxiety that Compton does. As Taylor Townsend, another African American player, rises in the rankings, it will be interesting to see if her Chicago background becomes a focal point of her story.

Race, class, and gender

Serena's physicality and muscularity leads to accusations that she is either not exactly a woman, or she is using steroids. Jaime Schultz described an incident in 2001 in which radio personality Sid Rosenberg said, "I can't even watch them [the Williams sisters] play anymore. I find it disgusting. I find both of those, what do you want to call them – they're just too muscular. They're boys" (2005, p. 346). Interestingly, even while accusing Serena and Venus of being so egregiously masculine as to be men, Rosenberg infantilizes them by calling them "boys."

This "gender shaming" continues to occur. In 2014, Shamil Tarpischev, the president of the Russian Tennis Federation, referred to Serena and Venus as "the Williams brothers" on a Russian talk show, and followed that comment by stating, "It's frightening when you look at them" (Clarey, 2014). To clarify, this was not a media personality or a nobody on Twitter. Tarpischev holds the position as president of his country's tennis federation and is a member of the International Olympic Committee.

Within days, the WTA had acted to fine Tarpischev $25,000, the maximum allowable under WTA rules, ban him from any involvement with the WTA, and moved to have him removed from the leadership of the Kremlin Cup, a WTA tournament that is held each year in Moscow (Clarey, 2014). Serena, who was playing the WTA Finals at the time, responded during a press conference:

> Q: This week the WTA gave a fine to Shamil Tarpischev for a remark he made about you and Venus. What's your reaction to that and the punishment he got?
>
> SERENA WILLIAMS: I think the WTA did a great job of taking initiative and taking immediate action to his comments. I thought they were very insensitive and extremely sexist as well as racist at the same time. I thought they were in a way bullying. I've done the best that I can do, and that's all I can say. So I just wasn't very happy with his comments. I think a lot of people weren't happy as well. But the WTA and the USTA did a wonderful job of making sure that – in this day of age, 2014 for someone with his power, it's really unacceptable to make such bullying remarks.
> (Serena Williams, 2014b)

I find it interesting that Serena referred to Tarpischev's comments as bullying, which she does multiple times. She is, indeed, naming what it is, especially given that he is in a powerful position, a more powerful position than Serena holds as a player. It brings the type of verbal bantering that Tarpischev engaged in under the auspices of bullying, a particular social phenomenon, rather than allowing it to remain an issue of personal differences that would keep his comments, and others, at an interpersonal level.

Race, class, gender, and hyperability

Serena's ability on the tennis court has established her as the greatest tennis player of all time.[5] However, her ability is seen as easy and second-nature, I contend, due to the prevalent stereotypes in sport that Black people are *naturally* athletic and physically dominant. Serena imposes her superiority and dominance through her play. The unsettling that this causes means that she does not get the accolades and respect that she should for being the greatest of all time.

Marking a cultural shift, however, this dismissal of Serena's ability began to slowly change during her second run at a Grand Slam in 2015, evidenced especially by the tickets for the US Open women's singles final (where Serena was expected to not only play, but complete the coveted Grand Slam – winning all four Grand Slam titles in a single year) selling out before the men's singles final, the first time in history that had happened at a Grand Slam event. The masses wanted to be there in person when Serena attained this achievement.

Race, class, gender, hyperability, and religion

Serena is a Jehovah's Witness. This is usually not readily apparent, except for when she wins a tournament and her first statement is always, "I want to thank my God, Jehovah."[6] In the pressroom, however, I observed a complete breakdown in understanding her religion (Williams, 2014a). She casually mentioned that she didn't celebrate her birthday during one answer and a (confused) journalist followed up on it. To this question, an uncomfortable (for me and one or two others, at least) debate occurred between Serena and the journalist. The transcript is as follows:

> SERENA: Ok. I'm 32, 33. I've never celebrated a birthday in my life. But I think that even if I did, I would be kind of trying not to at this point, just trying to forget it. Gosh. [laughter]
> ...
> Q: Serena, does that mean that you have never received a birthday present?
> SERENA: I have. I have. People give me presents but I don't celebrate them and people who know me don't. So, I've probably gotten like 15, 20 presents, but people mostly know that I don't celebrate it so they don't give me anything.
> Q: [cutting Serena off] So, literally, on the day of your birthday people who know you do not wish you a "happy birthday"?
> SERENA: [with a blank stare] Yeah. [awkward laughter from the press followed]
>
> (Williams, press conference interview, 2014a)

My guess is that this journalist had never heard of someone not celebrating birthdays. This, however, is a fundamental tenet of the theology of Jehovah's Witnesses. It should have come as no surprise, given how many titles Serena has won across her career and that she begins each champion's speech with "I want to thank my God, Jehovah." This journalist might be surprised to know that Christmas is not celebrated by Jehovah's Witnesses either because it is also a celebration of a birthday.

Serena Williams and intersectionality

In regards to Black athletes, they are simultaneously admired and controlled through a complex intersectional framework. As described previously, Ben Carrington explains that:

> the black athlete is ... positioned as a site for voyeuristic admiration – the black athlete is idolized for its sheer super-human physicality – but also controlled by a complex process of objectification and sexualization that once again renders the threat of negritude controllable to white patriarchy.
> (Carrington, 2010, p. 88)

Serena, then, can be seen as being voyeuristically admired for her hyperability, while also being controlled through mechanisms to contain her race, sex, gender, and class.

As previously described, Serena Williams is marked by her race, her sex, her gender, her class upbringing, her hyperability, and her religious beliefs. It cannot be said that Williams is triply (or more) oppressed however. Nira Yuval-Davis, in theorizing past assertions that Black women were triply oppressed, asserts "that there is no such thing as suffering from oppression 'as Black', 'as a woman', 'as a working-class person' ... Each social division has a different ontological basis, which is irreducible to other social divisions" (2011, p. 195). The reason that this attempt at reductionism is problematic is because, as Yuval-Davis further explains:

> Any attempt to essentialize "Blackness" or "womanhood" or "working classness" as specific forms of concrete oppression in additive ways inevitably conflates narratives of identity politics with descriptions of positionality as well as constructing identities within the terms of specific political projects. Such narratives often reflect hegemonic discourses of identity politics that render invisible experiences of the more marginal members of that specific social category and construct an homogenized "right way" to be its member.
> (Yuval-Davis, 2011, p. 195)

To be more specific, how do we understand the many intersections of Serena Williams without speaking of her identities as independent parts of her entirety? How do we see the interdependence of these identities?

The specific intersections that come to mind when I think of Williams are how race (Black) and sex (female) equal masculinity; race (Black) and class (lower-class) equal Compton, the picture of Blackness that is most dominant in

US culture; historically, race (Black) and class (lower and middle class) is at odds with tennis (white and upper class) and, arguably, currently still so; sex (female) and hyperability have led to Serena being accused of being a man or a woman on steroids; and race (Black) and hyperability equals a dismissiveness of Serena's tennis and mental skills as being "natural" Black physical prowess. Serena exists at various intersections, yet people don't see her as existing at intersections – they only see the specific identity categories – which is evidenced by people saying what seem to be very contradictory things. For example, popular discussions of Williams in regards to "sex + hyperability" and the "race + hyperability" categories are contradictory. Williams being believed to be on steroids (or actually accused of being a man) is contradictory to the belief that her abilities are entirely natural and easy for her to accomplish. The two equations cannot coexist. Contradictions such as this point to the complexity of intersectionality. The cultural linkage between sex and race causes difficulties for Black female athletes. Collins asserts that:

> The danger for Black women athletes does not lie in being deemed less feminine than White women because, historically, Black women as a group have been stigmatized in this fashion. Rather, for all female athletes and for Black women athletes in particular, the danger lies in being identified as lesbians. The stereotype of women athletes as "manly" and as being lesbians and for Black women as being more "masculine" than White women converge to provide a very different interpretive context for Black female athletes.
>
> (2005, p. 135)

Furthermore, intersectionality allows us to see Serena's religion as being invisible, even though it exists openly in the public.

Delia Douglas affirms that when the Williams sisters met tennis, it was an "interracial encounter between this Black family and the predominantly White culture of tennis" (2012, p. 132). Elaborating further, and pointing to the particular intersectional underpinnings of tennis as a sport, Douglas asserts that:

> In light of tennis's heritage of race, gender, and class elitism in the United States, the sport remains available to select groups, as evidenced by its enduring associations with resorts, country clubs, and tennis academies. Thus the arrival of two talented Black American female teenagers from the unlikely city of Compton, California, a location readily understood as [a] site of urban decay and gang violence, profoundly disrupted the White racial order (in addition to the class and geographic boundaries) of the Women's Tennis Association (WTA) tour.
>
> (2012, p. 131)

Indeed, Douglas points out that "it was widely believed that the sisters' refusal to comply with professional tennis's cultural codes of conduct was a sign of their contempt for the prevailing norms and cultural standards of the sport" (2012, p. 132), that these (Black) women ought to be conforming to (White) tennis mores, rather than there being inter-racial friction with both sides needing to find a way to coexist.

Serena's social activism, though it appears on the surface to be solely race-based in its focus, is, indeed, intersectionally-inflected. She does not hesitate to reach beyond the scope of what women should or should not be doing, nor is she afraid to acknowledge and fight for class-based issues as well, the kind of issues that would have been foregrounded during her upbringing in Compton, California. These identities that influence her all blur into one cohesive whole.

Furthermore, Serena eschews her celebrity status,[7] and rightfully so, since a celebrity status would remove the identities and the intersections that she is so eager to work within and across. It would especially distance her from lower- and working-class Black people, the backbone of the intersection where her social justice commitments lie. She is a celebrity, of course, but that does not mean that she avoids the hard work for social justice that happens in the trenches.

Serena Williams exists within a complex structure of contradictions that are a result of the various intersections that her identities make. The complexity is immense and involves Williams' race, sex, class, hyperability, and religion pushing against the white, upper-class culture of the world of professional tennis. Referring to Stuart Hall, we have an understanding of the formation and maintenance of specific identities and how they operate in the discursive realm. Using intersectionality, we can understand how the specific identities intersect to create other configurations. Furthermore, with both Hall and Patricia Hill Collins' framework of the matrix of domination, we can more clearly see how power operates across identities and intersections, as well as how identities and intersections operate within power structures.

Serena Williams as the greatest *activist* athlete of all time

On July 14, 2015, an article in *The Nation* offered readers the bold headline, "Serena Williams is Today's Muhammad Ali" (Zirin, 2015). Is she? What has made Muhammad Ali the standard by which other activist athletes are compared? And, why is the standard Serena is expected to attain male?

In laying out his argument, Dave Zirin explains what it means to be at the Muhammad Ali level of activist athlete, in his estimation, the highest level a person can attain. Zirin posits three standards for the activist athlete. First, the person needs to be the greatest in their sport. Just as Ali exclaimed, "I am the greatest!" and proved it time and time again, Serena exclaims that with every major championship she wins. Thus far, Serena has won 21 Grand Slam singles titles, which is "the same number every other active women's player has collected combined" (Zirin, 2015).[8] Second, the person "would have to be polarizing in a way that speaks to issues beyond the field: thrilling some people politically and enraging others with every triumph" (Zirin, 2015). Last, the person "would have to not just 'represent' or symbolize a political yearning but actually stand for something, and risk their commercial appeal by taking such stands" (Zirin, 2015). Indeed, related to the first standard, being the greatest, the third standard relies on greatness because there have to be endorsements, the risk to their commercial appeal, to be lost.

I would agree with these three standards for the activist athlete, though I have one reservation. These standards would exclude, in tennis, Althea Gibson and Arthur Ashe, who broke the color barrier for women's and men's tennis, respectively. They did become the best in their sports, and they were certainly polarizing for spectators and the tennis establishment; however, neither lost commercial appeal for their actions. Gibson played prior to the "open" era of tennis so there was no prize money and very little money to be made outside of tennis. Ashe was a tennis champion during the early years of the "open" era and he was able to ride the wave of mass commercial interests that entered men's tennis at the time.

Furthermore, there are difficulties in comparing a current athlete with an athlete from the past, especially given the different contextual spaces each inhabited. This erasure of the context in which Ali was "the greatest" causes the "historical amnesia" that David Andrews speaks of when he says:

> Ali corroborated his status as a cultural icon of historical proportions, while simultaneously erasing his threatening political stridency. Vague allusions to his controversial and outspoken past, coupled with the public sympathy derived from his apparent physical decline due to the ravages of Parkinson's Disease, gave Ali an aura of authentic individuality: a prized commodity in the culturally and politically myopic 1990s. As a result, Ali became a culturally resonant exemplar of postmodern American individualism and was thereby symbolically severed from his role as torchbearer for a collective struggle against various forms of American oppression.
>
> (2006, pp. 124–125)

Serena is being compared to Ali whose personal record has been subject to a "cynical form of superficial historical revisionism" (Andrews, 2006, p. 124), which has minimized his political activism and further valorized his in-the-ring accomplishments. Ali was an outsider, one of society's problems that needed correcting. This rogue to hero storyline occurred decades after Ali's retirement from boxing; however, there is an attempt to have this applied to Serena while she is still currently playing.

In *Black Sexual Politics* (2005), Patricia Hill Collins offers a rare analysis of Black women in sport. Collins claims that for all female athletes, and for Black female athletes in particular, the danger lies in being identified as lesbians. The stereotype of female athletes being "manly" and being lesbians converges with the stereotype of Black females being more masculine than their white counterparts. This convergence makes a field of landmines for Black female athletes. Black female athletes, then, must contend with racist, sexist, and homophobic stereotypes while competing in their given sports.

The positioning of Serena Williams in women's tennis for over the last decade has been interesting to look at. She performs very differently from the Black women who came before her in women's tennis. Mostly, the difference is that Serena looks like she belongs and is not just playing dress-up in tennis whites. Indeed, Serena displays Black performativity – playing off Butler's gender performativity – in which her actions are more conscious acting/production/reproduction of roles, in this case roles of Black women, with the knowledge that they are producing certain effects. Serena never allows the tennis establishment to get comfortable. As long as there is no comfort for Black people in the US, Serena will ensure that there is no comfort for the white world of tennis.

Conclusion

With the Throwbacks cohort, then, social activism became prominent, unlike in the Sustainers cohort. Amélie Mauresmo coming out as a lesbian in 1999 in the way that she did and the influx of women coaching men in professional tennis, are ways in which women are changing tennis from the inside. Venus Williams' fight for equal pay at the Grand Slam events required the recruitment of ministers of Parliament, and even Tony Blair, then the Prime Minister of Britain, to change the pay structure at Wimbledon. The Rainbow Flags Over Margaret Court Arena movement showed the influences of fan-based movements on society and even on players, notably Martina Navratilova and Laura Robson. Finally, Serena is the epitome of an activist athlete. In order to create the change that she is able to, she had to have a high status in tennis. She is both a great athlete and a great activist, balancing the two. After her loss in the 2019 Wimbledon singles final, Serena was asked in the press room about focusing only on tennis for the rest of her career instead of trying to balance tennis and activism. Serena responded by saying directly, "The day I stop fighting for equality and for people that look like you and me will be the day I'm in my grave," and then got up and left the room.

Notes

1 Pam Shriver, when I interviewed her, told me that Kim Clijsters was in the Throwbacks cohort (Shriver, private interview, 2015). I was confused by this because Clijsters has not been involved in any social activism, as far as I know. Clijsters did, however, show a clear move away from the individualism that had permeated women's tennis during the Sustainers cohort. In that way, yes, she belongs in the Throwbacks cohort. This chapter, though, is focused on social activism.
2 Part of this section is excerpted from my previously published article, "Judith Butler Redux – The Heterosexual Matrix and the Out Lesbian Athlete: Amélie Mauresmo, Gender Performance, and Women's Professional Tennis," published in the *Journal of the Philosophy of Sport*.
3 Surprisingly, in 1987 and 1988, women were actually paid more than the men at the Australian Open.
4 In 2016, Venus Williams, seeing the success that Serena had during her return to Indian Wells the previous year, also returned to Indian Wells.

5 Of course many would argue with me on this point, so I offer these facts:

Serena has won 23 Grand Slam singles titles across 20 years (the 1999 US Open was her first and 2017 Australian Open was her last … so far!). In addition, she has won 13 Grand Slam doubles titles, all with her sister Venus, and 2 Grand Slam mixed doubles titles. Across the 19 years, her competition was top-tier and always changing; players would rise in the rankings and then retire. Serena has played (and beaten) them all!

Steffi Graf won 22 Grand Slam singles titles across 12 years (the 1987 French Open was her first and the 1999 French Open was her last). In addition, she won 2 Grand Slam doubles titles. Steffi's primary competition during these 12 years was an aged Martina Navratilova and Monica Seles (whose career was cut short when Günter Parche, an overzealous Steffi Graf fanatic, stabbed her on court during a tournament and admitted to wanting to end the Graf-Seles rivalry so that Graf could play without competition).

Margaret Court won 24 Grand Slam singles titles across 14 years (the 1961 Australian Open was her first and the 1975 US Open was her last), which leads all players, male or female, in the history of tennis. In addition, Court won 19 Grand Slam doubles titles and 21 Grand Slam mixed doubles titles. Court, on paper, seems like an out-and-out winner in the GOAT (Greatest of All Time) competition; however, one caveat I would like to throw in is that only Australians played the Australian Open, because of the enormous cost of airfare, until the mid- to late-1980s. Of her totals, the Australian Open titles that Court won include 11 singles titles, 8 doubles titles, and 4 mixed doubles titles. For 11 of Court's 24 Grand Slam singles titles, then, the competition she faced was next to nothing. For those still not convinced, 4 of Suzanne Lenglen's French Open singles titles are not counted in her total of 12 Grand Slam singles titles because the French "Championships" were not open to foreigners. Lenglen is officially recorded as having won 8 Grand Slam singles titles. Logically, then, the same should be the case for Court. The Australian Open was open to everyone, but foreigners did not attend until the mid- to late-1980s; The French Open was closed to foreigners until 1925…. To-may-to, to-mah-to….

6 Venus, on the other hand, does not say anything like this or reference God publicly in any way.

7 When I (accidentally) referred to Serena as a "celebrity athlete" she corrected me: "I think that there is a lot of, I guess, quote/unquote celebrity athletes" (Williams, 2015c). I knew it was clunky and not what I meant to say right when I said it, but the press-room is a fast-paced world. Luckily for me, though, she found my overall question compelling and gave an illuminating answer.

8 This statement is true through the end of 2019. The active players who have won Grand Slam singles titles through 2019 are: Venus Williams (7), Maria Sharapova (5), Angelique Kerber (3), Victoria Azarenka (2), Petra Kvitova (2), Svetlana Kuznetsova (2), Garbiñe Muguruza (2), Naomi Osaka (2), Sloane Stephens (1), Simona Halep (1), Caroline Wozniacki (1), Ashleigh Barty (1), Sam Stosur (1), Bianca Andreescu (1), and Jelena Ostapenko (1). Angelique Kerber won the 2016 Australian Open, making the score: Serena (23), all other active players (32).

Conclusion

On March 20, 2016, Raymond Moore, the CEO of the Indian Wells tournament, stated during a press conference with the media on the morning of the tournament's women's final, that the women tennis players were "lucky" and owed a debt of gratitude to Roger Federer and Rafael Nadal for carrying the sport of tennis and allowing women to ride along. Specifically, Moore said:

> In my next life when I come back I want to be someone in the WTA, because they ride on the coattails of the men.... They don't make any decisions and they are lucky. They are very, very lucky. If I was a lady player, I'd go down every night on my knees and thank God that Roger Federer and Rafa Nadal were born, because they have carried the sport. They really have.
>
> (Rosenthal, 2016)

The imagery of a woman on her knees was not lost on Serena Williams, a player who many would argue has carried the sport of tennis as much as Federer or Nadal, if not more. Following her loss to Victoria Azarenka in the final at Indian Wells, Williams went on the offensive, stating: "There's only one way to interpret that. 'Get on your knees,' which is offensive enough, and 'thank a man'? We, as women, have come a long way. We shouldn't have to drop to our knees at any point" (S. Williams, March 20, 2016). Adding evidence to her statement by invoking the 2015 US Open women's final for which tickets sold out before the men's final, Williams asserted: "I'm sorry, did Roger play in that final? Or Rafa, or any man, play in that final that was sold out before the men's final? I think not" (Williams, 2016).

Moore sees hope in the future of the WTA, though. In an exchange during his press conference, Moore spoke of how a few of the emerging top female players are both competitively attractive and physically attractive:

> MOORE: But you know what? I think the WTA have a handful – not just one or two – but they have a handful of very attractive prospects that can assume the mantle. You know, Muguruza, Genie Bouchard. They have a lot of very attractive players. And the standard in ladies tennis has improved unbelievably.

Q: By attractive, you mean physically attractive or competitively attractive?

MOORE: No, no, no. I don't – I mean both. They are physically attractive and competitively attractive. They can assume the mantle of leadership once Serena decides to stop. I think they've got – they really have quite a few very, very attractive players.

(Rosenthal, 2016)

These statements from Moore, though shocking, follow Stacey Allaster's policies as CEO of the WTA from 2009–2015 of instilling a "strong is beautiful" advertising campaign, attempting to rid women's tennis of grunting, and changing the point structure and requirements for competition, which arguably was meant to strengthen the WTA by making its tournaments more on par with Grand Slam events. These changes actually diminished the WTA. Additionally, Steve Simon, the former CEO of the Indian Wells tennis tournament and now the current CEO of the WTA, continually refers to WTA players as "the girls." This culture of sexism is difficult to counter, even with strong visions of women's equality.

However, the issue of sexism goes back much further than 2009. In 1973, the WTA was created only after the male tennis players created the ATP, which denied women entry. Raymond Moore was one of the leaders of the ATP at that time; however, so was Arthur Ashe, Stan Smith, and others who are now considered respectable. The two tennis tours have always existed apart, with different leadership and revenue streams.

Steve Tignor, of *Tennis Magazine*, refers to this event as the "Original Split" (Tignor, 2016), and all of the issues of equal prize money for women's tennis emanate from this action 43 years ago. In September of 1972, during the first week of the US Open, male players huddled in a secluded stairwell and created the ATP, thus organizing all of the male players under one umbrella. The executive director of the ATP was Jack Kramer, tournament director of the Pacific Southwest Championships that the Original 9 would boycott the following year.

In May of 1973, the ATP called for a boycott of Wimbledon. Nikola Pilić was suspended by the Yugoslavian tennis association because, they claimed, he refused to play Davis Cup. The original suspension was for nine months, but this was reduced to one month; however, the Wimbledon schedule fell within that one-month time period. The ATP stated that if Pilić was not allowed to play, none should. As a result, 81 of the top players boycotted Wimbledon that year. Interestingly, three players – Ilie Năstase, Roger Taylor, and Ray Keldie – opposed the boycott and played anyway. The three players were issued fines by the ATP's disciplinary committee.

Despite having been denied representation with the ATP based solely on their gender, the women in tennis offered to support the ATP in their boycott of Wimbledon. Billie Jean King wrote in her autobiography of women's involvement in the boycott:

> Never mind that the so-called Association of Tennis Professionals would not admit female tennis professionals; I went to Arthur [Ashe] and the other leaders of the ATP, and I told them, "Look, we want to support you in this fight, so let's work together and if you do boycott Wimbledon, we're very likely to walk out with you." Now get the picture: the men have a dispute, and we are offering, free and clear, no strings attached, to stick our necks out and support them.... So it was utterly in the men's self-interest to accept our assistance. And did they? They wouldn't even respond. I was never able so much as to get the ATP leaders to sit down and explore matters.
>
> (Tignor, 2016)

Moore was a member of the ATP leadership at this time (Tignor, 2016). This issue of sexism, then, can be looked at as a long-standing culture within tennis, and not as an individual issue. Moore is not responding as an individual. He is one of the top executives governing professional tennis. He merely revealed the culture that the governing representatives already maintain.

Incidentally, with the ATP, apparently, not needing the help of women, King and the other women played Wimbledon that year. King won the triple crown at the 1973 Wimbledon: singles, doubles with Rosie Casals, and mixed doubles with Owen Davidson.

What the issue with Raymond Moore illuminates in regards to this project is two-fold. First, continued social activism in women's tennis is vitally needed still to combat sexism and other discriminatory practices. Moore's comments did not occur in a vacuum. The ease at which he spoke during the press conference points to the comfort level that he has with sexism, which means that those in his social milieu reflect that. His mistake within the world of tennis leadership was expressing that comfort with sexism publicly.

Second, this generational model of social activism within women's tennis works. Each of the players who responded, did so in ways which one would expect, given the cohort to which she belongs. For example, Billie Jean King from the Founders cohort stated via Twitter: "Disappointed in #RaymondMoore comments. He is wrong on so many levels. Every player, especially the top players, contribute to our success" (King, 2016). This is quintessentially the Founders cohort, focused on equality and speaking of "every player" without demarcating men and women.

Martina Navratilova, firmly based in the Joiners cohort, alluded to a women's boycott of Indian Wells when she said:

> It is really disheartening to see Ray Moore offer the extremely prejudiced and very old-fashioned statements regarding women tennis players. We have made it this far on our own, without help from male players, and will continue to do so. It would be hard to imagine any women wanting to go and play at Indian Wells if Moore stays as the tournament director.
>
> (Riach, 2016)

Given that Moore had voiced his opinion that women's tennis was second-rate to men's tennis, it would be impossible for him to continue as the CEO and tournament director for the Indian Wells tournament. Instead of a need to boycott Indian Wells, Moore resigned two days after making his offensive comments.

Victoria Azarenka, the champion at Indian Wells in 2016, and a member of the Sustainers cohort, spoke in press about Moore's comments. She said:

> Q: I must do my job and ask you whether you heard the comments that Mr. Moore made.
> VICTORIA AZARENKA: I did.
> Q: As a woman who has put all you have into this sport, could you reflect on those, please?
> VICTORIA AZARENKA: I think it's something that, again, we have to work through as women. Men don't get those comments. I don't want to address or insult anybody like we got a little bit. But I have just spoken to Paul, [sic] and he apologized. My thing is I don't understand any man comments in general towards women, because as simple as that, every single person on earth was brought and was born by a woman, right? Right?
> Q: Absolutely.
> VICTORIA AZARENKA: I think that's a good comment and I think people should remember that sometimes.
> ...
> Q: Do you think that Raymond Moore's apology is a little disingenuous given the nature of the comments he made just a few hours previously?
> VICTORIA AZARENKA: I'm trying not to think about it. As all my other comments, I'm not gonna bring somebody down. I'm just gonna rise above that. Today I think it was a great match. It was a great day for women's sport. Isn't it international happiest day or something like this? That's what I heard. Why can't we just be happy and enjoy and support each other, because that's what the world is missing a little bit. It's the support towards each other. Not just bashing and, oh, who is prettier or who is this, who has more, who has less. Let's just take care of each other.
>
> (Azarenka, March 20, 2016)

Though directly responding in regards to Moore, Azarenka is apolitical in her response. This "everyone should just get along" method without direct statements or a firm plan for correction is quintessential of the neoliberal moment we live in, and it most distinctly demarcates the Sustainers cohort from the other cohorts.

Serena Williams, on the other hand, being a member of the Throwbacks cohort, spoke directly of the impact of Moore's comments, how they were offensive, and offered ways to correct these issues of sexism in women's tennis. During Williams' press conference following her loss in the final at the 2016 Indian Wells tournament, she said:

Q: You just shared a beautiful moment on the court with CEO Raymond Moore, and he said earlier today, quote, if I was a lady player, I would go down every night on my knees and thank God that Roger Federer and Rafael Nadal were born. They have carried the sport. What's your reaction to that comment and the controversy it's created?

SERENA WILLIAMS: Well, I don't understand why I always have to answer questions about controversy like this (laughter.) Obviously I don't think any woman should be down on their knees thanking anybody like that. I think Venus, myself, a number of players have been – if I could tell you every day how many people say they don't watch tennis unless they're watching myself or my sister, I couldn't even bring up that number. So I don't think that is a very accurate statement. I think there is a lot of women out there who are more – are very exciting to watch. I think there are a lot of men out there who are exciting to watch. I think it definitely goes both ways. I think those remarks are very much mistaken and very, very, very inaccurate.

Q: Do you feel like there is maybe a misunderstanding behind how people are interpreting that in some way?

SERENA WILLIAMS: Well, if you read the transcript you can only interpret it one way. I speak very good English. I'm sure he does, too. You know, there's only one way to interpret that. Get on your knees, which is offensive enough, and thank a man, which is not – we, as women, have come a long way. We shouldn't have to drop to our knees at any point.

...

Q: You have led women, and Venus also, have led women through a lot of struggles. Are you surprised in 2016 that's issues and complaints and sexism are still cropping up?

SERENA WILLIAMS: Yeah, I'm still surprised, especially with me and Venus and all the other women on the tour that's done well. Last year the women's final at the US Open sold out well before the men. I'm sorry, did Roger play in that final or Rafa or any man play in that final that was sold out before the men's final? I think not. So I just feel like in order to make a comment you have to have history and you have to have facts and you have to know things. You have to know of everything. I mean, you look at someone like Billie Jean King who opened so many doors for not only women's players but women's athletes in general. So I feel like, you know, that is such a disservice to her and every female, not only a female athlete but every woman on this planet, that has ever tried to stand up for what they believed in and being proud to be a woman.

Q: What was your reaction when you saw it? You said you saw the transcript.

SERENA WILLIAMS: "Really?"

Q: How did it come to your attention?

SERENA WILLIAMS: (Laughter.) Actually, I love that quote. How did it come to my attention? Well, unfortunately, you know, sometimes we – if someone makes irrational comments or if something unfortunate goes on in the sport, you know, everyone hears about it. I'm on social media enough to hear about it. So, yeah.

(Williams, March 20, 2016)

The undercurrent of Serena's outrage is that she has driven the success of professional tennis as much as, or maybe more than, Federer and Nadal. Indeed, she even reminds us that tickets for the women's final at the 2015 US Open sold out before the tickets for the men's final. Fans were going to the women's final to see Serena win the coveted Grand Slam, and all four of the Grand Slam events in a calendar year. Unfortunately, Serena was beaten in the semi-finals, possibly succumbing to the pressure of the year-long quest; however, the ticket sales show us the importance and marketability of Serena Williams and of women's tennis.

In a surprise, Nicole Gibbs, the young Stanford University graduate who is making her way on the pro circuit after a hugely successful college tennis career, stepped into the Twitter fray as well, emerging from the Sustainers cohort and staking a claim at belonging to the Throwbacks cohort. Examples of her tweets, and there were many, included these three gems:

> Have received a lot of comments like WTA>ATP, I like women's tennis more, in light of Moore comments. Appreciated but misses the point....
>
> (Gibbs, 2016a)

> ... Not about who's better or what's more fun to watch. About equality. About supporting each other. I'm happy if we all succeed!!
>
> (Gibbs, 2016b)

> @ATPWorldTour, is the theory here tht @WTA players are stealing money out of ur pockets by being offered equal pay @ few tournies? #curious
>
> (Gibbs, 2016c)

Later, at a joint press conference with Billie Jean King (of the Founders cohort) and Chris Evert (of the Joiners cohort) regarding the issue of equal pay for women that came to a head at the end of the Indian Wells tournament, Gibbs was involved as well, leading the discussion to traverse the generational cohorts. A portion of the press conference transcript is as follows:

> NICOLE GIBBS: First of all, I just want to thank you guys for your words today. You guys have been such mentors to me throughout my career not just with your tennis, but also using your platform, which I think is so, so important. I was just talking to Jeff over here. I got into a little spat on Twitter last night. I wouldn't call it a spat but I was just hearing some negative opinions towards women on court with some statistics and some of my own thoughts about equality and finding a way everybody can support one another, like you said. I had multiple girls in the locker room come up to me and say, "Hey, I saw your tweets last night,

your messages, but my coach told me not to get involved, or I didn't think it was smart for me to get involved."

BILLIE JEAN KING: Really!?

NICOLE GIBBS: I'm not going to name names, but it's really disappointing. It's like, Okay, so you see me out there putting myself out there and trying to give myself an opportunity to use my platform, and you think, "Oh, I have an opportunity to use mine too but I'm not going to do that because maybe the media won't like it or maybe even men who are following me who have these opinions won't like it." I think there is far too much worrying about what other people are going to think when you're campaigning for equality as a woman. I think it's really important for us to do as you're saying, use our platform and really just fight the good fight.

BILLIE JEAN KING: What do you say to the ones that say they don't want to get involved or get committed to this?

NICOLE GIBBS: You know, I try not to be too heavy-handed because....

BILLIE JEAN KING: That doesn't work. You're right.

NICOLE GIBBS: Yeah, like you're saying, though, you can never really fully put yourself in someone else's shoes, so I'm not going to say, "You need to do this..." What I'll say is, "Hey, I would really appreciate some support on that." Or, "Hey, I'm writing a blog in the next couple weeks. Would you be willing to give a quote for that that's authentic and unfiltered?" I get a lot of positive responses, so I think it's appealing to people in a way that scares them.

CHRIS EVERT: If I could give you some advice: Never be fearful of telling your truth. I think that I am saying that because in my generation there was always so much fear about telling the truth and about consequences and about image and about how you'll look and how you'll sound. You know what? It's all wrong. So I admire you for speaking out as a current player. Just keep doing it.

NICOLE GIBBS: Thank you. Hopefully I can get past 74 in the world so I can have a little higher platform.

BILLIE JEAN KING: Doesn't matter. You have a platform because we're global now. We weren't global when we started. This is fantastic.

(King, Evert & Gibbs, March 23, 2016)

Afterwards, on Twitter, when Gibbs thanked Evert and King for letting her join in, Evert responded, "U r a future leader, girl.... You've got what it takes.. 👊, ✊, 👌" (Evert, 2016). What this illuminates is not only how a person can transition from the Sustainers cohort to the Throwbacks cohort, but also how members of the Founders cohort and Joiners cohort mentor players in the later generations. Through her tweets, Gibbs showed an interest in social activism in regards to equal pay, and she was quickly protected through mentoring by a few of the legends of women's tennis.

Thus, players from each of the cohorts responded in ways consistent with their cohorts. Billie Jean King, representing the Founders cohort, firmly advocated for equality for men and women. Chris Evert and Martina Navratilova, from the Joiners cohort, pointed out how it was, indeed, scary during the Joiners cohort – public outings of people, KGB following the players – and that it's not now, so people should speak up, along with an assertion that women will boycott next year's Indian Wells tournament. Victoria Azarenka, from the Sustainers cohort, just wanted the issue to go away and had no firm stance other than that we should all just get along with each other. Serena Williams, from the Throwbacks cohort, on the other hand, firmly pushed back against Raymond Moore. The cohort model that I created for this book ended up being a predictive model for former and current player behavior and responses. Time will tell if this just happened to be predictive for this instance, or whether the model really does have predictive qualities.

Despite the seeming differences across the generational cohorts, there is a common strand that ties the cohorts together. The cohorts are distinct on any given day; however, when controversy erupts, the cohorts merge together as one united force. Though the Joiners cohort was a project in identity politics, the Sustainers cohort was the ushering in of neoliberal politics, and the Throwbacks cohort is, primarily, an effort of current players working on social activism projects outside of tennis. The Founders cohort was the original fight for equality, no more and no less, but equality for women as for the men. This issue with Raymond Moore illuminated that the original strand that ties the cohorts together is the issue of equality.

Strengths and limitations of this study

One of the strengths of this study is that, in telling the story of social activism in women's professional tennis, the research and analysis is informed by an intersectional framework. This is rare in book-length scholarly work. Also, developing press conference participation as a research method is a strength, and I hope my experiences help other scholars whose work would benefit from press conference data.

Though using intersectionality to guide my research and analysis is a strength, I did not use it to its fullest extent, which makes its use also a limitation. My use in this study made it seem that intersectionality is something that someone carries along with them, like in their bag, and when one arrives to a particular location, "Ta da, look what I have in my bag." In the future, I will refrain from limiting intersectionality in this way. Though identity markers are one facet of society that one could analyze with intersectionality, there are other facets. For example, in a study of women's tennis, one needs to conceptualize the historical space of tennis – it being upper class, white, and male-dominated – in order to see the complexity. So, too, can one do an overlaying analysis of playing styles in tennis, where Chris Evert seemed docile and feminine because she stayed at the baseline and waited for the ball to come to her. Martina Navratilova, on the other hand, rushed the net in order to pick off shots and, thus, was viewed as aggressive and masculine. A full analysis of social activism in women's tennis would include three strands of intersectional analysis: identity categories, historical spaces, and playing styles.

Final thoughts

As the US women's national soccer team won the 2019 World Cup in a commanding fashion, it was clear how the activism in women's tennis has informed many of the women of the US soccer team. Their demands for equitable prize money have such power when, at the same time they are suing the US Soccer Federation, they show up to play their hearts out for the World Cup. Setting aside their grievances for the few weeks of the World Cup showed that these women are at the pinnacle of both professionalism and activism. Their message, also, was far-reaching, especially as the final whistle was blown and the chants in the stadium alternated between "USA, USA" and "Equal pay, equal pay." Indeed, Megan Rapinoe, who had been the first white athlete – male or female – to "take a knee" during the national anthem in a show of support for Colin Kaepernick in 2016, at a time when it was still a huge risk, emerged from the World Cup as a formidable member of the elite group of athlete-activists.

Epilogue

The Original 9, as a group, have not been inducted into the International Tennis Hall of Fame despite the argument that could be made that there would not be women's professional tennis as we know it today without their collective efforts. Indeed, Judy Dalton told me that, "I am proud to have been part of history but it would be nice to be treated sometimes as special, it seems that money is the top priority in the game today. No sense of what we did" (Dalton, 2015). And Billie Jean King stated:

> I have been very blessed in my life and career and I have no regrets. But the other members of the Original 9 have never been truly recognized for their role in tennis history. It is time we did something about that.
>
> (King, 2015)

These reflections from the Original 9 made me determined to work for their recognition.

On October 30, 2015, I wrote a formal letter to Stan Smith, president of the International Tennis Hall of Fame, to officially request that the Original 9 be included on the 2017 ballot of possible inductees. This seemed straightforward enough; however, things rarely appear as they are, and politics run deep.

Throughout my research, I have kept the members of the Original 9 updated on my findings, my theoretical insights, and my writing. When I sent the Original 9 the news that I had sent this letter to Stan Smith (along with a copy), my message was met with gratitude, but laced with a disbelief that the Original 9 would ever be inducted into the International Tennis Hall of Fame.

The skepticism on the part of the Original 9 stems from Smith's vocal admonishment of women making equal prize money in professional tennis. Rosie Casals described the underpinning of the Original 9's skepticism when she wrote:

> I know it's Stan Smith … funny. He played the Pacific Southwest in L.A., Jack Kramer's tournament that we boycotted. He won that tournament and was very much against the women getting equal prize money. When I won the tournament in Houston I won about $200 more in prize money than what Stan got for winning Kramer's tournament.
>
> (Personal correspondence, November 2, 2015)

Indeed, in 1970, as the #1 male player in the world, Smith did not have an admirable, or progressive, view of women's tennis. In an interview, when asked what his attitude toward women's tennis was, Smith's response was:

> You won't like my answer. I like to see a girl play until she is 20 and then quit the Pro circuit. There's a great opportunity for top girls to meet interesting people, visit other countries and get a variety of experiences. But I don't like to see a girl become hard and independent through too much competitive play. I would rather see her play socially and turn to something less physically demanding. There's always marriage, you know.
>
> (The WT Reporter, 1970, p. 47)

We can hope that Smith has become more enlightened to the accomplishments that women are capable of in the past four decades. The movement, or not, of my petition for the Original 9 to be included on the 2017 ballot for induction into the International Tennis Hall of Fame will depend on Smith's current views of the Original 9 and women earning comparable prize money in tennis.

To update, in 2018, the International Tennis Hall of Fame changed the petitioning process, effectively blocking me from being able to submit my annual request for the Original 9 to be included on the ballot. I have no doubt that if the Original 9 were put on the ballot, they would be inducted. As such, I have no qualms with continuing to push for their inclusion on the ballot.

Appendix

Methodological considerations—"Questions please." Press conference participation as a qualitative research method

Every press conference I attended began with the tournament media director or WTA on-site staff member saying, "questions, please," which, of course, sets journalists off to the races. Indeed, as Jim Denison and Pirkko Markula assert, "as one would expect, a press conference can't begin before a question has been asked: It's how the silence is broken" (2005, p. 321). Press conferences are used in sport as a venue for athletes and sports administrators to speak with the public through journalists as intermediaries to generate content for media industries. Press conference participation has been my primary method for collecting qualitative data from current professional tennis players for this book project on social activism in women's professional tennis. Press conferences are the only way to gain access to current players due to their celebrity status. Press conference participation as a research method is under-explored in the literature.

To attend press conferences requires media credentials. There is an art by which non-journalists do this for professional tennis tournaments, at which I have been somewhat successful. Once media credentials are obtained, there is an entire culture in the press room that needs to be respected in order to obtain further access to players beyond the press conferences, such as one-on-one interviews, and to increase the chances of obtaining media credentials at the tournament the following year.

I had attempted to work through the WTA to obtain a blanket press pass for the year (now two years) of my research; however, after almost a year of negotiating, a WTA staff member sent me a short, curt email stating:

> Thank you for the invitation for the WTA to participate in your research proposal. I have now reviewed the more detailed research proposal which you provided. While the research proposal is very interesting; the WTA is not able to provide the resources to support this research at present. Therefore, we are unable to accommodate your request. We thank you for your interest and wish you the best in your ongoing educational and future professional pursuits.
>
> (Personal communication, July 10, 2012)

Instead of having blanket access, I have had to apply for media credentials at each tournament that I want to attend. I had mixed success in attaining them, but huge success in the qualitative data that I was able to collect at tournaments once I had them.

There have been very few studies on using press conference participation as a research method for collecting qualitative data. *Presidential Press Conferences: A Critical Approach* by Carolyn Smith (1990) has been a useful book to describe the culture of the press conference and offer advice on its navigation, albeit in reference only to press conferences of US presidents. There have been a few articles on the culture of press conferences in various sporting contexts: Hockey (Gallmeier, 1988), baseball (Kelly, 1999), and rugby (Bruce & Tini, 2008). It is interesting, too, to think of the performance aspects of the press conference (Denison & Markula, 2005). Also, there have been more general articles that speak directly to the credentialing process for access to press conferences (Gabel & Feiser, 2001; Holton, 2012), tensions in the media center between journalists and others (Suggs, 2015), and public relations in regards to fan expectations and the promotion of the athlete (L'Etang, 2006; Summers & Morgan, 2008).

On my part, it has been a series of trials, and sometimes errors, being involved in press conference participation; however, the data that I have collected has been rich with information. With this book, I describe my process, my successes, and failures. Though my goal is to describe ways in which other academics can use press conference participation as a research method, my analysis of it will be a blend of observation of participation and autoethnography, since there are so few outside sources to rely upon. In regards to autoethnography:

> As an autoethnographer, I am both the author and focus of the story, the one who tells and the one who experiences, the observer and the observed.... I am the person at the intersection of the personal and the cultural, thinking and observing as an ethnographer and writing and describing as a storyteller.
> (Denzin, 2014, p. 19, quoting Ellis, 2009, p. 13)

Because using press conference participation was almost entirely experimental as a research method, the method is explained through a documentation of some of my experiences in the field. In addition, even though I was using press conference participation at tennis tournaments, the technique that I describe should be easily transferable to press conferences for other sports as well.

Gaining the coveted media credentials

Charles Gallmeier, who conducted fieldwork with a minor league ice hockey team, thought of his work as having four stages: "gaining entry; learning how to play one's role while there; establishing trust and rapport; and leaving the setting" (1988, p. 215). Of course, these four stages are not wholly distinct from each other. With tennis tournaments, one has to gain entry at each tournament and each tournament has a different set of media directors, players, and journalists, though there is often overlap. The four stages described by Gallmeier do, however, frame this section somewhat.

David Suggs describes the significance of the media credentials at a tournament succinctly when he writes:

> The media credential signifies status at a sporting event. Dangling from a lanyard or flapping from a belt loop, the small placard tells everyone who sees it that the bearer can go to restricted places, talk to coaches and athletes, record audio or video, and use designated work spaces. The credential symbolizes the legitimacy of media work, including access to sources and the freedom to publish.
>
> (2015, pp. 1–2)

In reality, press conferences are highly-controlled spaces where the same few journalists, who ask the same few questions of each player, attend. Few "outsiders" are allowed in this space. Furthermore, "in sports, journalists and organizations ... negotiate access through routines that have evolved over decades" (Suggs, 2015, p. 2). Indeed, Suggs notes that "the literature on the professional roles of journalists and public relations professionals in sports is extensive, but both it and the broader literature on the work of journalists curiously neglect the question of how journalists obtain and maintain access" (2015, p. 2). For professional tennis tournaments, it seems to be the case that being associated with a newspaper, magazine, or blog is sufficient for receiving media credentials upon request. Other sports may be more or less difficult to access. I am often categorized as "freelance" – meaning, apparently, that I am not affiliated with a media outlet – and, thus, often denied.

The media-tournament-player publicity machine can never be escaped. Tournaments want more exposure because it compels people to buy tickets and players want more exposure because it leads to more lucrative endorsement contracts. The media is the intermediary that facilitates this machine. Summers and Morgan explain further:

> The amount of money invested in and made by professional sport today and the complexity of those revenue sources has forged an important symbiotic relationship between the media, global PR activity, professional sport and the players and spectators of sport. Each needs the other to sustain an existence far beyond simply providing televised coverage of a sport. Players earnings increases, the cost of global competition rises, sponsors seek exposure to large audiences and fans thrive on the media and PR generated about sports people. This constant demand and supply of information, competition and excitement breeds heroes, villains, celebrities and superstars. Indeed, intrinsic to this commercialisation of sport is the creation of the "sport celebrity" as a product in their own right.
>
> (2008, p. 176)

Indeed, Jay Coakley agrees when he says, "each depends on the other for its commercial success and its prominent place in the popular culture" (Bruce & Tini, 2008, p. 108, quoting Coakley, 1998, p. 380). The media, as the intermediary between tournaments and players, gains access to both, through media credentials at events.

Furthermore, the interdependence between sports journalists and sports public relations personnel actually offers "a measure of control over what becomes sports news and how it is reported" (Bruce & Tini, 2008, quoting Lowes, 1999, p. 49). George Gabel and Craig Feiser assert that:

> because reporters and commentators must often obtain approval from private sports organizations to cover golf tournaments, basketball games, and other events, the credentialing process is often used to restrict traditional media outlets and stifle competition from information sources, other than those produced by the sports organization itself.
>
> (2001, p. 21)

This, however, has not been the case at tennis tournaments, where the dominant mainstream sports media are always present.

It's true that media directors at tennis tournaments have daunting tasks in selecting those who will gain access, and those they will deny. Avery Holton explains:

> Charged with the task of selecting who gets media access and who does not, gatekeepers must decide whom to trust with access. In terms of professional sports teams and media coverage, gatekeepers must decide who is admitted to the limited spaces available in press boxes, locker rooms, and other meeting areas. They must decide whom they can trust to speak with the athletes and representatives of their team. In doing so, they may consider an individual's employer or previous work for traditional reporters and mainstream bloggers. They may also consider an individual's past connection with the team. However, none of these considerations can be easily made for independent bloggers, who tend to be perceived as lacking experience and credibility. Thus, choosing who to trust and on what basis can be a daunting task.
>
> (2012, p. 46)

The selection, then, is based on who can be trusted to be around professional tennis players, many of whom are celebrities. Furthermore, Charles Gallmeier asserts that:

> To be successful in gaining entry to sport organizations, the ethnographer must make use of a "network of communicators" and a "network of legitimators;" the former provides the researcher with the "do's and don't's" so

that entrance into the subculture is less problematic, and the latter provides permission and serves as a "gatekeeper."

(1988, p. 216)

When I have asked for media credentials, I tell media directors that I was a former player and that Rosie Casals had been my coach (which she advised me to do). I also give a brief synopsis of my dissertation which lets them know the kinds of questions I will be asking the players. In the world of tennis, bloggers in the media center are just yet another venue for the dispersion of tournament information. It seems that if I had created a blog before beginning my dissertation research, I would have been granted media credentials at all of the tournaments to which I applied. As an academic writer, though, I struggled with the thought of maintaining a blog, especially when they are sometimes frowned upon in academic circles. In the end, I did not create a blog. I simply relied on my academic credentials and tennis network to gain access, with mixed results.

I was successful in receiving media credentials in 2012, during my pilot study for my dissertation, for the Washington Kastles and the Citi Open, both in Washington, D.C. This pilot study had a simple methodological question: Will press conference participation work as a research method for gaining qualitative data from current players? In 2014, with the start of my dissertation research, I requested and received media credentials for the Family Circle Cup in Charleston, South Carolina, the Citi Open, and the Western & Southern Open in Cincinnati, Ohio. I was denied access that year to the Miami Open in Key Biscayne, Florida, the Rogers Cup in Montreal, Canada, the Connecticut Open in New Haven, Connecticut, the Washington Kastles, the US Open in New York City, and the US Federation Cup matches which were held in Cleveland, Ohio, and St. Louis, Missouri. The media credential manager for the USTA even scolded me after Rosie Casals, my coach when I was a player, called her to request more information on why I was being denied credentials.[1] In 2015, I received media credentials for the French Open in Paris, France (for qualifying rounds), Washington Kastles matches, the Citi Open, and the Western & Southern Open. I was originally denied credentials for the 2015 Family Circle Cup; however, Stephan Fogleman, from *Tennis Atlantic*, gave me the opportunity to blog and live-tweet matches; thus, I was added to *Tennis Atlantic*'s already approved media credentials for the tournament. As one can see, it is a task to ask for credentials at each of these tournaments, and there is a high rejection rate for academic researchers, but it is worth the effort, as you will read.

The multi-sitedness of my study added richness and difficulty to it. Women's tennis is not simply maintaining the same culture each week as if the whole society gets transported to the next tour stop with no changes. George Marcus asserts that, "in practice, multi-sited fieldwork is ... always conducted with a keen awareness of being within the landscape, and as the landscape changes across sites, the identity of the ethnographer requires renegotiation" (1995, pp. 112–113). Indeed, in the early stages of my conceptualization of this project,

I assumed many facets of women's tennis would remain the same, that the multi-sitedness was simply a change of venue for the same cultural phenomena. However, each site had different tournament directors, different on-court officials, different players playing (or not playing) based on their schedules, etc. Indeed, my press conference credentials had to be individually negotiated with each tournament. This added a level of difficulty to my project; however, persistence seemed to prevail. All along, as I, the researcher, moved from site to site, I had to renegotiate my position and my relationships with those involved with the tournament at a given site.

Furthermore, tournaments can be in a player's home country, or the tournaments could be in a location where the player doesn't know the dominant language. A particular corporation may have purchased tournament sponsorship which obligates the players that corporation endorses to play in the tournament. Some top players are focused only on the Grand Slam events, while smaller tournaments are simply tune-ups for those larger tournaments. Players are engaged with each tournament in different ways.

Handling Rejection. Rejections arrive in one of two ways: very bluntly, or in a way that describes the difficulty in selecting whom to grant media credentials to and whom to deny. The latter type of rejection offers data that can be used. The former type of rejection, the blunt rejection, is sometimes off-putting. An example follows:

> Dear Kristi Tredway,
>
> Thank you for your interest in the Bank of the West Classic. A summary of your organization's credential request is listed below:
>
> Kristi Tredway, PRINT: Columnist – Denied
>
> Thank you for your interest in the Bank of the West Classic.
> (Personal communication, July 14, 2014)

This rejection offers no information to work with. I reply to all rejections to ask for more information. I do this to gather more data beyond the official rejection notice and there is a slim chance that I can change someone's mind. For example, when I replied following a rejection for the Rogers Cup tournament in Montreal, Canada, I received the following useful information:

> Unfortunately, we cannot allow media access to someone that is not covering the event for a specific media. Our facilities are quite small and we had to turn down some requests because we are running out of space. So, following our credential policy, when we do not have enough space for everyone, we prioritize medias with a larger reaching audience. Also, we want to be fair with everyone and only accept people related to a media for covering purposes.
> (Personal communication, July 9, 2014)

I reply to all notices of approval, too, with a short email expressing my gratitude. Politeness can never hurt. Besides, I want them to grant me access in the following years.

During one instance, I was annoyed at a rejection because the rejection did not seem to match the politics of the organization. During my pilot study in 2012, I had media credentials for the Washington Kastles matches. The Washington Kastles are one team that plays for WTT, and WTT is co-owned by Billie Jean King and Ilana Kloss, her partner, and CEO of WTT. For my dissertation study, I applied for credentials again in 2014. I was sent an email from the media director for the Washington Kastles that said:

> I received your credential request for this season. Are you a current member of the media? We are only able to credential media members due to league regulations.... If you are not a media member we are unable to grant a credential. I apologize for any miscommunication over the past two seasons.
>
> (Personal communication, June 30, 2014)

The part of this email that irked me was that I was denied "due to league regulations" and the "miscommunication over the past two seasons" meaning that I should have been denied access in 2012. I quickly sent an email to Billie Jean King, Ilana Kloss and Rosie Crews, the media director for WTT, explaining how the journalists who receive media credentials are always the same, writing for the same newspapers and magazines, and they ask the same questions of each player. I concluded by stating that, with this model, many important stories in tennis are never told and that is a shame. I never received a response to this email. Feeling brave (or, rather, feeling that I had nothing to lose), I requested credentials for the Washington Kastles again in 2015. To my surprise, I received an email back within 15 minutes from the same person who sent the above email, approving my credentials with no more information needed or hoops to jump through. He did, though, give me instructions to stay on topic (i.e., on the match instead of on my dissertation study), which was oddly blunt:

> You are granted a credential for the season. Please note that we are going to treat you the same as we would any member of the media as far as access, seating, etc. and we just ask that for any immediate pre-match and post-match media availabilities, you keep your questions related to that night's events/participants. etc.
>
> (Personal communication, July 6, 2015)

Instructions aside, the WTT seems to have had a change in their league regulations. Sending the email to King, Kloss and Crews was a gamble and it seemed to have paid off; however, I admit that it could have backfired.

At a tournament armed with media credentials

Negotiating a Space in the Media Center. The first rule of the media center is to not sit where the photographers sit if you are a writer, and, likewise, do not sit with the writers if you are a photographer. Also, too, the photographers and writers who are employed by the tournament have their own space that should not be intruded upon by "outsiders." On the first day, I always sit at the edge so that I can see the landscape of who is sitting where, then by midday or the next day, I can settle into a spot. I try to sit with those whose work is most similar to my own.

Tournament Entitlements. As a doctoral student who makes graduate student pay, I find the entitlements at tournaments to be fantastic. I appreciate the free food, courtside seats, free parking passes, and wi-fi access. Arguably, these entitlements are meant to secure positive responses from journalists which then, of course, transfers into their writing. David Suggs points out that "in sports media, the process of give-and-take has not been described in these terms, but scholars paint a picture of a media that is cozier with its sources and more willing to protect them than journalists on other beats" (2015, p. 5). The entitlements, and level of comfort, ensure this.

The entitlements change tournament by tournament. One tournament that I had credentials for offered a full hot meal buffet at lunch and dinner and even had a beer tap for use by all of the people in the media center.[2] One tournament offered only sack lunches and some hot food for dinners during late matches. One alternative that benefits the tournament is half-priced food cards that could be used at the various food vendors on site. The vendors make money, which makes the tournament amenities stronger, and there is a wide variety of food to choose from. Many journalists complained that there was no free food at this tournament, but I really enjoyed the variety and that the tournament was being supported.

Courtside seating is also tournament specific. One tournament allows those with media credentials to sit in any open seat in the stadium as long as you move when the ticket-holder for that seat arrives. This is completely reasonable. I have enjoyed some of the best seats for tennis that money can buy. At other tournaments, media credentials do not even matter for courtside seating and one needs a proper ticket for a seat, even when the stadium is almost empty. This creates a really depressing atmosphere. Players are sometimes playing in empty stadiums and journalists become cranky.

WTA Staff in the Media Center. During my first few tournaments, I was a bit terrified of the on-site WTA staff who sit in the back corner of the media center. They mediate between the players at the tournament and the journalists in the media center. When I arrived at my first tournament, I did not know the culture, nor the protocols, and I did not want to come across as a total idiot. In the end, though, the WTA staff have helped me gain as much access to players as they could. Luckily, they did not seem to tire of my many questions and they seemed at least somewhat interested in my project.

Deciding What Questions to Ask During the Press Conference. My first few press conferences were complete flops. I had a very specific question that I wanted to ask and, being very focused on consistency at the time, to assure validity with the responses, I would ask the question, for the most part, exactly the same each time. Looking back, the question was too long-winded and I was not yet aware of the ebb and flow of the press conference. It is difficult to simply change the subject in a press conference. It breaks the rhythm. However, the questions asked do offer incremental changes. I found that being flexible, and having a theme that I want to ask about instead of a specific question, allowed me to align the question that I really wanted to ask within the flow of the press conference.

Nothing terrible happened when I spoke in a way that disrupted the rhythm. Other writers, and of course the players, knew that I was new at press conferences. In that regard, I was given some leeway to flop without repercussions.

"The best press conference questions are those which compel a [person] to divulge a new piece of information about his [or her] public self" asserts Carolyn Smith (1990, p. 109). Furthermore,

> all press conference questions are not equal. A good press conference question is economically worded and accurately stated with an urgent warrant or other creative enticement so compelling that the [person] cannot avoid answering the question along the lines desired by the correspondent.
> (Smith, 1990, p. 110)

It takes years for press conference journalists to master how to deliver the perfect question.

According to Smith, every press conference question, in general, seeks one of seven different responses (1990, pp. 94–103). These are: questions of attitude, questions of consistency, requests for new information, questions for the record, questions that advocate a position, follow-up questions, and questions of attack.

Though Smith was describing press conferences with US presidents, this typology is easily transferrable to sport, though some I did not see used in tennis. Questions of attack are not used in press conferences at tennis tournaments. Furthermore, questions for the record are irrelevant for tennis players, and questions that advocate a position are not used, but it is understandable how these questions are useful when questioning political figures. At tennis press conferences, the types of questions asked are most likely questions of attitude ("How did you feel during the match?"; "Do you think that women at this tournament are given worse starting times than the men?"), and requests for new information ("I see that you have a new coach. How did this partnership come about?"). Additionally, follow-up questions and questions of consistency are asked to clarify the questions of attitude and the requests for new information previously asked.

One-On-One Interviews. The one-on-one interview with a player is an excellent way to gather deeper qualitative data. In the press room, one needs to follow the flow of the questioning, and it is difficult to ask a second question that might ask the player to delve deeper than with the first question. With one-on-one interviews, if I can get them, I can ask as many questions as I want, as long as the player remains interested.

Requests for one-on-one interviews go through the on-site WTA staff member(s). To request a player's time, I, along with everyone else, have to fill out a form and submit it to WTA staff at the tournament. The precarious issue with this form is that the last question asks what the topic of the interview will be. Of course, I would love to write what I am actually wanting to ask – questions specific to racism, homophobia, sexism, and the performances of different identities along with the freedom (or not) to perform the identities – but these questions have ways of making the WTA nervous. I often had to craft the phrase for what I wanted to talk about in very methodical ways that both ensured that I was truthful about what I wanted to discuss, while not triggering anyone's fears. Supposedly, too, WTA staff tell players what the journalist wants to ask about, and players can agree to speak or not. However, I had to ensure that my requests could get past the possible WTA vetting first.

One example is when I spent three days trying to conduct a one-on-one interview with Casey Delacqua in regards to this particular project that I was writing. Her perspective being Australian and being an out lesbian would have been a valuable asset to my research. Each day, an on-site WTA staff member would ask Delacqua if she wanted to talk to me. Each day, she hadn't decided, until she finally decided against it. Though Delacqua is out as a lesbian, she is extremely private. Even though I wasn't going to ask her about herself, but rather the politics around gay marriage in Australia and former player Margaret Court's homophobic rhetoric from her church's pulpit, Delacqua still would not do it. Of course, I was disappointed, but I could understand.

The Mixed Zone. The "mixed zone" is hated by journalists and players, but loved by on-site ATP and WTA staff and tennis fans. The mixed zone is an area where players can be interviewed directly after their matches, before they have entered the players' areas to shower, eat, have physiotherapy, etc. The player has to stand in this tiny area, still holding a heavy racket bag, with journalists' microphones surrounding him or her, all while being a post-match sweaty mess. When mixed zones are announced for players, there is usually a collective groan from journalists. Journalists have to leave the media center, which is usually located far away, ask their questions, and to the disdain of most, the interviews are not transcribed, as there is no transcriptionist in this area.

These complaints about the mixed zone have not only been waged by individual journalists. The International Tennis Writers Association (ITWA) has also weighed in on the topic. Their co-presidents issued a statement saying:

> We do not believe that a mixed zone is the right environment in which to have a meaningful discussion with players. Immediately after a match – especially a long match or one which the player has lost – is not the time or place to discuss issues other than what happened in the match or their next

opponent. In the modern world, where basic information on matches is instantly available to anyone with an internet connection, we need to communicate to our readers much more than simply how a match was won and lost. Mixed zones have also meant much wasted time for our members. While we are usually advised to go to the mixed zone immediately after matches, players themselves, understandably, often prefer to talk to us later, after they have showered. On many occasions our members have been left in mixed zones waiting for long periods for players to appear.... We believe that replacing press conferences with mixed zones is bad for us but also bad for the sport. Nobody gains from giving us less meaningful access to players.

(Fest & Newman, 2015)

The fans love that they can be near the player and hear the questions answered. The staff seems to appreciate that these are less formal, so less work, and, likely, it saves the tournament money by not having to use the transcriptionist as much.

Gaining Trust and Legitimacy in the Field. Charles Gallmeier, in describing his tactic for gaining the trust of those in the field, referred to his tactic as "the good boy" approach. He asserts:

To develop rapport with these networks, I used ... "the good boy" approach. This approach suggests not only taking precautions against trust violation, but also to become a positive influence in the setting. For example, I tried to stay out of people's way, especially the press, to avoid threatening their territory. I was sure to attend early morning practice sessions and all exhibition games and to always appear busy, taking notes in the press box, always appearing attentive, interested, working, and not just getting free tickets.

(1988, p. 218)

This approach has worked very well for me. I try to be as friendly as possible. I also make it clear that my writing is not a threat to those who are regularly in the press room by noting that, since my writing is for academic audiences, it will not appear in print for a year or more.

Luckily, too, my body still carries the markers of having been a professional tennis player in the past. When I conducted a one-on-one interview with Svetlana Kuznetsova, we were sitting in folding chairs with one chair between us. The change in her body language as we spoke was interesting to observe. When we first sat down and I was describing the context of my research study, and that I was an academic and not a journalist, she was interested. I had full eye contact, but her arms were crossed in front of her and her body was slouched and facing forward, not towards me. When I said that I had been a pro player, that Rosie Casals had been my coach, and that experience is what led me to this research study, her posture totally changed. She sat up and turned her body towards me and she maintained this position for the full interview. At first, I was surprised by her bodily shift, and a little nervous, but then I understood that I had her attention and she was showing me that she was comfortable and that I belonged.

When I arrived in my first press room, it was clear that the only time a person was allowed to speak to a player was after a media director or on-site WTA staff member said, "Are there any questions?" After a year in the field, I was finally trusted. In an email from an on-site WTA staff member, in regards to my request to speak to Serena Williams, I was told: "Serena's schedule is very tight.... Feel free to introduce yourself if you see her" (personal communication, August 15, 2015). I had finally been given the freedom to speak to players beyond the confines of the press room.

(Embarrassingly) Being Told the Culture of Players and Press. It is impossible to be in any research site for a length of time and not make awkward social gaffes. Charles Gallmeier describes his experiences in the field when he has made social gaffes and been reprimanded. He says:

> As a minimally socialized actor it was impossible to avoid making some mistakes. In fact, whether one is studying professional athletes or some other social world, it is not necessarily desirable to avoid committing every *faux pas*. Such norm violations are embarrassing but the mistakes and the reactions to them are ... valuable sources of information about the rule system which governs interaction in the setting.... My error revealed the norms operating in the press box.
>
> (1988, p. 219)

Indeed, it is both horrifying and comforting to be reprimanded by a player. Horrifying in that a superstar celebrity has just told you how you did something wrong. Comforting because you know what was wrong and how to not do it again. There are not the secret questions and the slow withdrawal of access, with upfront clarifications of the rules and expectations for me.

At one of my first forays into tournament press conferences, I spotted Venus Williams sitting on the sideline of the court while others were practicing, so I walked over to speak with her. Venus reprimanded me and, then, seeing what must have been horror on my face, described where I went wrong. The transcript is as follows:

> ME: Venus, can I ask you a question?
> VENUS: [not even looking up at me] No questions right now please.
> ME: [backing away] Oh, ok, sorry.
> VENUS: [looking right at me] I'm at team practice.
> ME: Ok.
> VENUS: Ok.
> ME: Thanks.
>
> (Personal communication, July 16, 2012)

Not knowing anything about the culture I was venturing into, Venus has the warm distinction of being the first superstar player that I spoke with for this study. I was so nervous around her then and I could hardly stutter out a question in the press conferences. Where I went wrong was asking Venus a question during team practice for the Washington Kastles while she was supporting her teammates during practice.

I am not sure if Venus remembers this – probably not, with the number of people she meets every day; however, since this day, she has been very warm towards me during press conferences. Usually, I receive direct looks from her with a friendly smile. By accepting that I had made a gaffe, and apologizing in a sincere manner very quickly through my body language, I believe that I gained legitimacy and trust from her which carried over into confidence speaking with other players.

When Tournaments Can't Control What Questions Journalists Ask, Nor How They Are Asked. Conversations in the press room sometimes go awry via cultural or language misunderstandings. I observed a person seemingly lose his media credential midway through a tournament, or possibly he was just too embarrassed to return, because of his question to a player, which was clunky and long-winded, and caused her embarrassment.

Though there are the heavyweights of tennis journalism who write for major newspapers or magazines and who travel the circuit much like the players, the media center at tournaments is often filled with people from local newspapers.

During a press conference with an up-and-coming player who had won an early round match, this journalist had the following interaction with the player:

QUESTION: Hello. Hey, how are you doing?
PLAYER: Hello.
QUESTION: I personally thank you very much for the interview yesterday. It was well received. I wrote about it in the black press. One thing I noticed about you, you seem to be having so much fun, and even when you seem to be exerting yourself, it's like fun. What is that about? [everyone chuckles] Talk to me about that just briefly, I mean because I love it. You seem to bring a kind of youthful, enthusiastic – and I say this very respectfully – poised game to it that's thrilling. To me it's good for tennis. I mean I like to see it. I mean I'm not going to eat your flesh, [everyone laughs] but keep doing what you're doing. You know, I'm serious. Keep doing what you're doing. I love it. It makes me want to come … and I'm saying like, wow, I'm an old man. I need to go to bed now, but I'm sitting here watching this young girl hitting this tennis ball. She's smiling. [everyone laughs] I mean come on, but I mean I love it. I say that respectfully, and I hope everybody else in the background feels the same way.
WTA STAFF MEMBER: [interrupting] Do you want to ask a question? [everyone chuckles]
QUESTION: But I mean – I'm sorry. Forgive me.
PLAYER: [awkwardly laughing] Why do I have fun on the tennis court? [everyone laughs]

(Family Circle Cup, April 8, 2015)

The player, appropriately, proceeded to correctly guess what the underlying question was and give an explanation of having fun while competing on the court. This question, though, closed down the press conference apart from another question from the same man. Nobody knew how to follow-up or move the press conference into a different direction after the question he posed. In all fairness, I thought that he simply cut his train of thought off at a very unfortunate time. It seemed like he was about to say, "It makes me want to come to the tournament" and that the tennis is so exciting that it keeps him up after his bedtime, but maybe I am wrong. It certainly was a huge social gaffe on his part.

Immediately following this press conference, the transcriptionist pulled a few of us aside and asked us whether what she heard was correct, what she should include in the transcript and what she should cut to make the transcript appropriate for the tournament archives. It was fascinating to be included in this group of people who wanted an accurate archive, but not a record of a player's possible embarrassment by a journalist.

The following morning, while sitting in the media center, this journalist sat a small plate of food next to where I was sitting, then he went to the back of the room, I assume, to get transcripts from the previous days' press conferences or the order of play for that day. I was not paying attention when he walked outside with an official from the media center. This journalist did not return for the rest of the tournament.

Dealing With Odd Behavior From Players. Odd behavior from professional tennis players, as with anyone, is a given from time to time. It is common for players to be late for scheduled press conferences, interviews and events. Those in the media center are accustomed to it. It is also common for players to rush to the press room the moment they are off the court after a loss, which can throw off the rhythm of the press room.

At a top-tier tournament that had both women and men, I decided to sit in on the men's press conferences so that I could compare the types of questions that men were asked versus what women were asked, and how they were asked. One day, while waiting for Andy Murray's press conference to begin, I decided to arrive a bit early to relax in the lounge area outside of the press conference meeting room where there was only me and a security guard. The security guard and I were watching the end of Novak Djokovic's match in which he lost soundly to someone ranked far lower than him. Literally, within a few minutes, Djokovic had made his way off the court and up the stairs to the press conference room. He burst through the door I was sitting beside and, having seen my badge (not that it said media), shouted to me, "I am starting my press conference now! Tell the ATP [which governs men's tennis]!" I had no idea what to do! Just as I wanted to hide behind the banner that said, "I'm just a grad student," I also wanted to explore this unexpected source of qualitative data. Luckily, I heard the security guard speak into his microphone on his shoulder that Djokovic had arrived and was demanding that his press conference begin. ATP personnel quickly arrived after that. Murray just had to wait until Djokovic finished his press conference. As with most of the examples I have described, one can never know when qualitative data will present itself.

Leaving the Field. I have now left the field. Charles Gallmeier, who described his own fieldwork as having four stages – "gaining entry; learning how to play one's role while there; establishing trust and rapport; and leaving the setting" (1988, p. 215) – uses a review of his fieldnotes to illuminate his leaving of his site for research. He says:

> During the disengaging period I experienced feelings of alienation, guilt, and real sadness. I had invested a great deal of time and energy in these relationships. When the research began, I was alone among strangers. But as the season progressed, I began to develop friendships with, and sympathy and understanding for these individuals. In short, I came to feel that I belonged. Feelings of disruption pertained not only to breaking relationships with the [players], but also to terminating the routine associated with the field research. Seven days a week for eight months I was either at the arena, riding the bus [to away games], or meeting the players after games at the team bar. Each evening I laboriously completed my daily field notes. Subsequently, I was obliged to reorient myself after the research ended.
>
> (1988, p. 229)

I conducted fieldwork in women's tennis beginning with my pilot study in July and August 2012 by having media credentials for the Washington Kastles of WTT and the Citi Open. I picked up press conference participation as a research method again for my research with the Family Circle Cup in March 2014 and ending with the Western & Southern Open in August 2015. During the 17 months of my research, I attended those two tournaments along with the Citi Open (July–August 2014, 2015), the Western & Southern Open (August 2014), Family Circle Cup (March 2015), the French Open (2015), and the Washington Kastles of WTT (July 2015). In between these tournaments, I was constantly staying aware of what was happening in the world of women's tennis through Twitter and media reports.

Leaving the field was difficult, and with every tournament, especially those I have "worked" before, I feel a pull to be there in the press room. I am not sure that anyone knows the right time to leave the field. It's probably always based on some external demand; for me, it was that I had enough data so I needed to complete my dissertation and move on. I have made friends, at least friendly acquaintances, with journalists, media directors, and WTA staff. I have also developed good rapport with players. I hope to continue in some capacity, with continued projects, even now that my dissertation is complete.

What scholars can gain from press conference participation

Many academic scholars rely on the documentation of press conferences for qualitative data, and direct quotes from athletes and those affiliated with sports.

The issue, however, is that those quotes are filtered through the analyses of various journalists. Scholars can fall into the trap of assuming that journalism is as unbiased as it claims to be. This, however, cannot be true. Any writing and any questions asked are going to have an angle of bias involved. When scholars choose to use press conference participation as a qualitative research method, the researcher, then, can know the journalists involved, thereby being aware of the biases and angles each journalist has, while also gaining an understanding of the atmosphere of the press conference. This, in turn, will allow the research to be more sound.

As academic writers, press conference participation can be a very valuable research method for sport sociologists in regards to Institutional Review Board (IRB) research compliance with US-based universities. Because press conferences are public, meaning that they are open to all of the journalists who have credentials to attend, and are moderated by the tournament's media director or an on-site WTA staff member, this research method does not need IRB approval apart from one instance. If the tournament is held outside of the US, the researcher needs to show compliance with the research standards of the country in which the tournament is held, despite my multiple efforts to explain that the people at the tournament are the same people who are at the US tournaments.

Notes

1 I have heard from a few prominent journalists that she is well-known for being very difficult and that the Fed Cup matches had, maybe, four journalists, so space was not an issue.
2 Sadly, it was only Bud Light. I do have standards, even if the beer is free.

Bibliography

Adams, W. L. (2011, July 2). Game, sex and match: The perils of female sports advertising. *Time*. Retrieved from: http://content.time.com/time/business/article/0,8599, 2081209,00.html

Ahmed, S. (2010). *The promise of happiness*. North Carolina: Duke University Press.

Alexander-Floyd, N. G. (2012). Disappearing acts: Reclaiming intersectionality in the social sciences in a post-black feminist era. *Feminist Formations*, 24(1), 1–25.

Alwin, D. F., & McCammon, R. J. (2003). Generations, cohorts, and social change. In J. T. Mortimer & M. J. Shanahan (Eds.), *Handbook of the life course*, (pp. 23–49). New York: Kluwer Academic/Plenum Publishers.

Anderson, E. (1999). *Code of the street: Decency, violence, and the moral life of the inner city*. New York: Norton.

Andrews, D. L. (2002). Coming to terms with cultural studies. *Journal of Sport and Social Issues*, 26(1), 110–117.

Andrews, D. L. (2006). *Sport – commerce – culture: Essays on sport in late capitalist America*. New York: Peter Lang.

Andrews, D. L. (in press: 2016). Sport and the politics of late capitalism. In A. S. Bairner, J. Kelly, & J. W. Lee (Eds.), *The handbook of sport and politics*. London: Routledge.

Antunovic, D., & Hardin, M. (2012). Activism in women's sports blogs: Fandom and feminist potential. *International Journal of Sport Communication*, 5(3), 305–322.

Anzaldúa, G. (1987). *Borderlands/La frontera*. San Francisco: Aunt Lute.

Arlington Arts Center. (2012). She Got Game, exhibition displayed January 13–March 18. Program retrieved from www.arlingtonartscenter.org/sites/default/files/pdfs/SHE% 20GOT%20GAME%20brochure.pdf

Associated Press. (1990, July 11). Court calls Navratilova poor role model. *Los Angeles Times*. Retrieved from http://articles.latimes.com/1990-07-11/sports/sp-420_1_poor-role

Associated Press. (2014, September 23). Toni Nadal: Men's game is different. *ESPN. com*. Retrieved from http://espn.go.com/tennis/story/_/id/11573619/rafael-nadal-coach-criticizes-selection-female-davis-cup-captain-spain

Austin, J. L. (1975). *How to do things with words* (2nd ed.). Edited by J. O. Urmson & M. Sbisà. Cambridge: Harvard University Press.

Austin, T., & Brennan, C. (1992). *Beyond Center Court: My story*. William Morrow & Company.

Australia 9. (2009). *Serena Williams vs. Kim Clijsters, 2009 US Open semi-finals*. Retrieved February 11, 2013, from www.youtube.com/watch?v=IXSFPnimclQ

Bibliography

Australian Christian Lobby. (2012, January 27). Rev Dr Margaret Court nominated as a National Living Treasure. *Australian Christian Lobby*. Retrieved from www.acl.org.au/2012/01/rev-dr-margaret-court-nominated-as-a-national-living-treasure/

Azarenka, V. (2016, March 20). Press conference. BNP Paribas Open.

Bayless, S. (1981). Martina Navratilova: Millionairess in search of happiness. *The Dallas Morning News*. Retrieved from http://news.google.com/newspapers?nid=1873&dat=19810801&id=5VIfAAAAIBAJ&sjid=G9IEAAAAIBAJ&pg=4998,652023

BBC Sport. (2006, April 25). Wimbledon defiant over equal pay. *BBC Sport*. Retrieved from http://news.bbc.co.uk/sport2/hi/tennis/4942608.stm

BBC Sport. (2014, June 22). Andy Murray: Amelie Mauresmo not planning radical overhaul. *BBC Sport*. Retrieved from www.bbc.com/sport/tennis/27956704

Belson, K. (2012, March 30). After howls of protest, WTA will address shrieks. *The New York Times*. Retrieved from www.nytimes.com/2012/03/31/sports/tennis/womens-tennis-association-to-tackle-excessive-grunting.html

Benokraitis, N. V. (1998). Working in the ivory basement: Subtle sex discrimination in higher education. In L. H. Collins, J. C. Chrisler, & K. Quina (Eds.), *Career strategies for women in academe: Arming Athena* (pp. 3–35). London: Sage.

Birrell, S. (2000). Feminist theories for sport. In J. Coakley & E. Dunning (Eds.), *Handbook of sports studies* (pp. 61–76). London: Sage.

Birrell, S., & Cole, C. L. (1990). Double fault: Renee Richards and the construction and naturalization of difference. *Sociology of Sport Journal, 7*(1), 1–21.

Birrell, S., & McDonald, M. G. (2012). Break points: Narrative interruption in the life of Billie Jean King. *Journal of Sport and Social Issues, 36*(4), 343–360.

Bonilla-Silva, E. (2006). *Racism without racists: Color-blind racism and the persistence of racial inequality in the United States*. Lanham, Maryland: Rowman & Littlefield.

Bonk, T. (1990, May 24). Tinling dies at 79 in England: Tennis: Historian of the women's game, he was both a fashion designer and liaison for the sport. *Los Angeles Times*. Retrieved from http://articles.latimes.com/1990-05-24/sports/sp-344_1_ted-tinling.

Bradley, P. (2003). *Mass media and the shaping of American feminism, 1963–1975*. Jackson: University of Mississippi Press.

Bradshaw, E. (2011, June 19). Rant time – Margaret Court, out dated and over rated. *WTA Tour Insights blog*. Retrieved from http://wtatourinsight.blogspot.com/2011/06/rant-time-margaret-cout-out-dated-and.html

Brake, D. L. (2010). *Getting in the game: Title IX and the women's sports revolution*. New York: NYU Press.

Briggs, S. (2014, September 23). Toni Nadal unhappy with appointment of Gala Leon as first female captain of Spain's Davis Cup team. *The Telegraph*. Retrieved from www.telegraph.co.uk/sport/tennis/11117240/Toni-Nadal-unhappy-with-appointment-of-Gala-Leon-as-first-female-captain-of-Spains-Davis-Cup-team.html

British Pathé. (1953). *Tennis fashions*. Available from www.britishpathe.com/video/tennis-fashions/query/teddy+tinling

British Pathé. (1967a). *London – Christine Truman's wedding dress*. Available from www.britishpathe.com/video/london-christine-trumans-wedding-dress/query/teddy+tinling

British Pathé. (1967b). Wimbledon fashion preview, www.britishpathe.com/video/wimbledon-fashion-preview/query/teddy+tinling

Broad, K. (2002). The gendered unapologetic: Queer resistance in women's sport. *Sociology of Sport Journal, 18*(2), 181–204.

Brown, R. M. (1973). *Rubyfruit jungle*. New York: Daughters.

Brown, R. M. (1984). *Sudden Death*. Bantam Books.

Brown, W. (2015). *Undoing the demos: Neoliberalism's stealth revolution*. Boston: MIT Press.

Bruce, T., & Tini, T. (2008). Unique crisis response strategies in sports public relations: Rugby League and the case for diversion. *Public Relations Review, 34*(2), 108–115.

Buechler, S. M. (1995). New social movement theories. *The Sociological Quarterly, 36*(3), 441–464.

Bunch, C. (1975). *Lesbianism and the women's movement*. Baltimore, MD: Diana Press.

Busfield, S. (2011, September 12). Serena Williams fined $2,000 for US Open final outburst. *The Guardian*. Retrieved from www.guardian.co.uk/sport/2011/sep/12/serena-williams-us-open-tennis-fine

Butler, J. (1990/2006). *Gender trouble: Feminism and the subversion of identity*. New York: Routledge.

Butler, J. (1993/2011). *Bodies that matter: On the discursive limits of "sex"*. New York: Routledge.

Butler, J. (1997). *Excitable speech: A politics of the performative*. New York: Routledge.

Butler, J. (1998). Athletic genders: Hyperbolic instance and/or the overcoming of sexual binarism. *Stanford Humanities Review, 6*(2). Retrieved from www.stanford.edu/group/SHR/6-2/html/butler.html

Cahn, S. K. (1994). *Coming on strong: Gender and sexuality in twentieth-century women's sport*. Cambridge, MA: Harvard University Press.

Carrington, B. (2010). *Race, sport and politics: The sporting black diaspora*. Thousand Oaks, California: Sage Publications.

Casals, R. (1970, October). The women: Up or down? *World Tennis Magazine*, 16–18.

Casals, R. (2015). Personal correspondence.

Casals, R. (2016). Personal correspondence.

Caudwell, J. (2006). Femme-fatale: Re-thinking the femme-inine. In J. Caudwell (Ed.), *Sport, sexualities, and queer/theory* (pp. 145–158). New York: Routledge.

Caudwell, J. (2011). Sport feminism(s): Narratives of linearity? *Journal of Sport and Social Issues, 35*(2), 111–125.

CBS Sports. (2011). *Serena Williams vs. Samantha Stosur, 2011 US Open final*. Retrieved February 11, 2013, from www.youtube.com/watch?v=px03E5NnPSU

CBSSports.com. (2012, January 13). Former champ Court stirs controversy ahead of Aussie Open. *CBS Sports*. Retrieved from www.cbssports.com/tennis/story/16847893/former-champ-court-stirs-controversy-ahead-of-aussie-open

Cho, S., Crenshaw, K. W., & McCall, L. (2013). Toward a field of intersectionality studies: Theory, applications, and praxis. *Signs, 38*(4), 785–810.

Clarey, C. (2007, February 22). Wimbledon to pay women and men equal prize money. *The New York Times*. Retrieved from www.nytimes.com/2007/02/22/sports/tennis/23cnd-tennis.html

Clarey, C. (2008, November 5). WTA rule may be made to be defied. *New York Times*. Retrieved from www.nytimes.com/2008/11/06/sports/tennis/06williams.html?_r=0

Clarey, C. (2014, October 17). Russian official is penalized for Williams sisters remark. *New York Times*. Retrieved from www.nytimes.com/2014/10/18/sports/tennis/wta-suspends-russian-official-for-comment-about-williams-sisters.html?_r=0

Coakley, J. J. (1998). *Sport in society: Issues and controversies* (6th ed.). New York: Irwin McGraw-Hill.

Collins, B., & Hollander, Z. (1994). *Bud Collins' modern encyclopedia of tennis*. Detroit: Visible Ink Press.

Collins, P. H. (1990/2000). *Black feminist thought: Knowledge, consciousness, and the politics of empowerment*. New York: Routledge.

Collins, P. H. (1998). *Fighting words: Black women and the search for justice*. Minneapolis: University of Minnesota Press.

Collins, P. H. (2005). *Black sexual politics: African Americans, gender, and the new racism*. New York: Routledge.

Collins, P. H. (2009). *Another kind of public education: Race, schools, the media, and democratic possibilities*. Boston: Beacon.

Collins, P. H. (2011). Piecing together a genealogical puzzle: Intersectionality and American pragmatism. *European Journal of Pragmatism and American Philosophy*, *3*(2), 88–112.

Collins, P. H. (2015). Intersectionality's definitional dilemmas. *Annual Review of Sociology*, 1–20.

Combahee River Collective. (1977). The Combahee River Collective statement. In B. Smith (Ed.) *Home girls: A Black feminist anthology* (pp. 264–274). New Brunswick, NJ: Rutgers University Press.

Court, M. (2012, January 25). Priority is to protect marriage. *Herald Sun*. Retrieved from www.heraldsun.com.au/opinion/priority-is-to-protect-marriage/story-e6frfhqf-1226252853390

Court, M., & McGann, G. (1976). *Court on court: A life in tennis*. London: W.H. Allen.

Court, M., & Oldfield, B. (1993). *A winning faith*. Family Reading Publication.

Crenshaw, K. (1989). Demarginalizing the intersection of race and sex: A Black feminist critique of antidiscrimination doctrine, feminist theory and antiracist politics. *University of Chicago Legal Forum*, 139–167.

Crenshaw, K. (1991). Mapping the margins: Intersectionality, identity politics, and violence against women of color. *Stanford Law Review*, 1241–1299.

Cullman, J. F. (1998). *I'm a lucky guy*. New York: Philip Morris.

Dalton, J. (2015). Personal correspondence.

Davis, A. Y. (1983). *Women, race, & class*. New York: Vintage.

Davis, K. (2008). Intersectionality as buzzword: A sociology of science perspective on what makes a feminist theory successful. *Feminist Theory*, *9*(1), 67–85.

Davis-Delano, L. R. & Crosset, T. (2008). Using social movement theory to study outcomes in sport-related social movements. *International Review for the Sociology of Sport*, *43*(2), 115–134.

Deford, F. (1984, July 9). A head to heed: Since the days when peach ice cream tasted like peach ice cream, Teddy Tinling's grace and sense of history have meant as much to tennis as his dress designs. *Sports Illustrated*. Retrieved from www.si.com/vault/1984/07/09/620433/a-head-to-heed.

DeMartini, J. R. (1983). Social movement participation: Political socialization, generational consciousness, and lasting effects. *Youth and Society*, *15*(2), 195–223.

Denison, J. & Markula, P. (2005). The press conference as a performance: Representing Haile Gebrselassie. *Sociology of Sport Journal*, *22*(3), 311.

Denzin, N. K. (2014). *Interpretive Autoethnography* (2nd ed.). Los Angeles: Sage.

Desmarais, F., & Bruce, T. (2008). Blurring the boundaries of sports public relations: National stereotypes as sport announcers' public relations tools. *Public Relations Review*, *34*(2), 183–191.

Dimitrov, R. (2008). Gender violence, fan activism and public relations in sport: The case of "footy fans against sexual assault". *Public Relations Review*, *34*(2), 90–98.

Donato, M. (1986, September 10). Yuki revisited: The London-based Japanese designer couldn't make the trip, but his elegant eveningwear is visiting Chicago, his "second hometown." *Chicago Tribune*. Retrieve from http://articles.chicagotribune.com/1986-09-10/entertainment/8603070560_1_fabric-dress-marshall-field

Douglas, D. D. (2002). To be young, gifted, black and female: A meditation on the cultural politics at play in representations of Venus and Serena Williams. Retrieved from School of Education, University of Otago: http://physed.otago.ac.nz/sosol/v5i2/v5i2_3.html

Douglas, D. D. (2005). Venus, Serena, and the Women's Tennis Association (WTA): When and where race enters. *Sociology of Sport Journal, 22*(3), 256–282.

Douglas, D. D. (2012). Venus, Serena, and the inconspicuous consumption of Blackness: A commentary on surveillance, race talk, and new racism(s). *Journal of Black Studies, 43*(2), 127–145.

Drath, E. (Director). (2011). *Renée* [Motion picture]. US: ESPN.

Drucker, J. (2015, August 25). Martina Navratilova: Tennis player who came in from the cold. *Huffington Post*. Retrieved from www.huffingtonpost.com/joel-drucker/martina-navratilova-the-t_b_8033450.html

Du Gay, P., Hall, S., Janes, L., MacKay, H., & Negus, K. (Eds.). (1997). *Doing cultural studies: The story of the Sony Walkman*. London: Sage.

Dunning, E. (1999). *Sport matters: Sociological studies of sport, violence, and civilization*: Abingdon, England: Taylor & Francis.

DuVernay, A. (Director). (2013). *Venus vs* [Motion picture]. US: ESPN.

Ellis, C. (2009). *Revision: Autoethnographic reflections on life and work*. Walnut Creek, CA: Left Coast Press.

EltonJohn.com. (September 10, 2018). Billie Jean King talks about Philadelphia Freedom. *Elton John.com*. Retrieved from www.eltonjohn.com/billie-jean-king-talks-about-philadelphia-freedom/

Equal Justice Initiative (2015, February 4). Serena Williams partners with EJI in historic return to Indian Wells tennis tournament. *Equal Justice Initiative*. Retrieved from www.eji.org/node/1036.

ESPN News. (2016, March 22). Djokovic criticized by Murray and Serena over equal pay. *ESPN News*. Retrieved from http://espn.go.com/tennis/story/_/id/15045951/novak-djokovic-criticised-andy-murray-serena-williams-equal-pay-stance.

Evans, C. (2008). Jean Patou's American mannequins: Early fashion shows and modernism. *Modernism/Modernity, 15*(2), 243–263.

Evening Independent (1972, July 8). Warning: Casals dressed down. *Evening Independent*. Retrieved from http://news.google.com/newspapers?nid=950&dat=19720708&id=TVhQAAAAIBAJ&sjid=u1cDAAAAIBAJ&pg=7375,1902523.

Evert, C. [ChrissieEvert] (2016, March 23). U r a future leader, girl.... You've got what it takes.. [Tweet]. Retrieved from https://twitter.com/ChrissieEvert/status/712838555048022016

Fanon, F. (1952/2008). *Black skin, white masks*: New York: Grove Press.

Feinstein, J. (1991). *Hard courts: Real life on the professional tennis tours*. New York: Villard.

Fest, S., & Newman, P. (2015). 2015 Co-presidents' message. *International Tennis Writers Association*. Retrieved from http://itwa.org

Festle, M. J. (1996). *Playing nice: Politics and apologies in women's sports*. New York: Columbia University Press.

194 Bibliography

Fink, J. S. (2012). Homophobia and the marketing of female athletes and women's sport. In G. B. Cunningham (Ed.), *Sexual orientation and gender identity in sport: Essays from activists, coaches, and scholars* (pp. 49–60). College Station, TX: Center for Sport Management Research and Education.

Finn, R. (1990, June 25), Rebel recalled in stately style. *The New York Times*. Retrieved from www.nytimes.com/1990/06/25/sports/rebel-recalled-in-stately-style.html

Finn, R. (1998, February 11). TENNIS: NOTEBOOK – FED CUP; King is back as captain as U.S. seeks revenge. *The New York Times*. Retrieved from www.nytimes.com/1998/02/11/sports/tennis-notebook-fed-cup-king-is-back-as-captain-as-us-seeks-revenge.html

Forman, P. J., & Plymire, D. C. (2005). Amélie Mauresmo's muscles: The lesbian heroic in women's professional tennis. *Women Studies Quarterly, 33*(1–2), 120–133.

Fraser, N. (1997). *Justice interruptus: Critical reflections on the "postsocialist" condition*. New York: Routledge.

Frye, M. (1978). Some notes on separatism and power. *Sinister Wisdom, 6.*

Gabel Jr., G. D., & Feiser, C. D. (2001). Sports credentialing and the battle over competitive coverage. *Communications Lawyer, 19,* 21–26.

Gallmeier, C. P. (1988). Methodological issues in qualitative sport research: Participant observation among hockey players. *Sociological Spectrum, 8*(3), 213–235.

Garrison, Z., & Smith, D. (2001). *Zina: My life in women's tennis*. Frog Books.

Geczy, A. & Karaminas, V. (2013). *Queer style*. London: Bloomsbury.

Genz, S. (2006). Third Way/ve: The politics of postfeminism. *Feminist Theory, 7*(3), 333–353.

Gever, M. (2003). *Entertaining lesbians: Celebrity, sexuality and self-invention*. New York: Routledge.

Gibbs, N. [Gibbsyyyy] (2016a, March 22). Have received a lot of comments like WTA>ATP, I like women's tennis more, in light of Moore comments. Appreciated but misses the point… [Tweet]. Retrieved from https://twitter.com/Gibbsyyyy/status/712429220169912320

Gibbs, N. [Gibbsyyyy] (2016b, March 22)…. Not about who's better or what's more fun to watch. About equality. About supporting each other. I'm happy if we all succeed!! [Tweet]. Retrieved from https://twitter.com/Gibbsyyyy/status/712429352290537473

Gibbs, N. [Gibbsyyyy] (2016c, March 22). @ATPWorldTour, is the theory here tht @ WTA players are stealing money out of ur pockets by being offered equal pay @ few tournies? #curious [Tweet]. Retrieved from https://twitter.com/Gibbsyyyy/status/712431714728091648

Gibson, A. (1958). *I always wanted to be somebody*. New York: Pyramid Books.

Ginn, L. (2012, January 17). King respects Court, disagrees adamantly with comments. *USA Today*. Retrieved from http://usatoday30.usatoday.com/sports/tennis/story/2012-01-17/billie-jean-king-talks-about-margaret-court-and-comments-about-gay-marriage/52623894/1

Glenn, E. N. (2002). Unequal freedom: How race and gender shaped American freedom and labor. Cambridge, MA: Harvard University Press.

Goolagong, E., & Collins, B. (1975). *Evonne! On the move*. Boston, Mass: Dutton.

Goolagong, E., & Jarratt, P. (1993). *Home! The Evonne Goolagong story*. Australia: Simon & Schuster.

Griffin, P. (1998). *Strong women, deep closets: Lesbians and homophobia in sport*. Champaign, IL: Human Kinetics.

Gross, K. N. (2006). *Colored Amazons: Crime, violence, and Black women in the City of Brotherly Love, 1880–1910*. Durham: Duke University Press.

Guilbert, S. (2004). Sport and violence: A typological analysis. *International Review for the Sociology of Sport, 39*(1), 45–55.

Guilbert, S. (2006). Violence in sports and among sportsmen: A single or two-track issue? *Aggressive Behavior, 32*(3), 231–240.

Halberstam, J. (1998). *Female masculinity*. Durham: Duke University Press.

Hall, S. (1996a). Introduction. Who needs "identity"? In S. Hall & P. du Gay (Eds.), *Questions of cultural identity* (pp. 1–17). New York: Sage.

Hall, S. (1996b). What is this "black" in black popular culture? In D. Morley & K.-H. Chen (Eds.), *Stuart Hall: Critical dialogues in cultural studies* (pp. 468–478). New York: Routledge.

Hall, S. (1996c). Race, culture and communications: Looking backward and forward at cultural studies. In J. Storey (Ed.), *What is cultural studies? A reader* (pp. 336–343). London: Arnold.

Hall, S. (1996d). On postmodernism and articulation: An interview with Stuart Hall (edited by Lawrence Grossberg). In D. Morley & K.-H. Chen (Eds.), *Stuart Hall: Critical dialogues in cultural studies* (pp. 131–150). London: Routledge.

Hall, S. (1998). Cultural identity and diaspora. In J. Rutherford (Ed.), *Identity: Community, culture, difference* (pp. 222–237). London: Lawrence & Wishart.

Harding, S. (1987). Introduction: Is there a feminist method? In S. Harding (Ed.), *Feminism and methodology: Social science issues*. Bloomington: Indiana University Press.

Harvey, D. (2005). *A brief history of neoliberalism*. Oxford: Oxford University Press.

Hebdige, D. (1979). *Subculture: The meaning of style*. New York: Methuen.

Heldman, G. M. (1970, November). Editorial: World Tennis Magazine signs 9 girls to pro contracts. *World Tennis Magazine*, 14–16, 48–49.

Heldman, J. M. (1967, June). Distinguished women in tennis: Nancy Richey. *World Tennis Magazine*, 18–19.

Heldman, J. M. (1968, January). Distinguished women in tennis: Judy Tegart. *World Tennis Magazine*, 40.

Heldman, J. M. (2015). Interview.

Heywood, L., & Drake, J. (Eds.). (1997). *Third wave agenda: Being feminist, doing feminism*. Minneapolis: University of Minnesota Press.

Heywood, L., & Dworkin, S. L. (2003). *Built to win: The female athlete as cultural icon*. Minneapolis: University of Minnesota Press.

Hobson, J. (2003). The "batty" politic: Toward an aesthetic of the black female body. *Hypatia, 18*(4), 87–105.

Holton, A. (2012). Baseball's digital disconnect: Trust, media credentialing, and the independent blogger. *Journal of Sports Media, 7*(1), 39–58.

hooks, b. (1984). *Feminist theory: From margin to center*. Boston: South End Press.

hooks, b. (1992). *Black looks: Race and representation*. Boston: South End Press.

hooks, b. (2016, May 9). Moving beyond pain. *The bell hooks Institute*. Retrieved from: www.bellhooksinstitute.com/blog/2016/5/9/moving-beyond-pain

Howard, J. (2006). *The rivals: Chris Evert vs. Martina Navratilova. Their epic duels and extraordinary friendship*. New York: Broadway.

Howson, N. (2014, June 10). Tennis reacts as Andy Murray appoints Amelie Mauresmo as new coach. *International Business Times*. Retrieved from www.ibtimes.co.uk/tennis-reacts-andy-murray-appoints-amelie-mauresmo-new-coach-1452125

Hylton, K. (2009). *"Race" and sport: Critical race theory*. New York: Routledge.

Bibliography

Institute of Chartered Accountants. (1897). *The accountant: The organ of chartered accountants throughout the world* (p. 36). General Index, 23. London: Gee & Co.

Jackson Jr., J. L. (2001). *Harlemworld: Doing race and class in contemporary Black America*. Chicago: University of Chicago Press.

Jamieson, L. M. & Orr, T. J. (2009). *Sport and violence: A critical examination of sport*. Boston: Elsevier.

Jenkins, S. (1991, April 29). Racket science: Billie Jean King has been a dynamo as a tennis champion, promoter, television commentator, businesswoman and feminist, but she may be even more compelling in her latest career: Teaching. *Sports Illustrated*. Retrieved from www.si.com/vault/1991/04/29/124076/racket-science-billie-jean-king-has-been-a-dynamo-as-a-tennis-champion-promoter-television-commentator-businesswoman-and-feminist-but-she-may-be-even-more-compelling-in-her-latest-career-teaching

Jones, A. (1971). *A game to love*. London: Stanley Paul.

JWfacts.com. (2015). United States Jehovah's Witness publisher statistics. *Facts About Jehovah's Witnesses*. Retrieved from www.jwfacts.com/watchtower/statistics-united-states.php

Kane, M. J. (2011, July 27). Sex sells sex, not women's sport: So what does sell women's sports? *The Nation*. Retrieved from www.thenation.com/article/sex-sells-sex-not-womens-sports/

Kaufman, M. T. (2004, May 1). Joseph F. Cullman 3rd, who made Philip Morris a tobacco power, dies at 92. *The New York Times*. Retrieved from www.nytimes.com/2004/05/01/business/joseph-f-cullman-3rd-who-made-philip-morris-a-tobacco-power-dies-at-92.html

Keeling, K. (2007). *Witch's flight: The cinematic, the Black femme, and the image of common sense*. Durham: Duke University Press.

Keese, P. (1973, July 20). Tennis decides all women are created equal, too. *The New York Times*. Retrieved from http://timesmachine.nytimes.com/timesmachine/1973/07/20/issue.html

Kelly, W. W. (1999). Caught in the spin cycle: An anthropological observer at the sites of Japanese professional baseball. *Public Culture*, *2*(2), 30–45.

Kennedy, E. L., & Davis, M. D. (1993). *Boots of leather, slippers of gold: The history of a lesbian community*. New York: Penguin Books.

Kincheloe, J. L. (2001). Describing the bricolage: Conceptualizing a new rigor in qualitative research. *Qualitative Inquiry*, *7*(6), 679.

King, B. J. (1968, December). A great idea from Florida. *World Tennis Magazine*, 32–33.

King, B. J. (2015, August 26). The legacy of the Original 9. *The Players Tribune*. Retrieved from www.theplayerstribune.com/billie-jean-king-women-tennis-history-original-9/

King, B. J. [BillieJeanKing]. (2016, March 20). Disappointed in #RaymondMoore comments. He is wrong on so many levels. Every player, especially the top players, contribute to our success. [Tweet]. Retrieved from https://twitter.com/BillieJeanKing/status/711670246227050496

King, B. J. & Brennan, C. (2008). *Pressure is a privilege: Lessons I've learned from life and the Battle of the Sexes*. New York: LifeTime Media.

King, B. J., & Chapin, K. (1974). *Billie Jean*. New York: Harper & Row.

King, B. J., & Deford, F. (1982). *Billie Jean*. New York: Viking.

King, B. J., & Starr, C. (1988). *We have come a long way: The story of women's tennis*. New York: McGraw-Hill.

King, B. J., Evert, C., & Gibbs, N. (2016, March 23). Press conference. Miami Open. Miami, FL.
King, S. (2005). Methodological contingencies in sport studies. In D. L. Andrews, D. S. Mason & M. L. Silk (Eds.), *Qualitative methods in sports studies* (pp. 21–38). New York: Berg Publishers.
Kleinman, S. (2007). *Feminist fieldwork analysis*. Los Angeles: Sage.
Kramer, J. (1970, November). A rebuttal to the editorial. *World Tennis Magazine*, 60.
Kuznetsova, S. (2014, July 28). Personal communication.
L'Etang, J. (2006). Public relations and sport in promotional culture. *Public Relations Review*, *32*(4), 386–394.
Lacy, B. (2011, December 7). Legend condemns gay marriage. *The West Australian*. Retrieved from https://au.news.yahoo.com/a/12256170/legend-condemns-gay-marriage/
Lake, R. J. (2014). *A social history of tennis in Britain*. New York: Routledge.
Laporte, R. (1971). The butch/femme question. *The Ladder*, *15*(9–10).
Leagle.com. (1973, February 7). *Heldman v. United States Lawn Tennis Association*. Retrieved from www.leagle.com/decision/19731595354FSupp.1241_11406/HELDMAN%20v.%20UNITED%20STATES%20LAWN%20TENNIS%20ASSOCIATION
Leagle.com. (1977, August 16). *Richards v. United States Tennis Association*. Retrieved from www.leagle.com/decision/197780693Misc2d713_1654/RICHARDS%20v.%20US%20TENNIS%20ASSN
Leeds Revolutionary Feminist Group. (1981). Love your enemy? The debate between heterosexual feminism and political lesbianism. Pamphlet retrieved from: https://docs.google.com/file/d/0B3dD4VR6trTUMzYzZTExNmMtY2FlMC00MjlhLTg1ZjItYjFhNGMzMWNlMGIx/edit?hl=en&authkey=CN6ixb8C&pli=1
LeGrand, C. (2012, January 12). Gays won't drive me from the Open, says Margaret Court. *The Australian*. Retrieved from www.theaustralian.com.au/news/nation/gays-wont-drive-me-from-open/story-e6frg6nf-1226242140162
Leibowitz, E. (2003). How Billie Jean King picked her outfit for the Battle of the Sexes match. *Smithsonian Magazine*. Retrieved from www.smithsonianmag.com/arts-culture/how-billie-jean-king-picked-her-outfit-for-the-battle-of-the-sexes-match-89938552/?no-ist
Leonard, D. J. (2004). The next M. J. or the next O. J.? Kobe Bryant, race, and the absurdity of colorblind rhetoric. *Journal of Sport & Social Issues*, *28*(3), 284–313.
Leonard, D. J. & King, C. R. (2011). *Commodified and criminalized: New racism and African Americans in contemporary sports*. Lanham: Rowman & Littlefield.
Lichtenstein, G. (1974). *A long way, baby: Behind the scenes in women's pro tennis*. New York: Morrow.
Little, A. (1988). *Suzanne Lenglen: Tennis idol of the twenties*. Wimbledon: Wimbledon Lawn Tennis Museum.
Lloyd, C. E., & Amdur, N. (1982). *Chrissie: My own story*. New York: Simon and Schuster.
Lloyd, C. E., & Lloyd, J. (1986). *Lloyd on Lloyd*. New York: Beaufort Books.
Lorde, A. (1984). *Sister outsider: Essays and speeches*. Berkeley: Crossing Press.
Lowes, M. D. (1999). *Inside the sports pages: Work routines, professional ideologies and the manufacture of sports news*. Toronto: University of Toronto Press.
Malcom, N. L. (2003). Constructing female athleticism: A study of girl's recreational softball. *American Behavioral Scientist*, *46*, 1387–1404.
Maloney, S. (2009, December). Margaret Court and Martina Navratilova. *The Monthly: Australian Politics, Society and Culture*. Retrieved from www.themonthly.com.au/

issue/2009/december/1295831572/shane-maloney/margaret-court-and-martina-navratilova

Mannheim, K. (1952). The problem of generations. In P. Kecskemeti (Ed.), *Karl Mannheim: Essays* (pp. 276–322). London: Routledge.

Marcus, G. E. (1995). Ethnography in/of the world system: The emergence of multi-sited ethnography. *Annual Review of Anthropology*, 95–117.

Matheson, A. (1975, July 16). Teddy Tinling goes to America, taking his splashy tennis dresses hung with baubles and sequins with him. *The Australian Women's Weekly*. Retrieved from http://trove.nla.gov.au/ndp/del/article/43458939

McCall, L. (2005). The complexity of intersectionality. *Signs*, *30*(3), 1771–1800.

McRobbie, A. (1980). Settling accounts with subcultures: A feminist critique. *Screen Education*, *34*, 37–49.

McRobbie, A. (2004). Post-feminism and popular culture. *Feminist Media Studies*, *4*(3), 255–264.

McRobbie, A. (2005). *The uses of cultural studies*. London: Sage.

McRobbie, A., & Garber, J. (1976/2006). Girls and subcultures. In S. Hall & T. Jefferson (Eds.), *Resistance through rituals: Youth subcultures in post-war Britain*. London: Hutchison.

Messner, M. A., Greenberg, M. A., & Peretz, T. (2015). *Some men: Feminist allies in the movement to end violence against women*. Oxford: Oxford University Press.

Mewshaw, M. (1993). *Ladies of the court: Grace and disgrace on the women's tennis tour*. New York: Crown Publishers.

Miller, T., McKay, J., & Martin, R. (2001). Courting lesbianism. In T. Miller (Ed.), *Sportsex*. Philadelphia: Temple University Press.

Mitchell, K. (2012, January 16). Laura Robson's gay rights stance reignites equality controversy. *The Guardian*. Retrieved from www.theguardian.com/sport/2012/jan/16/laura-robson-gay-rights-controversy

Moraga, C., & Anzaldúa, G. (Eds.). (1981). *This bridge called my back: Writings by radical women of color*. London: Persephone Press.

Muhammad, K. G. (2010). *The condemnation of Blackness: Race, crime, and the making of modern urban America*. Cambridge: Harvard University Press.

Muñoz, J. E. (1999). *Disidentifications: Queers of color and the performance of politics*. Minnesota: University of Minnesota Press.

Munt, S. R. (1998). *Heroic desire: Lesbian identity and cultural space*. London: Cassell.

Nash, J. C. (2008). Re-thinking intersectionality. *Feminist Review*, *89*(1), 1–15.

Nash, R. (2001). English football fan groups in the 1990s: Class, representation and fan power. *Soccer and Society*, *2*(1), 39–58.

Navratilova, M. (2012a, January 12). Press conference. Australian Open. Retrieved from www.ausopen.com/en_AU/news/interviews/2012-01-23/201201231327288553779.html

Navratilova, M. (2012b, January 27). Don't deny us same-sex marriage laws, says Martina Navratilova. *Herald Sun*. Retrieved from www.heraldsun.com.au/ipad/dont-deny-us-same-sex-marraige-laws-says-martina-navratilova/story-fn6bn88w-1226254744774

Navratilova, M. [Martina]. (2014, May 14). @KristiTredway There was no love lost between them, Margaret didn't really do anything of note to help the tour then. [Tweet]. Retrieved from https://twitter.com/KristiTredway/statuses/466613098749886464

Navratilova, M. [Martina]. (2014, May 15). @KristiTredway Yes, I couldn't believe they put us out on an outside court, women didn't get on the stadium till semis back then! [Tweet]. Retrieved from https://twitter.com/KristiTredway/statuses/466613098749886464

Navratilova, M. [Martina]. (2016, January 15). @KristiTredway no -played world team tennis instead- the French and Australian opens were not that big a deal then. Different now. [Tweet]. Retrieved from https://twitter.com/KristiTredway/status/688081553839251456

Navratilova, M. & Vecsey, G. (1985). *Martina.* New York: Knopf.

Newburrie, J. (2012). Petitioned Tennis Australia: Change the name of the Margaret Court Arena. *Change.org.* Retrieved from www.change.org/en-AU/petitions/tennis-australia-change-the-name-of-the-margaret-court-arena

Newman, P. (2013, June 18). Forty years on, Billie Jean King led the revolution that propelled women to greater equality. *The Independent.* Retrieved from www.independent.co.uk/sport/tennis/forty-years-on-how-billie-jean-king-led-the-revolution-that-propelled-women-to-greater-equality-8664164.html

Nowness (2011, September 1). Dewey Nicks: Strong is beautiful; The photographer serves up a slice of the biggest names in women's tennis. Retrieved from www.nowness.com/series/limber-up/dewey-nicks-strong-is-beautiful

Oberjuerge, P. (2009, March 19). No changing the Williams sisters' minds. *The New York Times.* Retrieved from www.nytimes.com/2009/03/20/sports/tennis/20tennis.html?_r=0

Parliament. (2006, June 28). Parliamentary business. Commons debate. Retrieved from www.publications.parliament.uk/pa/cm200506/cmhansrd/vo060628/debtext/60628-0002.htm

Peele, S. (2009, May 18). McEnroe: Serena's outburst was fine. *Psychology Today.* www.psychologytoday.com/blog/addiction-in-society/200909/mcenroe-serenas-outburst-was-fine

Perrotta, T. (2014, June 8). Men's tennis star Andy Murray hires Amelie Mauresmo as coach: Mauresmo to start with grass court season. *The Wall Street Journal.* Retrieved from www.wsj.com/articles/mens-tennis-star-andy-murray-hires-amelie-mauresmo-as-coach-1402234902

Perrotta, T. (2015, July 9). What to do about grunting in tennis? Maybe nothing. *The Wall Street Journal.* Retrieved from www.wsj.com/articles/what-to-do-about-grunting-in-tennis-maybe-nothing-1436467619

Pick, M. (2007). *Be dazzled! Norman Hartnell: Sixty years of glamour and fashion.* New York: Pointed Leaf Press.

Pieper, L. P. (2012). Gender regulation: Renée Richards revisited. *The International Journal of the History of Sport, 29*(5), 675–690.

Plymire, D. C. & Forman, P. J. (2000). Breaking the silence: Lesbian fans, the internet, and the sexual politics of women's sport. *International Journal of Sexuality and Gender Studies, 5*(2), 141–153.

Pollard, D. (2012, January 25). Court wrong on the issue of gay choice. *Herald Sun.* Retrieved from www.heraldsun.com.au/ipad/court-wrong-on-the-issue-of-gay-choice/story-fn6bfkm6-1226252771925

Pollard, D. (2014, August 15). Personal communication.

Popovich, N. (2015, September 11). Battle of the sexes: Charting how women in tennis achieved equal pay. *The Guardian.* Retrieved from www.theguardian.com/sport/2015/sep/11/how-women-in-tennis-achieved-equal-pay-us-open

Press Association. (2014, September 22). Rafael Nadal's coach queries move to appoint female Davis Cup captain. *The Guardian.* Retrieved from www.theguardian.com/sport/2014/sep/22/gala-leon-garcia-becomes-spain-first-female-davis-cup-captain-tennis

Rainbow Flags Over Margaret Court Arena. (ca. 2012). In *Facebook* [Society/Culture Page]. Retrieved from www.facebook.com/RainbowsOverMCA

Bibliography

Reinharz, S. (1992). *Feminist methods in social research*. Oxford: Oxford University Press.

Riach, J. (2016, March 21). Martina Navratilova: Female tennis players could boycott Indian Wells. *The Guardian*. Retrieved from www.theguardian.com/sport/2016/mar/21/navratilova-female-tennis-boycott-indian-wells?CMP=share_btn_tw

Rich, A. (1980). Compulsory heterosexuality and lesbian existence. *Signs*, *5*(4), 631–660.

Roberts, S. (2005). *A necessary spectacle: Billie Jean King, Bobby Riggs, and the tennis match that leveled the game*. New York: Crown Publishing.

Robson, D. (2009, March 11). Williams sisters unlikely to be penalized for missing event. *USA Today*. Retrieved from http://usatoday30.usatoday.com/sports/tennis/2009-03-11-williams-sisters-not-punished_N.htm

Rogers, I. (2015, July 5). Martinez to take over as Spain Davis Cup captain. *Reuters*. Retrieved from www.reuters.com/article/us-tennis-spain-davis-martinez-idUSKCN0PF0RP20150705

Rosenthal, D. (2016, March 20). Indian Wells CEO slams women's tennis, embarrasses himself with revolting & sexist comments. *CBS Los Angeles*. Retrieved from https://losangeles.cbslocal.com/2016/03/20/indian-wells-ceo-slams-womens-tennis-embarrasses-himself-with-revolting-sexist-comments/

Rothenberg, B. (2012, January 25). Grunting is loud, and so is response. *The New York Times*. Retrieved from www.nytimes.com/2012/01/26/sports/tennis/womens-tennis-tries-to-get-the-grunting-under-control.html?_r=0

Rothenberg, B. (2015, July 10). Tennis's top women balance body image with quest for success. *The New York Times*. Retrieved from www.nytimes.com/2015/07/11/sports/tennis/tenniss-top-women-balance-body-image-with-quest-for-success.html

Rottenberg, C. (2014) The rise of neoliberal feminism. *Cultural Studies*, *28*(3), 418–437.

Sackey, D. [donniejsackey]. (2016, March 22). @DjokerNole criticized by @Andy_Murray & @SerenaWilliams over equal prize $. Murray wins as he shades @Stako_tennis [Tweet]. Retrieved from https://twitter.com/donniejsackey/status/712417824833015808

Schultz, J. (2005). Reading the catsuit: Serena Williams and the production of blackness at the 2002 U.S. Open. *Journal of Sport & Social Issues*, *29*(3), 338–357.

Schultz, J. (2011). The physical activism of Billie Jean King. In S. Wagg (Ed.), *Key moments in sport: Critical essays on sporting milestones*. London: Routledge.

Sedgwick, E. K. (1993). Epistemology of the closet. In H. Abelove, M. A. Barale, & D. M. Halperin (Eds.), *The lesbian and gay studies reader* (pp. 45–61). New York: Routledge.

Sedgwick, E. K. (2008). *Epistemology of the closet* (2nd ed.). Berkeley, CA: University of California Press.

Seles, M. (1996). *Monica: From fear to victory*. New York: HarperCollins.

Shriver, P. (2015, April 9). Personal communication.

Shriver, P., Deford, F., & Adams, S. B. (1987). *Passing shots: Pam Shriver on tour*. New York: McGraw-Hill.

Smith, C. D. (1990). *Presidential press conferences: A critical approach*. New York: Praeger Publishers.

Smith, D. (2001, March 28). Williams' father says booing racially motivated. *USA Today*. Retrieved from http://usatoday30.usatoday.com/sports/tennis/stories/2001-03-26-williams.htm

Spencer, N. E. (1996). *America's sweetheart, Chris Evert: Celebrity femininity and tennis in postmodern America*. University of Illinois: Urbana-Champaign.

Spencer, N. E. (1997). Once upon a subculture. Professional women's tennis and the meaning of style, 1970–1974. *Journal of Sport and Social Issues, 21*(4), 363–378.

Spencer, N. E. (2000). Reading between the lines: A discursive analysis of the Billie Jean King vs. Bobby Riggs "Battle of the Sexes." *Sociology of Sport Journal, 17*(4), 386–402.

Spencer, N. E. (2001). From "child's play" to "party crasher": Venus Williams, racism and professional women's tennis. In D. L. Andrews & S. J. Jackson (Eds.), *Sport stars: The cultural politics of sporting celebrity* (pp. 87–101). New York: Routledge.

Spencer, N. E. (2003). "America's sweetheart" and "Czech-mate": A discursive analysis of the Evert-Navratilova rivalry. *Journal of Sport and Social Issues, 27*(1), 18–37.

Spencer, N. E. (2004). Sister Act VI: Venus and Serena Williams at Indian Wells: "Sincere fictions" and white racism. *Journal of Sport and Social Issues, 28*(2), 115–135.

Spencer, N. E. (2012). Foot fault! Interrogating social networking coverage of Serena's outburst at the 2009 U.S. Open. In C. Sandvoss, M. R. Real, & A. Bernstein (Eds.), *Bodies of discourse: Sports stars, media, and the global public*. New York: P. Lang.

Spry, T. (2001). Performing autoethnography: An embodied methodological praxis. *Qualitative Inquiry, 7*(6), 706–722.

Sreedhar, A. (2015, July 10). Women in the World: The inspiring story of how Venus Williams helped win equality for women players at Wimbledon. *The New York Times*. Retrieved from http://nytlive.nytimes.com/womenintheworld/2015/07/10/the-inspiring-story-of-how-venus-williams-helped-win-equal-pay-for-women-players-at-wimbledon/

Stabiner, K. (1986). *Courting fame: The perilous road to women's tennis stardom*. New York: Harper & Row.

Stoll, L. C. (2013). *Race and gender in the classroom: Teachers, privilege, and enduring social inequalities*. Lanham, Maryland: Lexington Books.

Stubbs, R. (2014, August 17). Personal communication.

Suggs, D. W. (2015). Tensions in the press box: Understanding relationships among sports media and source organizations. *Communication & Sport*.

Sullivan, M. (2015, July 13). Double fault in article on Serena Williams and body image? *The New York Times*. Retrieved from http://publiceditor.blogs.nytimes.com/2015/07/13/double-fault-in-article-on-serena-williams-and-body-image/

Summers, J. & Morgan, M. J. (2008). More than just the media: Considering the role of public relations in the creation of sporting celebrity and the management of fan expectations. *Public Relations Review, 34*(2), 176–182.

Sykes, H. (1998). Turning the closets inside/out: Towards a queer-feminist theory in women's physical education. *Sociology of Sport Journal, 15*(2), 154–173.

Symons, C. (2010). *The gay games: A history*. New York: Routledge.

Tedlock, B. (2005). The observation of participation and the emergence of public ethnography. In N. Denzin & Y. Lincoln (Eds.), *The Sage handbook of qualitative research* (3rd ed., pp. 467–481). Thousand Oaks, CA: Sage.

Tennis Australia. (2012, January 12). Tennis Australia statement. *Australian Open*. Retrieved from http://2012.australianopen.com/en_AU/news/articles/2012-01-12/201201121326330966849.html

The Independent. (2000, October 11). Equal prize money at Australian Open. *The Independent*. Retrieved from www.independent.co.uk/sport/tennis/equal-prize-money-at-australian-open-637129.html

The WT Reporter. (1968, October). Distinguished women in tennis: Julie M. Heldman. *World Tennis Magazine*, 58–59.

The WT Reporter. (1970, June). Interview with Stan Smith. *World Tennis Magazine*, 46–48.

Bibliography

The WT Reporter. (1971, July). Interview with Billie Jean King. *World Tennis Magazine*, 40–45.

Thomas Jr., R. M. (1990, May 24). Ted Tinling, designer, dies at 79: A combiner of tennis and lace. *The New York Times*. Retrieved from www.nytimes.com/1990/05/24/obituaries/ted-tinling-designer-dies-at-79-a-combiner-of-tennis-and-lace.html

Tignor, S. (2016, March 21). Unequal say. *Tennis Magazine*. Retrieved from www.tennis.com/pro-game/2016/03/unequal-say/57937/#.VvKUj8eFdGy

Timms, L. (1968, April). Poor little poor girls. *World Tennis Magazine*, 34.

Tinling, T. (1963). *White ladies*. London: Stanley Paul & Co.

Tinling, T. (1977). *The story of women's tennis fashion*. Wimbledon: Wimbledon Lawn Tennis Museum.

Tinling, T. (1979). *Love and faults: Personalities who have changed the history of tennis in my lifetime*. New York: Crown Publishers.

Tinling, T. (1983). *Sixty years in tennis*. London: Sidgwick & Jackson.

Tredway, K. (2014). Judith Butler redux – The heterosexual matrix and the out lesbian athlete: Amélie Mauresmo, gender performance, and women's professional tennis. *Journal of the Philosophy of Sport*, *41*(2), 163–176.

Tredway, K. (2015, July 18). Letters to the editor. *The New York Times*. Retrieved from www.nytimes.com/2015/07/19/sports/letters-to-the-editor.html?_r=0

Tredway, K. (2016). "The leaning tower of pizzazz": Ted Tinling, couturier for the women's professional tennis revolution. *Fashion, Style & Popular Culture*, *3*(3), 295–312.

Tredway, K. (2019). The Original 9: The social movement that created women's professional tennis, 1968–1973. In R. Lake (Ed.), *The Routledge handbook of tennis: History, culture and politics*. London: Routledge.

Tredway, K. (2019). Serena Williams and (the perception of) violence: Intersectionality, the performance of Blackness, and women's professional tennis. *Ethnic and Racial Studies*, pre-print available online.

Tredway, K. (2019). Rainbow Flags Over Margaret Court Arena: Commemoration vs. grassroots LGBTQ social activism at the Australian Open Tennis Championships. *Interactions: Studies in Communication & Culture*, *10*(1/2), pp. 71–90.

Tredway, K. & Liberti, R. (2018). "All frocked up in purple": Rosie Casals, Virginia Slims, and the politics of fashion at Wimbledon, 1972. *Fashion, Style & Popular Culture*, *5*(2), 235–247.

Tsing, A. L. (2005). *Friction: An ethnography of global connection*. Princeton: Princeton University Press.

USA Channel. (2004). *Serena Williams vs. Jennifer Capriati, 2004 US Open semi-finals*. Retrieved February 11, 2013, from www.youtube.com/watch?v=EnFVzqN6Ags

Wade, V., & Rafferty, J. (1984). *Ladies of the court: A century of women at Wimbledon*. New York: Atheneum.

Walby, S. (2007). Complexity theory, systems theory, and multiple intersecting social inequalities. *Philosophy of the Social Sciences*, *37*(4), 449–470.

Waldman, K. (2012, June 28). Long live the tennis grunt! *Slate*. Retrieved from www.slate.com/blogs/xx_factor/2012/06/28/grunting_and_tennis_why_the_case_to_ban_women_from_making_loud_noises_on_court_is_crazy_.html

Walsh, D. (2007, December 9). The big interview: Billie Jean King. *The Sunday Times*. Retrieved from http://cma.thesundaytimes.co.uk/sto/sport/tennis/article76764.ece

Ware, S. (2011). *Game, set, match: Billie Jean King and the revolution in women's sports*. Carolina: University of North Carolina Press.

Wertheim, L. J. (2001). *Venus envy: A sensational season inside the women's tour.* New York: HarperCollins.
Weston, K. (2002). *Gender in real time: Power and transience in a visual age.* New York: Routledge.
Whittier, N. (1995). *Feminist generations: The persistence of the radical women's movement.* Philadelphia: Temple University Press.
Whittier, N. (1997). Political generations, micro-cohorts, and the transformation of social movements. *American Sociological Review,* 760–778.
Williams, S. (2014, March 31). WTA All-Access Hour. Family Circle Cup, Charleston, SC.
Williams, S. (2014a, August 17). Press conference. Western & Southern Open, Cincinnati, OH.
Williams, S. (2014b, October 19). Press conference. BNP Paribas WTA Finals, Singapore.
Williams, S. (2015a, February 4). Serena Williams: I'm going back to Indian Wells. *Time Magazine.* Retrieved from http://time.com/3694659/serena-williams-indian-wells/
Williams, S. (2015b, June 29). Press conference. Wimbledon, London, England.
Williams, S. (2015c, August 19). Press conference. Western & Southern Open, Cincinnati, OH.
Williams, S. (2016, March 20). Press conference. BNP Paribas Open, Indian Wells, CA.
Williams, S., & Paisner, D. (2009). *Queen of the court.* London: Simon & Schuster.
Williams, V. (2006, June 26). Wimbledon has sent me a message: I'm only a second-class citizen. *The Times.* Retrieved from www.thetimes.co.uk/tto/sport/tennis/article2369985.ece
Williams, V. (2015, August). Press conference. Western & Southern Open, Cincinnati, OH.
Wilson, B. (2007). New media, social movements, and global sport studies: A revolutionary moment and the sociology of sport. *Sociology of Sport Journal, 24*(4), 457–477.
Wilson, B., & White, P. (2002). Revive the pride: Social process, political economy, and a fan-based grassroots movement. *Sociology of Sport Journal, 19*(2), 119–148.
Wilson, E. (2014). *Love game: A history of tennis, from Victorian pastime to global phenomenon.* London: Serpent's Tail.
Winker, G., & Degele, N. (2011). Intersectionality as multi-level analysis: Dealing with social inequality. *European Journal of Women's Studies, 18*(1), 51–66.
Woodward, K. (1997). Introduction. In K. Woodward (Ed.), *Identity and difference.* London: Sage.
WTA. (2013, June 27). WTA legends to be honored at historic 40th anniversary celebration. *WTA.com.* Retrieved from www.wtatennis.com/SEWTATour-Archive/Archive/PressReleases/2013/0627_40th_Anniversary.pdf
WTA Tour Rankings. (1997). Singles numeric. Retrieved from www.wtatennis.com/SEWTATour-Archive/Rankings_Stats/Singles_Numeric_1997.pdf
Yuval-Davis, N. (2006). Intersectionality and feminist politics. *European Journal of Women's Studies, 13*(3), 193–209.
Yuval-Davis, N. (2011). Beyond the recognition and re-distribution dichotomy: Intersectionality and stratification. In H. Lutz, M. T. H. Vivar, & L. Supik (Eds.), *Framing intersectionality: Debates on a multi-faceted concept in gender studies* (pp. 155–169). London: Routledge.
Zirin, D. (2015, July 14). Serena Williams is today's Muhammad Ali. *The Nation.* Retrieved from www.thenation.com/article/serena-williams-is-todays-muhammad-ali/

Index

AARP 85
ability 7, 11; *see also* hyperability
Acts Amendment (Lesbian and Gay Law Reform) Act (2002), Australia 142
Adams, Katrina 90, 94
advertising 40, 48, 50, 58, 61, 96; "strong is beautiful" campaign 30, 97, 105, 120, 163
aesthetic masculinity 85–90
age 7, 11, 15
Ahmed, S. 21
Alexander-Floyd, N. G. 9
Ali, Muhammad 28, 71, 97, 158, 159
All England Lawn Tennis and Croquet Club 130, 132
Allaster, Stacey 106, 163
Alves, Mariana 115, 116
Alwin, D. F. 31n1
Amanmuradova, Akgul 102
amateurism/amateur players 2, 35, 38, 42–43
American Indian feminism 31n2
American Lawn Tennis magazine 36
American Tennis Association (ATA) 35, 36
Anderson, Janet 132–133
Andreescu, Bianca 161n8
Andrews, D. L. 95, 97, 159
androgyny 85–86, 87, 92n12
anti-grunting policies 30, 97, 104, 105–106, 108, 120, 163
Anzaldúa, G. 18
appearance fees 42
Asderaki, Eva 116–117
Ashe, Arthur 37, 50, 66n9, 159, 163
Associated Press 37, 126, 139, 140
Association of Tennis Professionals (ATP) 103, 135, 163–164
Austin, J. L. 91n4

Austin, Tracy 26
Australian Championships/Australian Open 42, 92n13; and equal prize money 128, 129–130; *see also* Rainbow Flags Over Margaret Court Arena
Australian Tennis Association 47
autobiographies 26
autoethnography 174
Azarenka, Victoria 105, 161n8, 165, 169

Baker, Beverly 54
Ban deodorants 129
Barman, Fred 74
Barnett, Marilyn 27, 79, 80
Barr body test 75, 77
Barrett, A. 38
Bartkowicz, Jane "Peaches" 42, 43, 44, 47, 48, 60
Barty, Ashleigh 161n8
baseline players 68, 89, 90
"Battle of the Sexes" tennis match 27, 28, 30, 41, 58, 63–65, 120n4
Bayless, S. 84
Becker, Boris 138
Beijing tournament 103, 104
Belson, K. 106
Benson & Hedges 49
Beyoncé 96
bias and angles, press/journalists 188
Billie Jean King National Tennis Center 97
Birrell, S. 16, 17, 18, 27, 76, 77–78, 80
bivalent collectivities 22
Black activism 65
Black (female) athletes: body of 111, 113–115 (objectification and sexualization 114, 156); identified as lesbians 115, 157, 159; masculinity 157, 159
Black feminism 18, 31n2, 67

Black lesbian culture 87, 88
Black Lives Matter 65
Black Power movement 28
Black tennis players 35–37, 68, 90–91, 94; prize money 2, 37; unapologetic Blackness of Williams sisters 108–110, 120; *see also* Garrison, Zina; Gibson, Althea; Keys, Madison; Stephens, Sloane Townsend, Taylor; Williams sisters; Williams, Serena; Williams, Venus
Black women 9
Blair, Tony 133, 160
blogs/bloggers 175, 176, 177
body 8; *see also* Black (female) athletes, body of; muscularity
Bolardt, Antonin 73
Bollettieri, Nick 105
Bonk, T. 57–58
Borg, Bjorn 71
Bottini, I. 18
Bradley, P. 64, 65
Bradtke, Nicole 149
Brennan, C. 134
Bridge Cohort 5
Brinkman, Jeanie 74
Bristol-Myers 129
British Hard Court Championships (1968) 2, 38
Broad, K. 86
Brown, Rita Mae 18, 79, 80, 81, 91n5
Brown, W. 94–95
buccal smear test *see* Barr body test
Bueno, Maria 46
bullying 145, 154
Bunch, C. 18
butch-femme lesbian culture 86–87, 88, 89
butch lesbian hero 140
Butler, J. 8–9, 19, 27, 78, 81, 124, 125, 160

Cahn, S. K. 89, 127, 128
Camus, A. 53
Capriati, Jennifer 115
Carillo, Mary 106, 116
Carlos, John 28
Carrington, B. 112, 113–114, 119, 156
Casals, Manuel 44
Casals, Maria 44
Casals, Rosie 24, 26, 29, 30, 41–42, 43, 44–45, 47, 48, 62, 71, 81, 171; doubles titles 44, 46; on Ted Tinling 57; tennis dresses 52, 61; and Virginia Slims circuit 59, 60

Casals, Victoria 44
Caudwell, J. 22
CBS-TV 50–51
celebrity individualism 96, 98–100
celebrity status 68, 175; Serena Williams and 122, 158, 161n7
Chambers, D. 33
Chapin, K. 81, 82, 83
Charleston, South Carolina 151
China 97, 100, 103–104, 108
Cho, S. 22
Cincinnati premier event 103
Citi Open 177, 187
Clarey, C. 152, 154
class 6, 7, 11, 15, 17, 18, 22, 40, 41; Serena Williams and 151, 153–154, 156, 157, 158; *see also* upper-classness
Clijsters, Kim 116, 152, 160n1
closetedness 124
clothing: color allowed on 55; and femininity 52, 53, 58; ready-to-wear 55–56; Serena Williams 27, 110–111; white only 52, 53, 54–55, 61; Wimbledon 33–34, 51–52, 53–55, 61; *see also* fashion; Tinling, Ted
coaching male players 134, 137–141
Coakley, J. J. 176
Cobb, Jelani 134
Coetzer, Amanda 101
Cold War 71, 75, 91
Cole, C. L. 27, 76, 77–78
collective activism 2, 40, 67
collective identity 4, 5
collective memory 4, 5
Collins, B. 51
Collins, P. H. 7, 11, 13–15, 18, 109, 115, 158, 159
color-blind racism 14, 30, 109, 110, 111, 114
Combahee River Collective 18
communism 75
Compton, California 153, 156, 157, 158
Connecticut Open 177
Connolly, Maureen 55
corporate sponsorship 48–51, 59, 60
corporatization 1, 2, 30, 93–108, 119, 121, 122; effects on women's professional tennis 96–97; in society 94–95; and sport 95–96; of Women's Tennis Association (WTA) 93, 94, 96, 100–103, 108
Court, Barry 82, 83

Index

Court, Margaret 25, 26, 44, 45, 60, 66n8, 81–85; Billie Jean King on 81, 82, 145, 149–150; on Billie Jean King 81–82; and Bobby Riggs tennis match 63, 85; as Christian minister 85, 141, 142–143, 151; distancing from women's liberation and feminism 83; Grand Slam titles 81, 161n5; and homosexuality 84–85, 123, 141, 142–144, 145–151; nomination as "national living treasure" 141, 144, 150
Crenshaw, K. W. 11
Cullman, Howard 49
Cullman III, Joseph 41, 42, 47, 48–51, 59, 60, 64, 66
Cullman Sr., Joseph 49
cultural domain of power 13, 14
cultural identity 10
Czechoslovakia: Martina Navratilova's defection from 67, 71–76; Prague Spring era 72; Russian invasion of (1968) 72; Velvet Revolution (1989) 72

Daily Telegraph 126, 127
Dallas Morning News 84
Dalton, Judy (née Tegart) 24, 25, 26, 29, 42, 43, 44, 45, 47, 48, 58, 60, 171
data collection and analysis 26–28
Davenport, Lindsay 101, 125–126, 128
Davis, A. Y. 18, 31n2
Davis Cup 139
Davis, K. 11
Davis, M. D. 87
Deford, F. 61, 80
DeMartini, J. R. 3, 4
Deng Xiaoping 103
Denison, J. 173
Denzin, N. K. 174
difference 9, 11, 12
Dior, Christian 54
disciplinary domain of power 13, 14
discrimination 61–62, 83
discursive construction of identities 8, 9–10
Djokovic, Novak 138, 186–187
Douglas, D. D. 9, 27, 157
Drake, J. 19
Drath, E. 76
dress *see* clothing; fashion
Drucker, J. 73, 74
Du Bois, W. E. B. 90
Dubai premier event 103
Dubček, Alexander 72

Durr, Francoise 62
DuVernay, A. 129, 132, 134
Dworkin, S. L. 19

Earley, Brian 116, 117
Eaton, H. 35
economic equity *see* equal prize money
Edberg, Stefan 138
Ellesse 56
empowerment 11, 93, 105
Enberg, Dick 118
Engzell, Louise 116
Equal Justice Initiative 113, 152
equal prize money 1, 2, 31, 40, 67, 91, 163, 167–169; Australian Open 128, 129–130; French Open 128, 132; men's efforts for 134, 135–136; and Original 9 (Founders cohort) 29–30, 41, 42, 68, 80, 121; US Open 128, 129; Venus Williams and 122–123, 130–134, 160; Wimbledon 128, 130–134, 160; and Women's Tennis Association (WTA) 131
equality 16, 41, 121, 145, 146, 149, 164; marriage 121, 123, 141, 142, 150; racial 65; of tournaments offered 42, 43
Erakovic, Marina 102
Escañuela, José Luis 140
ethnicity 6, 7, 11, 15
Evans, C. 34
Evening Independent 61
Evert, Chris 53, 69–71, 99, 103, 126, 167, 168, 169; Grand Slam titles 30, 67–68; and Martina Navratilova rivalry and friendship 27, 28, 70–71; playing style 68, 70, 89, 169; on Ted Tinling 57; WTA presidency 101

"Fair Go, Sport!" program 144
Falconi, Irina 102
Family Circle Cup 177, 187
fan-based movements *see* Rainbow Flags Over Margaret Court Arena (2012)
Fanon, F. 112, 114
fashion: couture 33–34, 40, 51–58, 60–61; ready-to-wear 55–56; *see also* clothing; Tinling, Ted
Federation Cup 45–46, 47, 139, 177
Federer, Roger 130, 135, 138, 162
Feinstein, J. 27–28
Feiser, C. D. 176
femininity 19, 52, 53, 58, 86, 88, 107
feminism xiii, 1, 16–22, 68, 83; American Indian 31n2; Black 18, 31n2, 67; lesbian

18, 67, 87; liberal 16, 17, 19, 20, 21, 43; Marxist 17–18; neoliberal 17, 20–22, 97; and popular culture 93; postfeminism 17, 19–20, 22, 65, 96, 120; radical 17; second-wave 16–18, 19, 20, 22, 41, 43, 65, 68, 85; socialist 17, 18; sporting 22; third-wave 17, 19–20, 22, 93, 96; "women's lob" feminism 1, 42, 43
feminist content analysis 26
feminist research 23
Fernandez, GiGi 90
Fernandez, Mary Jo 90, 102
Fernández-Ladreda, Fernando 140
Ferrer, David 137, 139
Ferrero, Juan Carlos 139
Fest, S. 182–183
Fink, J. S. 107
flaneur lesbian form 140
Flood, C. 28
Fogleman, Stephan 177
Forman, P. J. 27, 123, 125–126, 127
Fornaciari, Sara 101, 102
Founders cohort 2, 5–6, 16, 29–30, 32, 39, 40–66, 68, 80, 121, 122
Fraser, N. 22
Frazier, D. 18
Frazier, Joe 71
Fred Perry (company) 56
freedom 95
French Championships/French Open 34, 42, 177, 187; and equal prize money 128, 132
Friedan, B. 18, 20, 43
Fromholtz, Diane 77

Gabel Jr., G. D. 176
Gallmeier, C. P. 174–175, 176–177, 184
Gannon, Joy 54
Garrison, Zina 26, 90, 94, 109
gay marriage *see* marriage equality
Geczy, A. 53
gender 6, 7, 11, 15, 17, 18, 67, 68, 75, 76–78, 124; as "anchor point" 13; as bivalent collectivity 22; "gender shaming" 154; and lesbian culture 85–87, 88–90; performance 9, 160; Serena Williams and 154, 156, 157
generational cohorts 3–6, 28, 31n1; *see also* Founders cohort; Joiners cohort; Sustainers cohort; Throwbacks cohort
Genz, S. 19–20
Gever, M. 86, 128

Gibbs, Nicole 167–168
Gibson, Althea 2, 29, 33, 35–37, 39, 40, 41, 50, 109, 159
Ginn, L. 149
"girl power" 93
Glenn, E. N. 13
globalization, of Women's Tennis Association (WTA) 96–97, 100, 103–104
golf 92n10
Gonzalez, Pancho 50
Goolagong, Evonne 26, 55
Gorringe, Chris 130
Graebner, C. 46
Graf, Steffi 30, 94, 96, 98–99, 102, 161n5
Grand Slam tennis tournaments 37, 42–43, 103; *see also* Australian Championships/Australian Open; French Championships/French Open; US National Championships/US Open; Wimbledon
Green, Tyler 148
Greenberg, M. A. 5, 31n1, 94
Gronert, Sarah 78
grunting 30, 97, 104, 105–106, 108, 120, 163
Guerrant, M. 46

Halberstam, J. 87, 88, 89
Halep, Simona 161n8
Hall, S. 7–8, 9–10, 12–13, 158
Harding, S. xii, xiii, 23
Harvey, D. 95, 100–101, 102, 103–104, 108, 122
Haydon Jones *see* Jones, Ann (née Haydon)
Hebdige, D. 41
Heldman, Gladys M. 1, 41, 42, 44, 47, 48, 59, 62, 63, 66
Heldman, Julie 24, 26, 42, 43, 44, 45–46, 46, 48, 60, 63
Heldman, Julius 48
Herald Sun (Melbourne newspaper) 126, 141, 145, 146–147
Hester, W. E. 77
heteronormativity 16, 67, 68
Heywood, L. 19, 22
hindrance rule 105, 116
Hingis, Martina 101, 125, 126, 127, 149
Hobson, J. 110–111
Hogan, P. 44, 60
Holton, A. 176

homophobia 10, 79–80, 86, 107, 123, 124, 125, 126, 127, 145, 159
homosexuality 78–79, 81; Margaret Court's admonition of 84–85, 123, 141, 142–144, 145–151
hooks, b. 18, 96
Howard, J. 28, 69, 70, 72–73, 73, 76, 77
Howson, N. 138
Huffman, Sarah 81
human rights 146, 147, 149
Hy-Boulais, Patricia 101, 102
Hylton, K. 114
hyper-femininity 107
hyperability, Serena Williams 155, 156, 157, 158

IAAF (International Amateur Athletic Federation) 75
identification 9, 12, 13
identities 3, 6, 7–13; as "anchor points" 13; collective 4, 5; cultural 10; discursive construction of 8, 9–10; historicity of 10; performance of 8–9, 78
identity markers xiii, 6, 22, 68, 169
identity politics xii, 10, 13, 22, 67, 68, 90, 91, 93, 121, 122–123, 156, 169
Indian Wells tournament 103, 111–113, 151–153, 162, 164–165, 169
individual activism 2, 67
individualism 19, 20–21, 40, 93, 94, 95, 108, 110, 121, 122; celebrity 96, 98–100; Serena Williams 115–119, 120
Institutional Review Board (IRB) research compliance 188
institutional structures 14
International Amateur Athletic Federation (IAAF) 75
International Lawn Tennis Federation (ITLF) (later International Tennis Federation (ITF)) 62, 67, 106, 128
International Tennis Hall of Fame 45, 46, 57, 58, 171, 172
International Tennis Writers Association (ITWA) 182–183
interpersonal domain of power 13, 14
intersectionality xii, xiii, 2–3, 6–7, 11–13, 28–29, 37, 41–42, 68, 110, 133, 169; and matrix of domination 13, 14–15, 158; Serena Williams and 156–158
Italian Open 39
ITLF/ITF *see* International Lawn Tennis Federation

ITWA (International Tennis Writers Association) 182–183
Jackson Jr., J. L. 109
Jarratt, P. 55
Jefferies, S. 18
Jenkins, S. 137
Jews 50
John, Elton 56–57
Johnson, Jack 119
Johnson, W. 35
Joiners cohort 2, 6, 16–17, 30, 32, 39, 67–92, 121, 122, 169
Jones, Ann (née Haydon) 2, 29, 33, 37–39, 40, 41, 55, 65
Journal of the Philosophy of Sport 128
journalists/press 124, 126–127, 175; bias and angles 188

Kaepernick, Colin 170
Kane, M. J. 107
Kaplan, Carrie 48
Karaminas, V. 53
Kaufman, M. T. 49, 50
Keeling, K. 88
Keese, P. 129
Keldie, Ray 163
Kellmeyer, Peachy 63
Kelnberger, Joseph G. 129
Kennedy, E. L. 87
Kerber, Angelique 161n8
Key Biscayne tournament 103, 177
Keys, Madison 109, 153
King, Billie Jean 1, 24, 26–27, 31n5, 41, 42, 43, 44, 45, 47, 48, 50, 71, 108, 126, 141, 179; abortion 81–82; on ATP Wimbledon boycott (1973) 163–164; "Battle of the Sexes" tennis match 28, 30, 41, 58, 63–65, 120n4; and Chris Evert 69–70; as coach for Tim Mayotte 137–138; as delegate to Sochi Olympics (2014) 97; and Elton John 56–57; Grand Slam titles 46; homophobic family 79–80; lesbianism 27, 67, 79–80, 81, 84, 91, 125, 140; on Margaret Court 81, 82, 145, 149–150; marriage to Larry King 79, 80, 82; on need for women's liberation and feminism 83; and prize money 39, 129, 130, 133–134, 167, 168–169; repoliticization of 96, 97–98, 119; on sexist remarks of Raymond Moore 164; on Ted Tinling 57–58; tennis dresses 58, 61, 63–64; on unionization 61–62

King, Larry 79, 80, 82
King, Rodney 153
Kirgin, Margaret Goatson 64
Kleinman, S. xiii
Kloss, Ilana 179
Kramer, Jack 48, 59, 163
Krantzcke, K. 46
Kruger, Johnette 101
Kschwendt, Karin 101
Kullman, Ferdinand 49
Kuznetsova, Svetlana 24, 148, 161n8, 183–184
Kvitova, Petra 161n8

Labat, Florencia 101
Lacoste 56
Lacy, B. 142
Lake, R. J. 15–16
Latina lesbian culture 87
Laver, Rod 39, 130, 144
LaVoi, Nicole 107
Lawn Tennis Association (LTA) 38
Leeds Revolutionary Feminist Group 18
legal structure of society 14
LeGrand, C. 144
Lemigova, Julia 89
Lendl, Ivan 138
Lenglen, Suzanne 2, 29, 33–35, 39, 40, 52, 57
Leo Burnett advertising agency 50
León, Gala 139, 140
Leonard, D. J. 114
lesbian feminism 18, 67, 87
lesbianism and lesbian culture 27, 67, 79–81, 90, 91, 107, 160; Amélie Mauresmo and 31, 122, 123–128, 140; Billy Jean King and 27, 67, 79–80, 81, 84, 125, 140; Black and Latina 87, 88; Black women athletes identified as lesbians 115, 157, 159; butch-femme 86–87, 88, 89; butch lesbian form 140; and closetedness 124; Conchita Martinez and 140; flaneur lesbian form 140; and gender 85–87, 88–90; "gender fuck" fashion 89; heroic lesbian form 140, 141; Margaret Court's admonition of 84–85, 123, 141, 142–144, 145–151; Martina Navratilova and 67, 68, 75, 80–81, 84–85, 85–86, 87–88, 89, 90, 125; see also LGBTQ (lesbian, gay, bisexual, transgender, queer) politics
LGBTQ (lesbian, gay, bisexual, transgender, queer) politics 17, 68, 79, 121, 122; see also lesbianism and lesbian culture; Rainbow Flags Over Margaret Court Arena
Li Na 96–97, 103, 104, 108
liberal feminism 16, 17, 19, 20, 21, 43
liberalism 20
Lichtenstein, G. 27
Lieberman, Nancy 79, 80, 86, 92n8
Lloyd, Chris Evert see Evert, Chris
Lloyd, John 53
Lopez, Feliciano 139–140
Lorde, A. 18

Majoli, Iva 1–2
male players, support for women 135–141; equal prize money 134, 135–136; hiring women as coaches 134, 137–141
Maleeva, Magdalena 99
Mandlíková, Hana 73
manliness 52
Mannheim, K. 3–4
Marble, A. 36
March on Washington (1963) 65
Marcus, G. E. 177
marketing 40, 48, 122
Markula, P. 173
Marlboro cigarettes 50, 51
marriage equality 121, 123, 141, 142, 150
Marriage Equality Amendment Bill, Australia 142
Martin, R. 123, 126, 127
Martínez, Conchita 137, 139–140, 141
Marxist feminism 17–18
masculinity 91, 115, 124, 126, 127, 128; aesthetic 85–90; Black female athletes 157, 159
Mateik, Tara 120n4
Matheson, A. 56
matrix of domination 13–16, 158
Mauresmo, Amélie 27, 86, 130, 141; as coach for Andy Murray 137, 138–139; lesbianism 31, 122, 123–128, 140, 160; muscularity 123, 125–127, 128
Mayotte, Tim 137–138
McCall, L. 11, 13
McCammon, R. J. 31n1
McDonald, M. G. 27, 80
McEnroe, John 71, 116, 118
McGann, G. 82, 84, 142
McGuire, Bart 129–130
McKay, J. 123, 126, 127
McNeil, Lori 90, 94
McRobbie, A. xiii, 19, 21, 22, 65, 96
Medalie, George Z. 48

media 175–176; *see also* press/journalists; social media; television
media credentials 173, 174–179
Melville Reid, Kerry 25, 42, 43, 44, 46, 47, 48, 60, 77
member checking 29
memory, collective 4, 5
men *see* male players
Messner, M. A. 5, 31n1, 94
Mewshaw, M. 28
Mexico City Olympic Games (1968) 47, 75
military, homosexuality within 78
Miller, T. 27, 123, 126
Mitchell, K. 148
Moore, Raymond 162–163, 164–165, 166, 169
Moraga, C. 18
Moran, Gussie 51, 54
Morgan, M. J. 175
Movement Cohort 5
Moyá, Carlos 139
Ms. Magazine 81
Muguruza, Garbiñe 161n8
multi-sited fieldwork 177–178
multicultural politics 13
Munt, S. R. 140–141
Murray, Andy 135–136, 137, 138–139
muscularity: Amélie Mauresmo 123, 125–127, 128; Martina Navratilova 75, 86; Serena Williams 154

NAACP (National Association for the Advancement of Colored People) 151
Nadal, Rafael 135, 139, 162
Nadal, Toni 139
Nash, J. C. 6
Nastăse, Ilie 39, 44, 129, 163
Nation, The 158–159
nation/nationality 6, 7, 11, 15, 17, 67, 68, 75–76, 90, 91
National Association for the Advancement of Colored People (NAACP) 151
National Living Treasure title, Australia 141, 144, 150
National Organization of Women 18
National Trust of Australia 141, 144
Navratilova, Martina 25, 30, 52, 68, 70–71, 91, 103, 123, 124, 169; androgyny 85–86; and Chris Evert rivalry and friendship 27, 28, 70–71; coaching by Billy Jean King 137; defection from Czechoslovakia 67, 71–75; early life in Czechoslovakia 71–72; Grand Slam titles 68; intersectional identities 68, 75–76; and lesbianism and lesbian culture 67, 68, 75, 80–81, 84–85, 85–86, 87–88, 89, 90, 125; muscularity 75, 86; playing style 68–69, 70, 87, 89, 169; and Rainbow Flags Over Margaret Court Arena 141, 148–149, 151, 160; response to Margaret Court's statement on homosexuality 146–147; and sex/gender discourse 68, 75–76, 85–86; on sexist remarks of Raymond Moore 164; on Ted Tinling 57; tennis debuts outside Czechoslovakia 72–73; US citizenship 71, 74, 75; US permanent residency card 71, 74
Nelson, Judy 81
neo-conservatism 19
neoliberal feminism 17, 20–22, 97
neoliberalism 20, 94–96, 100–101, 102, 104, 108, 110, 120, 122, 169
New York Daily News 79, 84, 86
Newcombe, John 144
Newman, P. 62, 182–183
Nicks, Dewey 107
Norman, P. 28
Novotna, Jana 101

Obama, Barack 65, 97, 110
objectification 19, 114, 156
Olympic Games: Cold War era 75; Mexico City (1968) 47, 75
one-to-one interviews 173, 181–182
"open" tennis 2, 35, 37–39, 41, 43
opposition 12, 13
oppression 41
Original 9, 1–2, 24–25, 27, 28, 29–30, 39, 40, 41, 42, 43–47, 48, 65–66, 94; accomplishments of 58–59; depoliticization of 96; and International Tennis Hall of Fame 171–172
Osaka, Naomi 117, 161n8
Ostapenko, Jelena 161n8
other/othering 9–10, 11

Pacific Southwest Championships, Los Angeles 43, 48, 59
Parche, Günter 99, 161n5
Patou, J. 33, 34
patriarchy 16, 17, 18, 87
pay 34–35; under the table 37, 42; *see also* prize money
Peretz, T. 5, 31n1, 94

performance: gender 9, 160; and identity 8–9, 78
Perrotta, T. 105, 138, 139
Peters, Roumania and Margaret 36
Petkovic, Andrea 16
Philadelphia Freedom team 56–57
Philip Morris cigarette company 48–51, 59
Phillips, Tim 130–131
Pieper, L. P. 75
Pierce, Mary 102, 127
Pigeon, Kristy 24, 26, 42, 43, 44, 46, 47, 48, 58, 60
Pilić, Nikola 163
playing styles: Chris Evert 68, 70, 89, 169; Martina Navratilova 68–69, 70, 87, 89, 169; *see also* baseline players; serve-and-volley players
Plymire, D. C. 27, 123, 125–126, 127
Pollard, D. 143, 150
popular culture, and feminism 93
postfeminism 17, 19–20, 22, 65, 96, 120
power/power relations 3, 6, 7, 8, 11, 22, 28, 89, 96; domains of power 13–15, 122, 158
press conference participation as research method 173–188; being told the culture of players and press 184–185; dealing with odd behavior from players 186–187; deciding what questions to ask 181; gaining media credentials 173, 174–179; gaining trust and legitimacy in the field 183–184; gains for scholars from 187–188; handling rejection 178–179; leaving the field 187; mixed zone 182–183; negotiating a space in the media center 180; tournament entitlements 180, 180; when questions go awry 185–186; WTA staff in the media center 180
press/journalists 124, 126–127, 175; bias and angles 188
privatization 94, 95
prize money 35, 93, 103; and amateur players 35, 38; Black players 2, 37; disparity 2, 38, 39, 40, 42, 43, 59; equality *see* equal prize money
Professional Cohort 5
professionalization 34–35
public relations (PR) 175, 176

queer culture 89

race 6, 7, 9, 11, 15, 17, 18, 40, 41, 68, 90–91, 108; as "anchor point" 13; as bivalent collectivity 22; Serena Williams and 151–158
racial discrimination 61, 62
racial equality 65
racial segregation 36–37
racism 9, 10, 14, 35–37, 111–115; color-blind 14, 30, 110, 111, 114; Serena Williams and 111–114, 151–153
radical feminism 17
Radicalesbians 18
Rafter, Pat 144
Rainbow Flags Over Margaret Court Arena (2012) 25–26, 31, 123, 141–151, 160
Rapinoe, Megan 170
Raskind, Richard *see* Richards, Renée
recognition 22
redistribution 22
Reinharz, S. 23–24
religious beliefs 17; Margaret Court 85, 141, 142, 145; Serena Williams 155–156, 157, 158
representation 2, 9, 16, 67, 121
research methods and design 22–26; questionnaires 24–26; semi-structured interviews 22–23, 23–24
Riach, J. 164
Rich, A. 18
Richards, Renée 27, 30, 67, 76–78, 91
Richey, Nancy 42, 43, 44, 46, 48, 60
Riggs, Bobby 28, 30, 41, 63, 64–65, 84, 120n4
Roberts, S. 28, 69, 128–129
Robinson, Jackie 28, 37, 50
Robson, Laura 25, 123, 136, 141, 148, 151, 160
Rogers Cup 177
Rogers, I. 140
Ramos, Carlos 117, 118
Rosenberg, Sid 154
Rosenthal, D. 162–163
Rosewall, Ken 38, 144
Rottenberg, B. 20–21
Rubin, Chanda 90, 94
Russell, B. 28

Sackey, Donnie 135, 136
Safarova, Lucie 102
Sampson, Julie 55
Santana, Manuel 50
Scarsbrick, Brian 144
Schiavone, Francesca 102
Schultz, J. 27, 110, 111, 154

212 Index

Scott, Eugene 76
Scott, Larry 131–132, 152
second-wave feminism 16–18, 19, 20, 22, 41, 43, 65, 68, 85
Sedgwick, E. K. 124, 128
segregation: racial 36–37; sex 16
Seles, Monica 26, 102, 161n5; grunting 105; stabbing of 30, 96, 98, 99–100, 161n5
self-governance 104, 108
self-reflexivity xii–xiii
semi-structured interviews 22–23, 23–24
Sergio Tacchini (company) 56
serve-and-volley players 69, 87, 88, 89, 90
sex 8, 9, 17, 67, 68, 75, 76–78, 85, 91, 107, 121, 124, 156, 157
sex segregation 16
sex testing 75, 76
sexism 9, 10, 83, 162–167
sexuality 6, 7, 11, 15, 17, 18, 22, 67, 68, 91; *see also* homosexuality; lesbianism
sexualization of Black athletic body 114, 156
Sharapova, Maria 105, 161n8
Shriver, P. 24, 25, 26, 27, 29, 31, 98, 101, 121, 160n1
Simon, Steve 163
Smith, Barbara 18
Smith, Beverly 18
Smith, C. D. 174, 181
Smith, D. 152
Smith, Stan 163, 171–172
Smith, T. 28
soccer 170
social inequalities 6, 7, 11, 14, 20, 21
social justice 6, 21, 31, 108, 120, 122; Serena Williams and 110, 113, 123, 151, 152, 158
social media 2, 121
social movements: collective identity and memory 4, 5; continuity 4–5; definition of 4; Founders cohort 5–6; generational cohorts within 3, 4–6, 28; Joiners cohort 6; organizational approaches to 4; political process approaches to 4; recruitment and cohort turnover 4–5; Sustainers cohort 6
socialist feminism 17, 18
Soviet Union (USSR) 71, 75
Spanish Davis Cup Team 137, 139–140
Spanish Tennis Federation 140
speech acts 124
Spencer, N. E. 27, 41, 111, 153

Spirlea, Irina 102
sponsorship, corporate 48–51, 59, 60
sporting feminism 22
Stabiner, K. 27
Stakhovsky, Sergiy 135–136
Stanford Humanities Review 125
Starr, C. 1
Stephens, Sloane 109, 153, 161n8
Stockton, D. 44
Stosur, Samantha 102, 116, 118, 161n8
Stove, Betty 62
"strong is beautiful" advertising campaign 30, 97, 105, 106–108, 120, 163
structural domain of power 13, 14, 15
Stubbs, Rennae 24, 25, 27, 144, 147–148, 150
subcultures 27, 41
subject 8
subjectivities 7, 8
Suggs, D. W. 175
Sukova, Vera 73
Summers, J. 175
survey research 23, 24
Sustainers cohort 2, 6, 17, 30, 32, 68, 90, 91, 93–120, 122, 165, 169

Talbert, Bill 129
Tarpischev, Shamil 154
Tauziat, Nathalie 101
Taylor, Roger 163
Tegart, Judy *see* Dalton, Judy (née Tegart)
television 50–51
Tennis Atlantic 177
Tennis Australia 26, 144, 147, 149, 150
third-wave feminism 17, 19–20, 22, 93, 96
Thomas Jr., R. M. 51
Throwbacks cohort 2, 31, 32, 39, 121–161, 169
Tignor, S. 163, 164
Tiley, Craig 149
Time magazine 112
Timms, L. 38
Tinling, Ted 26, 33, 34, 41, 42, 47, 48, 66; and "Battle of the Sexes" match 63–64; fashion design for women's tennis 47, 51–58; London fashion house 52–53; move to Philadelphia 56–57; as player liaison 53, 54, 57; and Suzanne Lenglen 34, 52, 57; and Virginia Slims tour 53, 60–61; and Wimbledon 51–52, 53–55, 57
Title IX legislation xi, 63
Tobacco and Allied Stocks, Inc. 49
Toronto/Montreal premier event 103

tournaments: equality/availability 42, 43, 93; "international" 103; premier 102–103; WTA and structure of 102–103; *see also* Grand Slam tennis tournaments; *and names of individual tournaments*
Townsend, Taylor 109, 153
Trailblazers 29, 33–39
trans movement 121
Truman, Christine 38, 53
Tsing, A. L. 89
Tsurubuchi, Shino 116
Turnbull, W. 44, 46
Turner, L. 45

unapologetic Blackness 108–110, 120
unions *see* Women's Tennis Association (WTA)
United States Lawn Tennis Association (USLTA) (later United States Tennis Association (USTA)) 30, 35, 36, 37, 48, 62, 91; sanctioned tournaments 59; and sex testing 77
upper-classness 15–16, 42, 67, 68, 83–84, 157, 158, 169
US Clay Court Championships 46
US Hard Court Championships 44
US National Championships/US Open 36, 42, 59; and color on clothing 55; and equal prize money 128, 129; location 92n13; Serena Williams and 108, 115–119; televising of 50–51 USLTA/USTA *see* United States Law tennis Association
USSR (Soviet Union) 71, 75

Van Roost, Dominique 101
Vecsey, G. 71–72, 73, 74
Vicario, Arantxa Sanchez 102
Virginia Slims cigarettes 51
Virginia Slims circuit 41, 44, 48, 49, 53, 59–61, 62
Volkov, Alexander 138

Wade, Virginia 26, 38, 55
Walby, S. 22
Waldman, K. 105
Walker, Andrew 106
Walsh, D. 79–80
Wambach, Abby 81
Ware, S. 27
Washington, Booker T. 90
Washington Kastles 177, 179, 187
Werdel-Witmeyer, Marianne 101

Wertheim, L. J. 28
Western & Southern Open 177, 187
Weston, K. 87, 88
whiteness 16, 67, 68, 83, 157, 158, 169
Whittier, N. 3, 4, 5, 6, 28, 31, 33, 40, 67, 93–94
Wightman Cup 47
Wild, Linda 101
Williams sisters 27, 37, 90, 91, 94, 114, 157–158; intersectional identities 110; social justice agenda 110, 113, 120; unapologetic Blackness 108–110, 120; *see also* Williams, Serena; Williams, Venus
Williams, Richard 152, 153
Williams, Serena 26, 29, 30, 102, 114–115, 121, 127, 169; Black aesthetic and style 109; and celebrity status 122, 158, 161n7; and class 151, 153–154, 156, 157, 158; clothing 27, 110–111; constraints on her individualism 115–119, 120; and gender 154, 156, 157; Grand Slam titles 108, 158, 161n5; as greatest *activist* athlete 158–160; hyperability 155, 156, 157, 158; and Indian Wells tournament 111–113, 151–153; and intersectionality 156–158; outbursts on court 115–118; physicality and muscularity 154; protest of the Confederate Flag (2000) 151; and race/racism 111–114, 151–158, 156, 158; religious beliefs 155–156, 157, 158; and rules of tennis 115–119; and sexism 162, 165–167; social justice work 110, 113, 123, 151, 152, 158; and "Strong is Beautiful" campaign 107–108; and US Open 108, 115–119
Williams, Venus 29, 31, 102, 108, 111, 112, 122, 127, 151–152, 153, 160n4, 161n6; and equal prize money 122–123, 130–134, 160; Grand Slam titles 161n8
Wilson, E. 15, 54
Wimbledon 37, 42, 43, 47; ATP boycott of (1973) 163–164; dresses and dress codes 33–34, 51–52, 53–55, 61; prize money 39, 128, 130–134, 160
womanhood, redefining of 76–78
women's liberation movement 1, 28, 40, 67, 83, 86–87, 150
"women's lob" feminism 1, 42, 43
Women's Tennis Association (WTA) 1, 25, 27, 30, 40, 41, 61–63, 67, 76, 97–98, 149, 154, 162, 173; anti-grunting

Women's Tennis Association (WTA) *continued*
policies 30, 97, 104, 105–106, 108, 120, 163; CEO (chief executive officer) 102; corporatization of 93, 94, 96, 100–103, 108; and equal prize money 131; founding of 98; globalization of 96–97, 100, 103–104; "international" tournaments 103; Players Association 101, 102; Players Council 102, 106; premier mandatory events 102–103, 112; presidents 101; restructuring of 93, 100–103, 119–120; and sex testing 77; "strong is beautiful" advertising campaign 30, 97, 105, 106–108, 163; tournament structure 102–103

Woods, Tiger 110
Woodward, K. 7, 9, 10
work–family balance 20–21
World Team Tennis (WTT) 179
World Tennis magazine 1, 42, 47, 48
Wozniacki, Caroline 161n8
WT Reporter 58, 172
WTA *see* Women's Tennis Association (WTA)
WTA Tour 62, 63
Wuhan tournament 103, 104

Yuval-Davis, N. 22, 156

Zeigenfuss, Valerie 42, 43, 44, 47, 48, 60
Zirin, D. 158–159